Praise for *The Shadow Market*

"Remarkable."

Financial Times

"Dense and disturbing ... Weiner succeeds in making the case that something fundamental has changed in the world with the rise of Eastern and Middle Eastern economies, and that is worth paying attention to."

The New York Times Book Review

"Weiner out-hustles the global influence peddlers."

Vanity Fair

"Alarming ... A bleak survey of how flush authoritarian governments deploy financial means to achieve geopolitical ends."

Bloomberg BusinessWeek

"Unnerving [and] consistently engaging ... A revealing – and troubling – overview of the uses of money and power at the international level."

Kirkus Reviews

"Weiner has interesting stories to tell about the antics of hedge funds and so-called 'private equity' businesses ... and the new great game of 'energy diplomacy'."

The Guardian

"Weiner explains how the US is ceding dominance to countries with more cash and less debt. His book explains how to succeed as an investor in the world of the shadow market."

Worth

"Captivating."

Crain's Chicago Business

"Informative [and] admirably lucid."

Publishers Weekly

THE
SHADOW
MARKET

How Sovereign Wealth Funds Secretly Dominate
the Global Economy

Eric J. Weiner

ONEWORLD

A Oneworld Book

First published in trade paperback by Oneworld Publications 2011
This updated edition published 2011
Reprinted 2011

Originally published in the United States of America by Scribner,
A Division of Simon & Schuster, Inc., in 2010

ISBN 978–1–85168–822–7

Typeset by Jayvee, Trivandrum, India
Cover design by Jamie Keenan
Text designed by Erich Hobbing
Printed and bound by CPI Group (UK) Ltd, Croydon, CR0 4YY

Oneworld Publications
185 Banbury Road Oxford OX2 7AR, England

Learn more about Oneworld. Join our mailing list to
find out about our latest titles and special offers at:
www.oneworld-publications.com

For Paige
Who always believed

Contents

THE
SHADOW
MARKET

Between the idea
And the reality
Between the motion
And the act
Falls the Shadow

—T. S. Eliot, "The Hollow Men"

The Future Happened Yesterday

Do you ever get the feeling that something's happened in the global economy that we don't fully understand? That while we have been focused on fixing the wounded economy and worrying about lost jobs and battered bank accounts, the world was changing in important but nearly imperceptible ways? You'd be right. It did. Enormous economic changes are taking place around the globe, many of them hidden in plain sight, others just plain hidden—kept from the press, the government, and, most of all, the everyday investor. Ever since 2008, when the global financial crisis hit, the economic world as we know it has been flipped on its head. Countries and corporations that once dominated the planet have been decimated. Meanwhile, other powers have risen in their place and asserted themselves globally. The truth is that, no matter how much belt-tightening we do or how soon company profits and employment levels recover, we won't be returning to "normal" any time soon.

While Western economies tanked in 2009 and 2010, nations like China and the small oil-rich states of the Persian Gulf, which still had plenty of wealth on hand, suddenly discovered that they were *really* rich compared to the rest of the world. So they started using their cash to seize geopolitical power. Wealth and influence crept to the East. Meanwhile, Western nations literally didn't have the money to save themselves from the financial contagion they had started. American banks and investment institutions flat-out didn't have the capital to rescue the financial system themselves. In

1

late 2008, the US government was desperately trying to stave off an economic panic. That autumn, as the stock market reeled and the largest banks stared at insolvency, the US Treasury Department sent envoys to China, Singapore, Abu Dhabi, Kuwait, and Saudi Arabia looking for investments of hundreds of billions of dollars. But America's envoys were completely rebuffed. The problem was that each of these countries already had been burned by the earlier failures of major US investment banks like Lehman Brothers and Bear Stearns; they had little appetite for taking on more American risk.

Today we are presented with tangible proof that the era of American economic hegemony is over. The West's fiscal policies and patterns of consumption over the past few decades have left us with untenable amounts of debt. For decades, the bulk of the liquidity in the global capital markets was provided by multinational banks from the US, the UK, and Japan. But today the global need for investment capital far outstrips the cash that the world's largest banks can provide. Instead much larger entities with deep reserves of wealth have emerged to keep the markets flush: a loosely configured, unregulated global "shadow market" that supplies the money that the world needs to grow. With remarkable stealth, this network has largely supplanted the United States as the pacesetter for the global economy. The development of this shadow market means that a new global economic force is at play—one that we'll all have to contend with for decades to come.

"The last two hundred years of world history have been a major historical aberration," says Kishore Mahbubani, dean of the Lee Kuan Yew School of Public Policy in Singapore and one of the world's leading authorities on the new wave of globalization. "This is a key point that people in the West have a hard time wrapping their minds around. From the year 1 to the year 1820, China and India consistently had the two largest economies in the world. When you think about it, it's quite amazing that a small continent like Europe was able to conquer and colonize the world. In many ways this global domination by the West continued for a surprisingly long time. But I think it's finally coming to a natural end. So the challenge for the West is, will it accept its loss of power in the global system or will it resist the transfer of power?"

WHAT IS THE SHADOW MARKET?

The shadow market isn't a physical entity. It has no headquarters, bourse, or formal leadership. It isn't even a single zone of exchange in the way that we typically define a financial market. Rather, it's the invisible and ever-shifting global nexus where money mixes with geopolitical power. In specific terms, the shadow market is a collection of unaffiliated, extremely wealthy nations and investors that effectively run the international economy through their prodigious holdings of stocks, bonds, property, currencies, and other financial instruments, which they keep in largely unregulated investment vehicles such as hedge funds, private equity funds, and government-run sovereign wealth funds, as well as in vast government-owned holding companies. A 2009 McKinsey Global Institute study concluded that, as of late 2008, more than £8 trillion in assets was controlled by such oil-rich states as Saudi Arabia, Kuwait, and Abu Dhabi; the wealthy Asian nations of China, Japan, and South Korea; and hedge funds and private equity funds. What's more, McKinsey predicted that the assets of nations in Asia and the Persian Gulf are poised to grow by more than 50 percent within five years.

This pile of capital is the basis for the shadow market's power, for liquidity is the key to a functioning market. Looking back more than a century, nearly every world financial crisis has been caused by a sudden lack of liquidity—typically during tough economic times, when fear sets in among investors. At that point, banks and other finance companies start hoarding cash rather than investing it or lending it out, which, as the West learned in 2008, can strangle the economy rather suddenly.

In a capitalist world, the most powerful entities are those that provide the most liquidity. Since wealthy sovereign nations have the deepest pockets, they're in the best position to provide the liquidity the market needs. In practical terms, this transformation can be seen in major property transactions throughout Europe and the United States, where shadow market countries have been eagerly snapping up trophy properties for what they consider to be bargain basement prices from their previous highs before Western economies started tanking. In Britain, for example, Middle Eastern nations have been active investors because the remaining legacy of colonial bonds makes property here especially appealing. "There is a strong British influence in the [Persian] Gulf," says Fadi Moussalli, the Dubai-based head of Middle Eastern and North African operations for the global real estate investment consulting firm Jones Lang LaSalle. "There is a strong British lobby here and very close economic ties, cultural ties, historical ties. These countries were former British colonies. So there's a huge focus on Britain when it comes to investing."

For example, Moussalli points to the Shard London Bridge, the skyscraper designed to be the tallest building in western Europe, as the kind of project that likely would never get off the ground without Persian Gulf oil wealth. When the £2 billion plan nearly unraveled in late 2008 as the Qatari development group constructing the tower started to miss its funding targets, the financiers putting together the deal realized that the magnitude of the shortfalls was too large for any single bank to handle. The usual fix—gathering a consortium of lenders—would be too slow and cumbersome. So they quietly asked their home country for help. Specifically, they tapped Qatari Diar, the property company owned by Qatar's sovereign wealth fund, for a generous loan of an "undisclosed amount"—reportedly £430 million—that assured the Shard would be built.

The nation of Qatar has been aggressively investing in central London property from London Bridge to Knightsbridge. Over the past few years, Qatari investment vehicles have spent billions of pounds on properties such as Harrods department store, the Chelsea Barracks, the US embassy building at Grosvenor Square, the Canary Wharf financial district, and numerous London apartment buildings and hotels. And Qatar has expressed interest in helping the UK to finance and develop the facilities needed for the 2012 Olympic Games.

"Real estate investing in the West in 2010 is really about the financial crisis," Moussalli says. "Everything that the [Persian] Gulf States and other rich countries are buying today has the smell of blood and flesh and distress in it. Real estate is trading at a discount from its highs of 2007. So this is an opportunity to benefit from the global market dislocation. I don't think they're overpaying for these properties. A lot of these guys are my clients–they are shrewd, they are tough negotiators, and they squeeze every vendor down to get their price. And right now they're timing the real estate market in the West and building their portfolios."

Working together, the members of the shadow market could supply enough capital to stave off any global economic calamity. They have that much money at their disposal. But the catch is that the members are reluctant to work together to solve global problems. Instead they prefer to protect their own interests and zones of influence first. So, wealthy neighbors in the Persian Gulf, such as Abu Dhabi and Kuwait, will readily cooperate on different projects and initiatives. But those same Persian Gulf nations are far less likely to go along with a country like China or Singapore. America once could use its commanding position as the world's unquestioned economic leader as a galvanizing force behind cooperative solutions to global financial problems. It steered many of the key decisions among the Group of Seven nations, or G7, the collection of leading economies consisting of Canada, France, Germany, Italy, Japan, the UK, and the US. But neither the US alone nor the G7 together can dominate this market. Instead they now has to play by someone else's rules.

To get a sense of what this loss of financial control means, recall again the crisis of 2008, when the United States sought help from shadow market countries and was rebuffed. To the shadow market, it was too late to bail out America. As Lou Jiwei, head of the China Investment Corporation (CIC), China's primary sovereign wealth fund, bluntly told the Clinton Global Initiative conference in Hong Kong in December 2008, "China can't save the world. It can only save itself." And that's precisely what China and the other wealthy shadow market countries did.

Starting in late 2008, China pumped £400 billion of capital into its own economy in a stimulus plan to bolster the Chinese stock market and the country's businesses. Throughout the Middle East, neighboring countries bailed each other out, the most notable of which was Abu Dhabi's financial rescue of Dubai, which ran into serious investment trouble and almost collapsed. In Kuwait, the country's sovereign wealth fund set up a special multibillion-dinar investment vehicle that was only allowed to buy shares of local companies in order to prop up the Kuwait Stock Exchange, which had fallen nearly 40 percent.

None of these expenditures involved permanently saddling the nations with unmanageable levels of debt. Remarkably, China didn't even have to dip into its stock reserves during the crisis. The shadow market countries had the financial or natural resources to support their own economies. The cash-strapped West, on the other hand, couldn't possibly embark on such significant capital-intensive projects. It simply didn't have the money in its coffers. So their economies suffered—mightily.

QUESTION: HOW BIG IS THE SHADOW MARKET?
ANSWER: BIGGER

So how has this mighty new shadow market emerged seemingly overnight? Consider a few key points:

- China, Japan, and other wealthy nations hold vast investments in global currencies. For instance, as of July 2010 China's central bank, the People's Bank of China, announced that it controlled roughly £1.6 trillion in foreign exchange reserves, which are held by a government-run agency called the State Administration of Foreign Exchange, or SAFE. In 2006 China passed Japan as the world's largest owner of foreign exchange reserves. By 2009, SAFE's foreign exchange investments accounted for nearly a third of the world's total currency holdings. Still, China and Japan aren't alone. Other

6

major holders of foreign exchange reserves around the world include Russia, India, South Korea, and Brazil. Combined, they're sitting on trillions and trillions too.

- For most of the twentieth century, the bulk of America's public debt was held by US-based institutions, such as mutual funds and corporate and government pension funds. But since 2007, more than 60 percent of American debt has been owned by nonresident foreign investors and independent governments—primarily rich Asian nations such as China, Japan, and Singapore. China, the largest owner of US Treasury securities in the world, held £600 billion worth of American debt as of April 2010.

- Sovereign wealth funds (SWFs) are now a global phenomenon. These government-owned investment vehicles are managed separately from a country's debt and currency reserves. As of December 2010, roughly £2.5 trillion in global capital was managed through different SWFs, up from £600 billion in 1999, according to the Sovereign Wealth Fund Institute. The largest funds belong to oil-rich nations and industrial powerhouses such as Abu Dhabi, Saudi Arabia, China, Singapore, Kuwait, Russia, and Norway. Abu Dhabi's primary SWF still has more than £300 billion in assets even after taking a severe hit during the most recent financial crisis and contributing billions to bail out neighboring Dubai. That's a lot of cash. Abu Dhabi is hardly alone. The International Monetary Fund (IMF) projects that the total assets managed through SWFs will rise to more than £6.5 trillion within the next few years as the size and number of funds explodes. Fast-growing countries such as India and Brazil are developing plans for their own funds. Indeed, SWFs have become the height of fashion in global finance. An example can be found in the fallout of the massive BP oil spill in the Gulf of Mexico. As the cost of the cleanup escalated, the value of BP shares was sliced in half. By July 2010, BP executives had become concerned that the weakened company was vulnerable to a takeover. They needed financial help, fast. So who did they approach? Not Western banks of the governments of the United States or the United Kingdom. Instead, they reached out to the real arbiters of liquidity in the financial markets, the sovereign wealth funds in Abu Dhabi, Kuwait, Qatar, and Singapore, each of which owned a small position in BP. Then CEO Tony Hayward flew out to meet personally with "key business partners." Kuwait rejected the request out of hand, but the others remained noncommittal. So why did BP executives choose this tack? Because they knew that these SWFs controlled enough cash to easily help the company out of a tight spot in the shortest amount of time. That's the essence of the shadow market's power.

- Foreign investors account for 40 percent of all property deals in the United Kingdom. In fact, these investors are gobbling up prime properties as quickly as they can: They have bought 70 percent of the London residential property sold at a price tag of £5 million or more. More than half of current home purchases in prime central London neighborhoods are made by overseas buyers, and overall, roughly one in ten London home buyers is a second-home buyer from the Middle East.

- The spending spree on trophy properties has hit very close to home. In September 2008, when Abu Dhabi's sovereign wealth bought Manchester City Football Club for £200 million, it marked the first time that a foreign *government*, as opposed to a wealthy foreign investor, has owned a premier European football club. Since then, the club's Abu Dhabi ownership has spent lavishly to pursue star players from all over the world.

- Private unregulated investment vehicles such as hedge funds and private equity funds now set the tone for the behavior of the financial markets. Hedge funds are unregulated mutual funds that often capitalize on complicated trading schemes to generate profits. Private equity funds, on the other hand, like those owned by ultrasecretive New York firms like the Blackstone Group and the Carlyle Group, are designed to take over undervalued businesses, clean up the books, streamline the operations, and resell them for a tidy profit. As of January 2011, hedge funds and private equity funds controlled more than £2.5 trillion in assets. Obviously, that's a smaller pile of capital compared to the vast sums commanded by such superrich countries as China, Abu Dhabi, Singapore, and Kuwait. Still, these funds' innovative and sophisticated investment techniques have given them levels of influence far beyond their size and scope, leading the shadow market herd into new sectors, securities, and asset classes.

- To put all of these numbers and statistics in a broader context, consider that the McKinsey Global Institute estimates that by 2013, the governments of countries in Asia and the Persian Gulf, global hedge funds, and private equity funds will control more than a combined £12.5 trillion in assets. How much money is that? Consider that the gross domestic product (GDP) of the United States is expected to be around £10.6 trillion in 2013, and the GDP of the European Union is expected to be around £12 trillion, according to estimates by the IMF. In other words, a financial force larger than both the US and the European economies will be at play in the capital markets. And this dwarfs the UK, which is expected to have a GDP of just £1.7 trillion. On its own, China's central bank, which controls more than £1.3 trillion in assets, is already the largest single investor in the world, bigger than any major multinational money management firm, from Barclays Bank to Fidelity Investments to State Street Corporation to BlackRock. And numerous other wealthy nations aren't far behind China. When you consider everything on the table, there's really only one conclusion: The shadow market soon will be the most powerful financial force on the face of the earth—if it isn't already.

- Numerous Western industries have been gutted—retail, car

manufacturing, industrial manufacturing, and the media, to name a few—and consumers have struggled with joblessness, high debt levels, and stagnant incomes. As a result, the US and the UK have stumbled around in a general sense of fear and stasis and political impotence. But not the shadow market. It's kept moving forward. In particular, many of the shadow market countries have launched an unprecedented scramble to buy the world's resources while they're still available. China has been insuring itself future access to oil, minerals, food, and anything else it cannot supply for itself. The number of deals around the globe is staggering, and, in some countries, the presence and power of Chinese companies have effectively created neocolonial relationships, with Chinese corporations and officials calling the shots within their own overseas fiefdoms. China also has forced its way into ownership of the world's cutting-edge technologies in engineering, computers, and high-end manufacturing. For example, in October 2010, China unveiled the world's fastest supercomputer, the Tianhe-1A, which can make more than 2.5 thousand trillion calculations per second.

What makes the shadow market truly different, and more dangerous, than any financial force the world has ever known is the fact that it consists primarily of independent governments—many of them rivals of the US, UK, and other Western nations and all willing to use their capital to advance political, rather than financial, aims. For centuries, Western powers have practiced a corporate form of capitalism in which power was derived from the development of newer and bigger companies. The government's involvement in the nation's economic system extended to regulation and taxation, but other than that, it typically tried to get out of the private sector's way. The system was so successful that economists and political scientists came to the conclusion that a capitalist economy naturally led to a politically democratic government on the symbiotic grounds that once people tasted economic freedom, they'd demand the political variety as well.

The shadow market, however, has turned all of that upside down. For the most part, the countries of the shadow market have employed capitalist strategies to amass their fortunes. But even though they've used capitalist tools, many are hardly "free" countries politically or economically. Instead they adopted a nationalistic form of capitalism where the state created companies and investment funds that could participate in the global economy. But the money generated by these entities doesn't belong to the company, its workers, or its shareholders, the way in America IBM's profits belong to IBM or in Britain Tesco's profits belong to Tesco. Instead most of the money from these companies and investment vehicles rolls up to the state, giving the government the power to determine how to deploy the bulk of the capital generated by its economy.

That's why the shadow market's rise has fundamentally changed the way we view the economic world. It's not just corporate greed that we have to watch out for anymore, it's geopolitical power plays as well. Major investors can have completely divergent agendas from the countries where they're investing, and sometimes they can make financial moves that have more to do with politics than economics. This helps explain why in June 2009 China jumped at the chance to pay £700 million for forty-five million shares of Morgan Stanley to go along with stock it had bought earlier. The purchase gave China a combined 10 percent ownership stake in Morgan Stanley, which was in addition to its 10 percent stake in Blackstone Group. Now China certainly could turn a profit from its Morgan Stanley position. But investment returns didn't appear to be what the deal was about. Instead let's say that one day in the not-too-distant future, China develops an even greater problem with America's dollar policy. Well, it's one thing for China to approach the US Treasury Department as a rival superpower. But it's quite another to do it as the owner of 10 percent of Morgan Stanley and 10 percent of the Blackstone Group, not to mention the holder of about £1.3 trillion worth of US currency reserves and debt instruments.

To make matters even more complicated, there's practically

no regulatory oversight of the shadow market's activities. Why? Because its deals often take place in foreign countries and therefore are cloaked under the different financial rules established by each country. So we regularly have no idea what's happening until after it's happened. The potential for conflicts of interest can be right on the surface. Yet there's little or nothing we can do about it.

Not that the Western governments are all that interested in clamping down on the shadow market's activities right now. Indeed, the global economy has become so intertwined that our future success is tied to the shadow market's continued support. As Brad Setser, an economist in the Obama administration's National Economic Council, stated in an influential September 2008 report for the Council on Foreign Relations called *Sovereign Wealth and Sovereign Power*: "The United States' main sources of financing are not allies. Without financing from China, Russia, and the [Persian] Gulf States, the dollar would fall sharply, US interest rates would rise, and the US government would find it far more difficult to sustain its global role at an acceptable domestic cost."

In other words, through these investments, we've become entwined with rival nations in conflicting and potentially dangerous ways that we never could have imagined just five years ago. That's why Michael McConnell, the former director of national intelligence, told the US Congress in his 2008 threat assessment report that one of his most serious concerns about America's long-term security is "the financial capabilities of Russia, China, and the OPEC countries, and the potential use of their market access to exert financial leverage to achieve political ends."

These fears have never been more on target and never more true than today. As we are about to see, the countries and entities that comprise the shadow market have been very busily pursuing their new world order, changing the global economy more rapidly than most of us could ever imagine.

CHAPTER 1

Money Is a Weapon

Tuesday, 17th March 2009, was a typically brisk, rainy weekday in late-winter Washington, DC. Other than an unusually angry wind gusting in off the Potomac River, events were fairly quiet in the district, just another normal business day.

But about thirty miles north of the White House, at the Johns Hopkins University Warfare Analysis Laboratory in Laurel, Maryland, things were far from normal. There, a group of America's top military and intelligence officials had come together in secret to watch the work of several dozen innocuous-looking men and women who were gathered in a large war room around a series of V-shaped tables. For the most part, the military and intelligence leaders kept their eyes trained on a bank of video screens, on which deadly conflicts from across the globe were playing out. To their dismay, the United States was losing over and over again.

Fortunately these battles weren't real. Instead they were part of a new war game exercise unlike anything the Pentagon's military strategists had ever come up with. While these types of planning events typically involve strategic bombing campaigns and deployments of fighting forces, this one ignored all that. Instead it was based exclusively on economics. The weapons were dollars, bonds, and stocks. And the grunts on the ground were government economists, academics, hedge fund traders, and Wall Street banking executives. The idea was to simulate what would happen if the world disintegrated into a series of full-fledged financial wars. And as the battles played out over the two-day exercise, America's military brass continually found that their hands were tied. There was no way for America to win. Regardless of what happened in the world and how the United States responded to it, they ultimately ended up losing—to China. The results presented a deeply sobering reality for our veteran war strategists.

"Basically what we saw was that China can hurt us in all kinds of ways because of their enormous amount of financial reserves and our huge national debt," says Paul Bracken, a professor of management and political science at the Yale School of Management and a leading expert on financial warfare. "What's probably most troubling is that they don't even have to really do anything to influence us. They can just go to the fundamental insight of game theory, which is that you only have to be able to threaten to do it to have an effect. The key is having something to back up the threat. And China has that with its capital and our debt."

THE FUTURE IS NOT A GAME

Although the Pentagon technically considered the clandestine exercise "unclassified," there are no official records of it available to the public. The Warfare Analysis Laboratory will confirm only that the event took place. The US Defense Department won't discuss it. And most of the military officials and civilian financial experts who participated and *were* willing to speak insisted that their conversations remain "on background." Few would allow their names to be used publicly. Clearly this was a hush-hush operation.

That said, several of the participants believe that it's important for the public to understand the emerging threats we face in the new economic world. So they were eager to explain in general terms how the war games worked: Several dozen economists and finance professionals divided themselves into teams representing different countries and regions, such as the United States, China, eastern Asia, and so on. They then holed up for two days in a room facing a massive digital wall awash with economic data that were constantly being updated. Several of the participants said the scene reminded them of something out of the 1964 Cold War dark comedy *Dr. Strangelove or: How I Stopped Worrying and Learned to Love the Bomb*.

The teams were overseen by a group of neutral proctors who presented different potential geopolitical and financial scenarios, such as a belligerent nuclear threat by North Korea or Iran or a dramatic move up or down in natural gas prices. The proctors then judged each team's response. The participants were told to use all of the resources at their disposal to gain global economic dominance while reacting to these events. Meanwhile, leaders from different branches of the US armed forces and intelligence community anxiously watched the proceedings and took reams of notes about what was going on.

The war games themselves were nothing like what one might imagine based on what we've all seen in movies and on television, where distressed military officers and nuclear technicians frantically run around the White House situation room trying to stop a multinational disaster before it engulfs the world. Instead these proceedings were calm and deliberative, devoid of emotional outbursts or shouting matches. Each team methodically went through its options and their consequences before responding. America and Russia, once the world's lone superpowers, were unintentionally inhibited in their responses because they were continually drawn into costly diverting struggles that sapped their economic strength. At the same time, China showed a surprisingly nimble ability to use its vast holdings of currency and debt reserves as a powerful cudgel against the rest of the world, particularly the United States.

"China showed that she could be very sophisticated in the financial markets and use them to her advantage," Bracken says.

"For example, China could simply move the maturity of some of its Treasuries from ninety to sixty days and it would send shock waves through the New York Stock Exchange without affecting China that much. We know that and the games showed it."

In fact, whenever America did something that China didn't approve of, China started dumping a small portion of its dollar-based assets, which included US Treasury bonds and other holdings in addition to currency. These sales, representing just a tiny fraction of China's overall dollar portfolio, would flood the financial markets with US currency and cause its value to plunge as demand suddenly dried up. In America, this drop in the value of the dollar would trigger just enough economic chaos to force political leaders to rethink their policies and appease the Chinese. In the meantime, China still could hold on to enough US currency and debt to make life difficult for Americans whenever it desired. That's why China was the unequivocal winner at the end of the two days. It wound up being the richest country on earth and could use that power to get what it wanted.

Specifically, China used its vast capital reserves to buy clandestine relationships with several nations, especially Russia, and gain influence over the entire Far East region.

In the case of Russia, the Chinese team coveted its neighbor's rich supply of natural resources as a partial solution to the demands of its rapidly growing economy. Meanwhile, the Russian team was eager to get its hands on China's capital to pay for possible military interventions along its western border. So China and Russia worked together on secret arrangements that funded Russia's geopolitical incursions while funneling valuable natural resources into China. Meanwhile, the US team had no idea this collusion was going on until the deals were done.

"People left the room thinking that the US lost sight of what the hell it was trying to do," Bracken says. "The problem was the US had the wrong objective, which was to demonstrate leadership to the world without regard to its cost. So we got into a conflict with

Russia and spent a lot of money we didn't have. And China won because we lost sight of how much money we had and our deficits got too high. China, for its part, played a more businesslike strategy. It locked up resources, played conservatively, and did pretty much all the things it's doing in the world today. I think the key was China didn't set out to be a global superpower. It was just interested in taking care of China."

Even more troubling to America's military and intelligence strategists was how the games revealed a fundamental misunderstanding of the West's seemingly codependent financial relationships with China and the other wealthy countries that hold a lot of US and European currency and debt. As it turns out, these relationships aren't so simple. For instance, it's no secret why China has roughly $2 trillion in various US holdings. It holds these assets for financial security. As China's national wealth has grown, it has eagerly acquired these positions because the dollar and US debt have long been considered among the safest investments in the global financial markets. Why? Because the US economy is the largest and most diverse in the world, so investors have traditionally considered it extremely unlikely that the country would default on its financial obligations. In the meantime, the reason that the United States so eagerly accepted China's capital was that we needed the money. As a result, China became America's banker.

The catch was that the United States always assumed that there was a twist in the financial relationship that gave it some leverage. There's an old financial proverb attributed to the billionaire oil magnate J. Paul Getty that goes: "If you owe the bank $100, that's your problem. If you owe the bank $100 million, that's the bank's problem." In other words, if you owe a lender a relatively small sum, it can control your relationship and make life difficult for you because a loss on your loan means little to the institution. But if you owe a lender a lot of money, *you* control the relationship, because your lender has a vested interest in keeping you afloat, even during hard times, since it eventually needs to get its cash back. After all, if the economy collapsed, its investments would lose value too. So everybody would be poor. What would be the point of that?

Of course, this perspective is in many ways just an economic extension of the foreign policy doctrine of mutually assured destruction. The idea, which became popular during the Cold War, is that as long as two military superpowers have enough weaponry to annihilate each other, neither will be willing to strike first. So the countries end up in a deadly stalemate.

Over the past decade, as US and European debt load has sky-rocketed, the concept of mutually assured destruction has become the central economic metaphor for the West's financial dilemma. With the economy weakening, foreign interests, particularly China, have provided the West with needed investment capital. As a result, they've also amassed those increasingly sizable ownership positions in US and European government debts, corporate bonds, shares, and currencies—especially the dollar. One would think that this encroaching foreign influence would deeply concern the West. But the sad truth is that our economic conditions have eroded so dramatically that we've become willing, even eager, to accept money from anyone who can provide it. In historical terms, this is a recent development, and we're still getting acquainted with the painful reality of what's happened. But the bottom line is that we've deluded ourselves that foreign nations that own trillions of dollars, pounds, and euros of debt and currency reserves are actually our partners, not rivals.

This belief, of course, assumes that there are only two choices for a country that owns a tremendous amount of its rival's financial reserves: keep them or dump them. The economic war games, however, revealed a third option. As it turns out, if Country A owns a lot of Country B's currency and debt and doesn't like Country B's foreign policy, all Country A has to do is sell a trickle of its holdings, signal its "lack of confidence" in Country B as an investment, and let the international financial markets do the rest, destroying the value of Country B. Call this concept the weapon-ization of global capital. Eventually the pressure will build until Country B's government relents. If not, the value of its currency and stock market will plummet into free fall, which can trigger any number of economic catastrophes—from runaway inflation to a prolonged recession—that no government wants to confront. This isn't a partnership at all. Country A, in essence, has an eco-nomic weapon of mass destruction that it can point squarely at Country B whenever it wants.

For the West, this means that the sheer size of our national debts—and the fact that it's largely held by many of our global rivals—has reduced our potential geopolitical influence, because we really are controlled by the countries that have invested in us. They, in effect, are our shareholders.

While this outcome may be shocking to some, the sad truth is that many members of the US intelligence community weren't all that surprised (although the decisiveness of China's financial dom-inance did catch just about everyone off guard). The reality is that many government experts have been planning for this possibility for some time. The idea of holding economic war games came up during former president George W. Bush's first term, long before Michael McConnell, Bush's top intelligence official, spelled out the potential threats in a February 2008 risk assessment report to the US Congress. "Public statements by Chinese leaders indicate that Beijing perceives itself as being in the midst of a twenty-year 'win-dow of opportunity' favorable to China's growth, development, and rise of influence," McConnell told the Senate Armed Services Committee. "As China's influence grows, Beijing probably will increasingly expect its interests to be respected by other countries."

So, really, how stunned could the people who've been exam-ining these projections for years have been by the results of their economic war games? Indeed, the entire concept behind the exer-cise, which the Pentagon spent more than two years developing, was to figure out America's vulnerabilities, not its strengths. The planners operated under the presumption that the United States had put itself in a significantly weakened position, perhaps permanently. As one intelligence veteran who helped organize the event put it, "You don't spend all this time and money studying an issue unless you think there might be a problem. It's like, you don't go to a mechanic unless you think there's something wrong with your car. And surprise, surprise, we found out that there's something really wrong with our car."

Speaking to various national intelligence specialists, it becomes clear that several related developments over the past decade have magnified the seriousness of America's weakened financial condition. The main change is the way that the technology revolution has shrunk the world, at least metaphorically, and completely transformed the global capital markets.

Today information moves around the planet in a fraction of a second. Since markets feed on information, the primary effect of these technological advancements has been to open up the global financial markets, and particularly Wall Street, to anyone who might want to participate. Now small, wealthy countries like the Persian Gulf oil states can easily buy and sell piles of stocks, bonds, and currencies all day, every day. The process is much easier than it ever was before. And it's enabled them to spread their sovereign wealth all over the world as major investors in ways they never thought possible, while becoming wildly rich in the process. Meanwhile, large nations that are loaded with capital can amass unprecedented war chests filled with stocks, bonds, real estate, and foreign currency reserves, which they can use to get the resources that their populations require.

To understand the geopolitical significance of this enormous global transformation, consider that US intelligence officials estimate that by around 2030 China will surpass America and become the largest national economy on earth. Today China produces about 75 percent of its energy from coal, while the United States generates about 65 percent of its energy from oil and natural gas.

Coal-powered energy is typically a dirty business that pollutes the atmosphere far more than energy generated by oil and gas, not to mention renewable, environmentally friendly energy sources such as solar and wind power. The nation's leadership realizes this and is beginning to shift China to a more petroleum-based power system that also incorporates alternative energy sources. And it's doing so largely by using the country's mounds of capital to strike deals with oil- and gas-producing nations, from Russia to Venezuela, which will give the Chinese people access to needed reserves.

China's development guarantees that in the near future, the global demand for oil and gas is going to increase sharply as the country's economy expands. And from the West's perspective, this means that China presents a formidable competitor for a limited resource that still largely powers our enormous economy. We're going to have to compete for the resources we need. As one finance expert who participated in the war games predicts, "Our next major global conflict will be over access to energy resources. That's the fault line. It's almost inevitable that we'll butt heads with China over it."

BEHOLD THE DOLLARIZED GLOBE

The global battle for natural resources is nothing new in the history of human civilization. For thousands of years, gaining control of precious resources has been the driving force behind the expansion of geopolitical empires, from the Greeks and the Romans to the French and the British. Nation-states have consistently used their militaries for economic purposes, securing access to different foods, spices, metals, and minerals, blockading one another's ports, and enforcing embargoes. But in general, historical global trade disputes were relatively simple affairs. The biggest empire with the most military strength and broadest reach dominated the world.

This changed after World War II, when the United States emerged as a new kind of global power. In America, the world had an empire based on commerce and finance rather than geographical expansion. Although the United States maintained a network of military bases across the globe, it didn't, for the most part, physically conquer other countries. Instead it would meddle with other countries' political leadership to create new markets for its burgeoning capitalist economic system. Along the way America ushered in a brand-new system of international finance, one based on the buying and selling of financial instruments rather than hard goods. And that, in the end, wound up transforming the world.

Consider America's immediate predecessor, the British Empire. At the dawn of the twentieth century, the British Empire encompassed about thirteen million square miles of land mass, or about one-fourth of the face of the earth, scattered throughout Asia, Africa, the South Pacific, and North America. It controlled roughly a quarter of the planet's population and was considered the largest and most sophisticated empire in the history of mankind. Still, its strength was based on the classic geopolitical model of conquering new territory to acquire critical resources and create new markets to trade goods.

The first factor that distinguished the United States from Britain was that America was a contiguous empire with a rich assortment of natural resources within its borders; by the 1880s, it already had much of what it needed to feed, clothe, and shelter its population and had begun the process of commercially linking the East and West coasts. As a result, when the US started to emerge as a global economic power in the late nineteenth century, it wasn't particularly interested in cobbling together a large collection of overseas colonies. This self-sufficiency lasted until the mid-twentieth century, when oil emerged as the one precious resource the US could not control.

The second differentiating factor between the United States

and its predecessors was that America was largely a "private sector" empire driven by a capitalist instinct rather than an imperialist instinct. Although the United States ultimately established an enormous government superstructure in Washington featuring what former president Dwight Eisenhower famously termed the "military-industrial complex" in 1960, the nation at its core remained ideologically predisposed toward creating an inviting environment for commerce rather than expanding its geopolitical power. Indeed, prior to World War II American foreign policy pursued isolationism, not imperialism. The United States really just wanted to be left alone. So instead of invading countries, America's demands generally focused on prying open trading markets for the growing businesses that sold its goods and services.

Even when you look at America's imperial incursions, they were typically based on advancing the cause of commerce and trade. For example, consider its hold on the Panama Canal Zone, which began in the early twentieth century under Republican president and former war hero Theodore Roosevelt. Back in the mid-nineteenth century, when the idea of building a canal that would enable ships to cut across Central America and move from the Atlantic Ocean to the Pacific Ocean without going all the way around the tip of South America first gained popularity, the area belonged to Colombia. France, which had tremendous success building the Suez Canal in Egypt, first tried to create a canal in the Panamanian territory starting in 1880. But the French gave up after nine years. Roosevelt, however, refused to let go of the concept. It was too important to America's economic interests—and particularly to the nascent oil companies that were transporting petroleum from California to the East Coast and needed to reduce their shipping time. Something had to be done.

First Roosevelt tried to pay off the Colombian government to gain access to the land. But that failed. So he sent a battleship armed with marines down to the isthmus. Their orders were to cooperate with a collection of Panamanian rebels who wanted to break away from Colombia and form their own independent country. Within months, the US and Panamanian fighters forced Colombia to grant the territory its independence. Then Roosevelt and the new Panamanian government quickly signed a ninety-nine-year lease that gave the United States access to a fifty-mile-long, ten-mile-wide strip of land where American engineers could construct a canal. That's the way American economic diplomacy often worked before World War II.

After World War II, economic conditions around the world changed. Europe was physically decimated, and the United States, which by now had become the richest country in the world by most statistical measures, could afford to help rebuild the continent with the $12.4 billion European Recovery Program, also known as the Marshall Plan. US aid bought America a lot of diplomatic goodwill following the war, which it deployed in our new conflict against an emerging political and ideological rival: the communist empire of the Soviet Union. The Cold War dramatically changed economic warfare strategy, largely because the old ways didn't work anymore. The Soviet bloc didn't need to trade with the West, other than to gain access to technological advances. So the classic economic warfare tactics such as blockades and embargoes were irrelevant. Instead the two rivals engaged in a series of violent proxy wars along the front lines of smaller countries like Korea and Vietnam.

Meanwhile, US companies thrived in the postwar global economy. In an unofficial way, they helped serve as American ambassadors, promoting free-market capitalism by spreading out and selling their products all over the planet. The soldiers in this fight were desirable high-profile brands like Coca-Cola and Disney. In addition, the US financial community started loudly preaching the logic of using the financial markets to capitalize on compounded interest, showing the world how it could invest on Wall Street and make money off its money rather than just save it or spend it. America's major multinational banks—Chase Manhattan and Citicorp, J. P. Morgan and Goldman Sachs—provided liquidity throughout the world. And combined, these private-sector interests helped convert a large portion of the planet to accepting some form of American-style free-market economic ideology.

So by the time the Soviet Union formally collapsed in 1991, the United States had become the pacesetter for the rest of the world and established a new level of global stability. As the journalist and foreign policy expert Fareed Zakaria explained in 2008 in *Newsweek*: "Since the late 1980s, the world has been moving toward an extraordinary degree of political stability. The end of the Cold War has ushered in a period with no major military competition among the world's great powers—something virtually unprecedented in modern history. It has meant the winding down of most of the proxy and civil wars, insurgencies and guerrilla actions that dotted the Cold War landscape. Even given the bloodshed in places like Iraq, Afghanistan, and Somalia, the number of people dying as a result of political violence of any kind has dropped steeply over the past three decades."

Meanwhile, the United States cemented itself as the planet's lone economic superpower. America possessed an enviable number of major corporations producing a broad spectrum of products and providing a diverse array of services that were in high demand across the globe. Plus, US companies could find all the money they needed to grow in the country's intricate financial markets. Not surprisingly, numerous developed nations tried to mimic America's success and restructured their economies around Wall Street–style financial markets as well. Japan, in particular, rose from the ashes of World War II to become the world's second biggest economy largely by emulating America's strategies. But Japan was hardly alone. Indeed, looking at the world as a single financial entity, following the fall of the Soviet Union the global economy experienced previously unseen levels of growth and prosperity, as Zakaria also noted: "Over the past quarter century, the global economy has doubled every 10 years, going from $31 trillion in 1999 to $62 trillion in 2008. Recessions have become tamer than ever before, averaging eight months rather than two years. More than 400 million people across Asia have been lifted out of poverty. Between 2003 and 2007, average income world-wide grew at a faster rate (3.1 percent) than in any previous period in recorded human history."

Of course, during this period of radical worldwide growth, the United States continued to expand its financial reach. Soon the dollar replaced gold as the most stable financial instrument on earth in the eyes of international investors. In many ways, it became the closest thing we had to a global currency. As a result, more dollars were traded outside of America than were available in the nation's own domestic money supply. And by the 1990s, most of the devel-oped world had adopted capital markets modeled on those in the United States as key ingredients of their economic systems.

In many ways, we're now living in the global, free-market cap-italist society that America's big bankers and financiers always dreamed of. Today, more and more countries are freeing their companies to participate in Western financial markets and cre-ating their own capital markets to raise money for their develop-ing businesses. Money flows across the planet far surpass the value of worldwide physical trade. In 2007 the total value of all global imports and exports was $25 trillion (£12.5 trillion) for the entire year. Meanwhile, the world's currency markets, the largest finan-cial market on the planet, traded $3 trillion *a day*. And that figure doesn't even include all the cash moving around in other capital markets in search of investments in stocks, bonds, mutual funds, hedge funds, and so on. In short, more than America itself, Amer-ican-style capital markets have conquered the world.

Unfortunately, this development has brought its own set of consequences that one never could have foreseen. By linking the world's financial markets, a small spark in a relatively obscure corner of the globe can suddenly become a worldwide conflagra-tion. So more than ever, having access to lots of capital has become an essential factor in keeping a modern economy humming, particularly in difficult times. This means that the wealthier a country is, the better equipped it will be to handle the increasing number of financial crises we're bound to see as the global market economy continues to expand. We used to worry about an important country's economy collapsing because it could hurt the financial markets. Today, after the financial crisis in 2007 and 2008, we're more concerned about a hiccup in the markets wrecking an otherwise solvent nation. The game has changed permanently. The capital markets have taken over.

WHY THE TWENTY-FIRST CENTURY BEGAN IN 1995

To understand how these new linkages in the global financial system can quickly spread economic crises across the planet and how it takes the power of liquidity to stop a global contagion in its tracks, just look back to 1995 and America's response to the devaluation of the Mexican peso. Former US treasury secretary Robert Rubin has called the "tequila crisis," as it became known, the first real financial crisis of the twenty-first century. Rubin's point was that the fiasco that ensued following Mexico's decision to devalue the peso offered a stark example of the dangers posed by the evolution of the twenty-first-century global financial system.

In the early 1990s, the Mexican economy seemed to be stable and growing. The government and private sector were creating jobs. Global emerging-markets investors were eagerly pouring capital into the country, looking to strike it rich. And the nation's once cash-starved treasury was building up unprecedented stockpiles of foreign currency reserves. At the end of 1993, Mexico had $25 billion (£16 billion) worth of reserves, compared to just $6 billion in 1989. In the eyes of the global financial markets, this was a country on the rise.

But starting in early 1994, conditions changed drastically. First, in January, the Mexican government was forced to put down a bloody armed rebellion by Zapatista guerrillas in Chiapas, a poor agrarian state bordering Guatemala. Then, in March, Luis Donaldo Colosio, the immensely popular presidential candidate for the ruling Institutional Revolutionary Party (also known as the PRI) and the presumed next president of Mexico, was assassinated. The party named Ernesto Zedillo, a relatively unknown figure outside his country, as Colosio's replacement in the August election. Meanwhile, the mayhem continued. In June Alfredo Harp Helú, a fifty-year-old billionaire Mexican banking magnate, was kidnapped in Mexico City and held by gangsters for more than three months. His family ended up paying $30 million (£19 million) for his release. Then, in September, just a month after Zedillo won the presidential election, José Francisco Ruiz Massieu, the secretary-general of the PRI and a former Mexican deputy attorney general, was gunned down in front of the party's Mexico City headquarters.

Naturally, with all this instability, the global financial markets started to see Mexico as a far riskier investment. This had a devastating effect on the country's economy. The value of the peso tumbled, and Mexican interest rates shot up. To support the peso, the Mexican government decided to raid the nation's stockpile of foreign currency reserves. From February to December 1994, Mexico's reserves fell from $30 billion to less than $6 billion. And to make matters worse, Mexico owed $23 billion in tesobonos, short-term debt securities that the government had sold to get quick access to capital. By late autumn 1994, conditions were so grim that the financial markets were rife with bets on when Mexico would collapse.

In December, Mexico's leaders decided that the country had to reduce the value of the peso by 15 percent to realign the currency with financial reality. The peso historically had been valued on a "crawling peg" exchange rate tied to the US dollar. In 1993 the rate was around thirty American cents to the peso. But in 1994 Mexico spent roughly $15 billion maintaining this exchange rate. It couldn't afford to continue. So Mexican officials established a new lower exchange rate of twenty-five cents to the peso. But the plan didn't hold. Within days, the floor collapsed, and the peso was in free fall. Mexican officials had lost control of their currency.

Seeing no other option, on 22nd December the Mexican government decided to let the value of the peso "float" in the global capital markets. Almost immediately, it crashed, and Mexican interest rates started running wild. By the end of December, the peso was worth 35 percent less than it had been worth at the start of the month, and by January, its exchange rate had fallen to less than seventeen cents, a level not seen since the 1980s. To make matters worse, the government no longer could borrow money, even with bonds carrying interest rates of 20 percent, because lenders were petrified that they'd never see their cash again.

Meanwhile, in the rest of the global capital markets, all hell was breaking loose. Investments in emerging markets—from Latin American nations like Brazil and Argentina to more distant and seemingly unrelated countries like the Czech Republic and Thailand—dried up overnight. In the past, the problems in Mexico might have been considered an isolated issue involving a relatively minor currency. But now that the global financial markets had become intertwined, currency and bond traders saw Mexico's weakness as an ominous sign of things to come in other parts of the world.

For all the fears about emerging markets, the most important question raised by Mexico's economic implosion was, What would it mean for its neighbor to the north, the United States? Since so many international economies were tied to America, economists and finance experts were terrified that a peso meltdown would spread like a deadly virus across the Rio Grande and from there out to the rest of the world. Fortunately, Robert Rubin, the newly appointed treasury secretary, saw this as well and realized that America's only choice was to step in and stop the peso crisis before it crossed the border.

To do this, Rubin first had to convince then president Bill Clinton to arrange a dramatic and expensive intervention to save Mexico. Rubin argued that if the peso received no financial support, the Mexican economy would crumble. And this could have terrible consequences for the United States. Why? Mexico was America's third largest trading partner. That meant an economic crash there would directly hurt US businesses and hundreds of thousands of workers. In addition, the crisis was crippling global investments in developing markets around the world. At the time, roughly 40 percent of America's exports went to emerging-market countries. So the Mexican mess threatened US businesses and workers in other, less direct ways as well. In fact, a US Federal Reserve Bank study estimated that in the worst-case scenario, an economic disaster in Mexico could reduce the growth of America's gross domestic product by as much as 1 percentage point per year.

Regardless of Rubin's persuasiveness, there was no getting around the enormous cost of his plan. The Mexican rescue package was estimated at $40 billion (£25 billion), roughly $20 billion of which would have to come from the United States. These days that may not seem like a ton of money, but in 1994 the United States spent $28 billion on all of its different global intelligence programs combined. The entire budget for the Department of Education was $29 billion. And here Clinton was being asked to hand over that kind of money to another country. Not only that, but the US economy had somehow become tangentially linked to the weakness of the peso. To the president and his advisers, the whole notion seemed insane.

But as Rubin persisted, Clinton grasped the severity of the problem. Stepping over Congress, the president asserted his emergency executive authority to provide Mexico with $20 billion in loan guarantees. The IMF, in turn, put up nearly $18 billion, far more than it had ever lent to any entity in its fifty-year history. And Canada put up $1 billion. Almost miraculously, the effort started to work. Although the Mexican economy sank into a brutal recession in 1995, the infusion of capital enabled the country to return to the financial markets within a matter of months, reestablishing its own liquidity and ending the credit crunch. Indeed, between June 1995 and March 1996, Mexico raised roughly $8 billion from the sale of government bonds. The Mexican economy was on its way back to growth again.

Economists and politicians would take away countless lessons from the tequila crisis. But to any growing nation with aspirations for increased geopolitical influence, specifically countries like China, Russia, and the Persian Gulf oil states, the message was obvious: liquidity ruled. America, which was in a strong fiscal position at the time, had used its financial muscle to fix an economic meltdown in a neighboring country in order to protect its own economic interests. It was fortunate that the United States had the liquidity and the influence at the IMF to buy a solution before the real chaos hit. In this way, capital—or, more specifically, access to capital—had become a powerful weapon; one that moved much more rapidly than, and could possibly end up superseding, military might.

Of course, it was one thing for a growing country to gather enormous piles of assets as its economy expanded. But it was quite another thing to successfully put that capital to work in the global financial markets. This was the challenge for the wealthy countries of the burgeoning shadow market at the dawn of the twenty-first century: to take their mounds of reserves and invest them so that they could grow and benefit their populations, while also giving their governments increasing leverage over Western nations in need of cash. The only question for these countries was how to do it because they had such limited expertise in the ways of the modern financial markets. If only someone or something could help set the pace for them as investors; could provide a road map for turning a finite pile of money into a continuously regenerating supply of capital. All these piles of billions of dollars, as well as pounds and euros, needing a guiding hand. It didn't take long, of course, for the experts to arrive, eager to attack the future.

CHAPTER 2

How to Spend $4 Trillion

Rich foreign governments control impressive amounts of capital today, but they're relatively new to investing. Many investment officials for foreign governments know full well that they have a lot to learn to catch up with the most sophisticated players in the global financial markets. So rather than go it alone, the wealthy nations in the shadow market eagerly follow the "smart money," mimicking its moves and strategies, buying its expertise, and learning rapidly along the way.

In the shadow market, the smart money refers to the secretive managers of major private equity funds and hedge funds, who generally are considered the shrewdest investors in the world. The vast majority of these money managers are located in the United States and the UK. And they set the tone for the shadow market's behavior. Foreign governments have started buying sizable stakes in these private equity firms. For example:

- Over the last several years, China has invested £2 billion in the New York-based Blackstone Group and more than £600 million in the British private equity firm Apax Partners.
- Abu Dhabi has put £1.1 billion into the Carlyle Group and picked up a 40 percent stake in a fund operated by Apollo Management, the investment firm run by former Drexel Burnham Lambert investment banker Leon Black.

- Singapore has invested £4 billion in TPG Capital, the massive Fort Worth, Texas, private equity firm that was formerly known as Texas Pacific Group and is headed by the legendary investor David Bonderman.
- Kuwait has invested £500 million in the New York money manager BlackRock, which operates private equity and hedge funds. Kuwait also owns sizable stakes in major private equity firms such as Thomas H. Lee Partners, Oaktree Capital Management, and Kohlberg Kravis Roberts & Co. (KKR).

These private equity firms have used this money to execute their investment strategy, which, simply put, is to take over undervalued companies, streamline the operations, and then resell them for a profit. The foreign governments, in turn, have gained priceless access to some of the most sophisticated financial minds on the planet.

Firms controlled by these governments are also partnering with US investment specialists to set up their own investment funds. For example, an arm of China's sovereign wealth fund has formed a £1.8 billion private equity fund with Morgan Stanley, and the government of Shanghai created a joint venture with the Blackstone Group to establish a £466 million fund denominated exclusively in yuan. Meanwhile, the Korea Development Bank and KKR have solidified plans for a new private equity fund that would buy assets from "cash-strapped Korean companies," according to the private equities newsletter *AH Assets*.

Globally, private equity funds control about £1.6 trillion in assets and hedge funds control another £1 trillion. This combined $4-plus trillion—more than £2.5 trillion—makes these investment vehicles a significant but hardly overwhelming slice of the shadow market. However, their power is magnified multiple times over because of their influence over the behavior of the world's wealthiest foreign countries, each of which has hundreds of billions, if not trillions, of dollars in investment capital at their disposal. Wealthy countries have come to understand that it's not easy to successfully invest a pile of money in the modern financial markets. Take on too much risk, and you could squander your whole nest egg. Invest too conservatively, and you could miss out on the returns your rivals are enjoying.

That's where large private equity partnerships and hedge funds come in. They provide the investment expertise that these foreign countries require. A report by Chicago management employment firm Heidricks & Struggles noted that one of the clear employment trends in the financial industry in 2009 was Western investment professionals moving to international sovereign wealth funds. The firm said that it expected this pattern to accelerate in 2010. Chinese financial firms have held recruiting sessions in New York, London, and other cities and hired hundreds of workers with investment experience. Some SWFs in the Persian Gulf require that all of their new hires have previously worked at Western hedge funds or private equity firms.

Even more significant, these funds have supplied the models for wealthy nations to use to invest the riches that have fallen into their laps. They've given the shadow market its game plan.

OTHER PEOPLE'S MONEY

Let's look at how private equity operates in order to understand why SWFs are so eager to deploy its techniques. The term *private equity* is derived from the way that the partnerships operate, meaning that their investments in companies are negotiated in "private" rather than in "public" by buying stock through the stock market. The concept applies to a broad spectrum of financial activities, from venture capital (where early-stage developing businesses get much-needed backing from investors who want a significant long-range return and are willing to take on a lot of risk to get it) to mezzanine financing (where established companies are looking for short-term loans at better terms than they can get from a bank). But when most Wall Street professionals hear the phrase *private equity,* their first thought is "corporate takeovers." That's because this part of the business has turned out to be so lucrative that countless private equity shops have added it to their portfolios. In many circles, the expression *private equity* has simply replaced the 1980s term for corporate takeover: leveraged buyout, or LBO.

Whatever you want to call it—an LBO or private equity—the strategy of a buyout is still the same. The partners put their capital into a fund with other wealthy outside investors and then borrow money from banks and insurance companies to create a huge war chest. The lenders and outside investors are known as the fund's limited partners. With their cash in place, the private equity professionals then start using their fund to take over companies with the goal of cleaning up the financials and reselling them for a profit within about five years. Of course, the borrowed money— or what the financial world calls leverage—is the key to the success of these deals. With leverage, a small partnership can take over a much larger company while limiting its own financial exposure. And size is critically important to the private equity industry because large deals pay off much more handsomely than smaller ones.

A megabuyout, defined as a takeover costing more than £500 million, typically returns around 23 percent in its first year, compared to 11 percent for a deal that's worth less than £125 million, according to the National Venture Capital Association. This is the power of leverage: it can increase the return on an investment several times over. It helps explain why from 1996 to 2006 the average size of a buyout in the United States rose from £329 million to £828 million. And that doesn't include 2007, a record year for buyouts that featured the largest takeovers in history. In May 2007, Kohlberg Kravis Roberts bought the British drug store chain Alliance Boots for £11 billion. Then, in September 2007, KKR picked up the credit card processing company First Data Corporation for £13 billion. And finally, in October 2007, a consortium headed by KKR and David Bonderman's TPG took over the largest power generating company in Texas, TXU Corporation, for £16 billion. The TXU deal was the biggest corporate takeover of all time, and it remained that way through the financial collapse of 2008 and 2009. But the record probably won't last long. Once liquidity returns to the capital markets, and lenders regain their taste for risk and start looking for attractive investments, it's safe to assume that the megabuyouts will resume.

But regardless of the size of the deals, private equity can be a fabulously lucrative business because the partnerships have creative ways of making sure that they get paid—and paid well—before anyone else does. They immediately take 20 percent or more of the profits generated from each buyout. In financial parlance, this is called the partnership's "carried interest," and it's meant to give the private equity team a strong incentive for performance. It also reduces the fund's limited partners' take to 80 percent of the profits or less. In addition, private equity partnerships get an added management fee of 1.5 percent to 2.5 percent of the investment fund to cover the costs of administering the investments. Overall, it's a pretty sweet arrangement.

However, what's truly amazing is that private equity funds still are highly profitable ventures for investors, even with all the fees and the carried interest the partners grab for themselves. Limited partners in private equity funds can almost count on double-digit returns on their cash even in tough markets. From 1996 to 2006, private equity deals outperformed the Standard and Poor's (S&P) 500 index by a wide margin—in some years, by 15 percentage points or more. And in 2002, the highly difficult year following the 9/11 terrorist attacks, the S&P 500 fell about 10 percent. Meanwhile, the average private equity fund was slightly profitable, and the top quartile made nearly 10 percent. Even when the global financial markets bottomed out in late 2008 and 2009, the returns on private equity buyouts held up far better than the major stock market indices.

This explains why well-heeled investors and institutions have become increasingly interested in participating in private equity funds in recent years. In 1996 US private equity firms raised a total of £23.7 billion from investors for buyouts. By 2006, the figure was £160 billion and climbing. In other words, investors aren't being frightened off by private equity's high fees or carried interest. They just want a piece of the action.

PLUCKING NICKELS FROM THE AIR, A MILLION AT A TIME

Hedge funds, the other major investment vehicles that have influenced the investment decisions of the wealthy foreign governments in the shadow market, are different from private equity funds because they're not interested in corporate takeovers. Rather, they're trading vehicles that buy and sell a broad range of financial instruments: stocks, bonds, derivatives, currencies, and so on. In general, they profit by spotting price discrepancies in different financial markets and then exploiting those discrepancies, no matter how tiny, by trading securities in vast quantities over and over and over again. Many hedge fund traders describe what they do as "plucking nickels out of the air." Their logic is that a nickel may be worth a paltry five cents, but if you acquire enough of them over time, you'll become rich.

Of course, the wealthy governments in the shadow market also hold lots of stocks, bonds, currencies, and other financial instruments to trade in the financial markets. They just aren't nearly as nimble or savvy about it as the world's best hedge fund traders. So investment officials representing shadow market governments have begun actively seeking trading advice from influential hedge fund managers and have even started directly investing alongside them. For example, in June 2009, the China Investment Corporation decided to put a quarter billion pounds into a "fund-of-funds" hedge fund managed by its partner the Blackstone Group. A fund-of-funds investment means that the Blackstone hedge fund puts its money into other hedge funds run by other investment managers. Then, a month later, CIC said that it had hired Blackstone and Morgan Stanley to oversee capital that the SWF is investing in a collection of international hedge funds. This is how the shadow market is buying its way into the global financial industry.

Despite the shadow market's recent interest, hedge funds have been used for a long time. The first one was created by a man named Alfred Winslow Jones, a former writer for *Fortune* magazine who in 1949 launched an investment partnership called A. W. Jones & Co. The story goes that Jones had a key insight: that he could "hedge" his investments by using leverage to buy shares in a company while at the same time "selling short," or betting against, those same shares. If the price of the stock went up, Jones could profit from his leveraged position, and if the price fell, his short position would protect him on the downside. By themselves, the leveraged position and the short position were considered highly risky investments. But when paired together, they created a conservative trade. It wouldn't pay off in windfalls, but it wouldn't let investors lose their money, either. Jones saw this and decided to call his investment partnership a "hedged fund" because all of his investments would be hedged using his strategy. Eventually finance professionals and the business press dropped the *d* and referred to these investment partnerships as hedge funds.

Like so many legends, Wall Street's version of the hedge fund's creation offers a nice, neat story, but it's not altogether true. In this case, it ignores one crucial point. While investment partnerships may not have specifically used the term "hedged fund" or "hedge fund," the strategy of hedging investments existed long before Alfred Winslow Jones ever started dabbling in the financial markets. Indeed, Wall Street's first master at hedging trades—and probably the true creator of the hedge fund—was none other than Benjamin Graham, Warren Buffett's teacher and mentor, who's widely considered the father of "value investing."

As an investor, Graham was constantly looking for transactions that he considered riskless. He'd gotten burned in the 1930s during the Great Depression, and it stuck with him for the rest of his life. So he was petrified of losing money and closely evaluated the risk profile of every stock and bond his firm, Graham-Newman, bought. Graham's typical trades involved buying bonds in bankrupt companies and then selling short those companies' shares, or vice versa.

Trading strategies aside, what really makes hedge funds different from other, more common investment vehicles, like mutual funds, is that they've never really been regulated by the US Securities and Exchange Commission (SEC)—another important reason why they're attractive to major foreign investors like sovereign wealth funds. Hedge funds traditionally have been considered investment partnerships reserved exclusively for "qualified purchasers": meaning sophisticated financial players with at least several million pounds already invested in the markets. The idea was that everyone involved in such strategies knew what he or she was doing. And since the little people on Main Street weren't affected by them, the government saw no reason to get involved in overseeing them.

Hedge fund managers have long argued that this freedom from regulation provides them with the latitude they need to make their investment strategies work. But what the lack of oversight really has done is to hand them the ability to establish phenomenally lucrative payment schedules for themselves without anyone nosing around in their business. Like private equity firms, a hedge fund manager takes at least 20 percent of his fund's profits off the top, plus he collects an additional management fee of around 2 percent of the fund's total assets under management per year. So if you have a £50 million hedge fund (which is smaller than average) earning a 10 percent return in one year, you make £2 million that year—or £1 million from your fund's £5 million in profits, plus £1 million from your management fee. These outsized payment packages make the compensation plans at more heavily regulated investment outfits like mutual funds—which just collect management fees from their investors—appear downright penurious. However, this advantage is partly offset by the intense pressure hedge fund managers feel to justify their mammoth salaries with whopping returns for their investors.

Beyond this glaring lack of regulation, the single factor that truly transformed the hedge fund industry was the development of the computer. Using computer models, buying and selling stocks, bonds, commodities, and currencies became much faster and easier. Then, starting in the 1980s, traders began to experiment with technology to help them spot market inefficiencies that they never could have seen before. It was like pouring gasoline on Ben Graham's concept of riskless transactions and lighting a match. The business exploded. Suddenly, a computer could tell a trader that, say, the Thai baht was selling for slightly more in Singapore than in London. In the blink of an eye, that trader could buy baht in London and sell them in Singapore. The trades were so safe that the profits on each transaction were minuscule. But through the use of leverage, or borrowed capital, the trader could make the transaction over and over—furiously plucking nickels out of the air—until the returns piled up.

As technology made trading increasingly sophisticated, a new type of trader started to emerge at investment firms. Suddenly big-brained physicists and mathematicians from MIT and Harvard were showing up on trading floors, earning huge salaries to lead the global search for pricing anomalies to exploit, like the previous simple Thai baht example. Hedge funds became centers of financial innovation, remarkable profit-generating machines that seemingly churned out money without incurring any risk.

However, as it turns out, many hedge fund managers aren't nearly as clever or prescient as they'd like us to believe. Indeed, many high-profile managers were completely destroyed, or at least partially wiped out, when they couldn't see the collapse of the financial markets coming in 2008 and 2009. For example, Farallon Capital Management, a San Francisco hedge fund firm with £13 billion in assets, saw its largest fund lose more than 30 percent of its value in the downturn. The largest fund run by the Citadel Investment Group, a Chicago hedge fund firm with £6 billion in assets, lost 54 percent of its value. Perry Capital, run by investor and NYU professor Richard Perry in New York City, experienced its first-ever full-year loss in 2008, as its biggest fund was down 27 percent. And legendary investor John Meriwether, whose Long-Term Capital Management hedge fund nearly brought down the global financial markets in 1998, was forced to close up his new hedge fund, JWM Partners, after its flagship Relative Value Opportunity fund lost 42 percent of its value in 2008.

Then there's Bernie Madoff, best known in financial circles for his business as a NASDAQ "market maker"—meaning that his firm bought and sold NASDAQ stocks to facilitate trading. But Madoff also was quietly managing money for a select group of friends, wealthy individuals, and institutions. What was so notable about Madoff's money management business was his seemingly uncanny ability to post remarkable returns in good times and bad. In reality, as we all learned, the whole operation was a massive Ponzi scheme; Madoff kept his ruse going by paying his old investors with the money he brought in from new investors. But when the markets turned sour in 2008 and his investors started clamoring for their money back, his scam finally was exposed. In June 2009, Madoff was sentenced to 150 years in a US federal prison for his fraud. Most of his personal and professional assets have been liquidated. And his former investors are still fighting over what they're owed.

The discovery of Madoff's far-reaching crime was a true low point in the history of global finance. But that's the thing about the capital markets: they offer a constantly updating scorecard of winners and losers. And when you look at the historical performances of hedge fund managers, it's clear that some have far more reliable track records than others. For example, on the opposite end of the spectrum from Meriwether and Madoff are the other well-known and highly regarded hedge fund traders James Simons of Renaissance Technologies and John Paulson of Paulson & Co. While the rest of the financial world was falling apart in 2008, these two thrived. Was it an accident? Hardly. Paulson, in fact, started betting against the US housing market as far back as 2005, long before signs of a worldwide financial crisis appeared. He could just see that something was wrong, while other financial professionals continued to believe that everything was okay. In the end, he wound up personally taking home £1 billion in 2008.

Of course Paulson had Wall Street's help in securing his windfall. As the Securities and Exchange Commission later discovered, Paulson worked with Goldman Sachs to build a complex mortgage security that was specifically designed for him to bet against. The security was a form of a synthetic collateralized debt obligation. In simple terms, a collateralized debt obligation, or CDO, is a security whose value is based on the performance of a pool of loans, such as mortgages. A synthetic CDO is similar to a regular CDO except its value is based on derivatives like mortgage-backed securities that really are side bets on the performance of the pool of loans rather than the actual loans themselves. In essence, a synthetic CDO is one financial step removed from the pool of loans than a regular CDO.

According to the SEC, Paulson and Goldman structured their CDO to fail by loading it up with derivatives tied to junky high-risk mortgages. Goldman called the new debt security Abacus

2007-AC1 and aggressively marketed it to the firm's clients. Two outfits bought them, IKB Deutsche Industriebank AG and ACA Management LLC. But Goldman didn't tell its clients that Paulson had helped build Abacus and was shorting it on the other side. The synthetic CDO was so complex that even sophisticated financial minds couldn't spot the time bomb buried inside. With Goldman's help, Paulson had figured out a way to take the risk out of betting against the American real estate bubble. He made half a million pounds on the deal. And Goldman was only too happy to let Paulson do it since he paid the firm £7.5 million for the service and enabled Goldman to also make money betting against the US housing market. Meanwhile, the Abacus investors lost more than £500 million combined.

Unfortunately for Goldman Sachs, the SEC didn't view the Abacus CDO as a fair trade. Regulators argued that someone at Goldman should have told the firm's clients that the security had been specifically set up to explode. On 16th April 2010, the commission charged Goldman and its executive who headed the Abacus deal, Fabrice Tourre, with "defrauding investors by misstating and omitting key facts about a financial product tied to subprime mortgages as the housing market was beginning to falter." Goldman Sachs, once one of the most esteemed names on Wall Street, suddenly was considered a rogue firm and it would be forced to fight aggressively to avoid legal punishment. Paulson, on the other hand, walked away scot-free—richer, wiser, and with no legal entanglements. He wasn't even charged in the case. It turned out Paulson was only doing what a hedge fund manager was supposed to do to make money for his investors. Paulson was clever. But Goldman Sachs was crooked, according to the SEC.

This story offers a prime example of how the shadow market is able to operate by its own rules. In the United States, savvy hedge fund managers have been pushing the limits of financial regulation for decades. And it's here, in their trading prowess, their economic vision, and their ability to bully and game the global financial system that the most important hedge funds in America intersect with the wealthiest countries around the world. Because both are trying to use the capital markets to maximize the returns on their piles of cash. But these nations lack the technical trading abilities of their Wall Street rivals, so when it comes time for the countries of the shadow market to adjust their financial holdings—primarily changing their mix of foreign currency reserves, government-issued bonds, and commodities—they often take their cues from the most sophisticated hedge fund traders in the world. And symbiotically, major hedge fund managers, when devising their long-range outlooks, have to calculate what they think these rich countries are going to do with their financial holdings.

A case in point would be the active trading in gold during the first half of 2009. Like the rest of the global economy, the price of gold hit the skids in the autumn of 2008. It eventually leveled out in November, when gold's spot price—meaning the cash price in the commodities markets that changes from minute to minute—fell below $715 an ounce. But then something odd started to happen: the price of gold began to climb even as conditions in the overall global economy deteriorated further. Suddenly, by March 2009, the precious metal's spot price was up to $996 an ounce. That's a 40 percent increase in just four months. Although gold fluctuated a bit through the spring of 2009, by August, it was back around $950 an ounce. And by September, it had eclipsed $1,000 an ounce, a level the precious metal hadn't seen since May 2008.

What was going on? We can't know for sure, but it appears that some major players quietly entered the gold market and started buying the metal as a safety hedge against a potential collapse of the dollar. In April 2009, China revealed that it had been making substantial investments in gold for years—increasing its reserves by 76 percent since 2003—and called on the International Monetary Fund to sell its 3,217 tons of gold holdings so that the country could buy more. The specific details of precisely when China bought its gold and how much it paid are unknowable because all of its purchases were made in private deals that were beyond the disclosure requirements of global commodities exchanges. Meanwhile, throughout the spring of 2009, the commodities markets were rife with rumors that oil-rich countries like Saudi Arabia, Singapore, and Norway were moving substantial chunks of their cash reserves into gold. "It's difficult to know exactly what China or countries in the Middle East are doing when it comes to gold because you're relying on them to report their holdings," says Mark O'Byrne, the executive director of GoldCore, a precious metals dealer and investment advisory firm based in Dublin. "But anyone with half a brain assumed they were buying. They would have had to be financially illiterate not to do it."

Then, in May 2009, Paulson & Co. posted a relatively bare-bones filing listing its recent purchases, as required by the Securities and Exchange Commission. The document showed that Paulson's funds had made substantial investments in gold and gold-production companies over the previous six months. In particular, Paulson's holdings in the Gold Trust, a fund that directly tracks the day-to-day price of gold bullion, now represented nearly 30 percent of the firm's total portfolio. For Paulson, this was a huge, bullish bet on the price of gold.

So what really happened? Did all of these countries independently decide to pile into the gold market? Did they follow Paulson's lead? Did they communicate with one another or seek Paulson's advice? Or did Paulson simply anticipate that an international gold rush was coming and try to capitalize on it? Even though we can see the shadow market's symbiosis right in front of our eyes, the truth is that we really don't know what these countries and investment funds were up to and why. And in almost all cases, we won't know until well after the deeds are done. Because at the end of the day, that's the one key rule of the shadow market: keep as much activity as possible hidden.

SILENCE IS GOLDEN

All of the different players that interact within the shadow market—the hedge fund traders, the private equity investors, and the superrich independent nations with cash to burn—come to the world of finance from different perspectives. Some view it as a means for gaining geopolitical power. Others look at it as a way of monetizing their natural resources. And still others see it as a way to generate profits. But there's one area where they almost all agree. And that's their desire to operate in absolute secrecy.

The analogy would be an enormous worldwide game of poker. If you had a seat at that table, would you want to show everyone your hand? But with the increased interconnectedness of the financial markets, it's important to know in general terms what others are up to—if for no other reason than we want to prevent another international financial disaster. However, it's difficult for the United States and other Western nations to tell the newly powerful countries dominating the shadow market to open up their financial books so that the world can have increased investment "transparency." That's just not a pill these governments are going to swallow easily.

Indeed, in October 2007, the International Monetary Fund spearheaded an effort to establish a code of conduct for sovereign wealth funds, which at the time were busy buying up stakes in key Western companies. The IMF's point in developing these so-called best practices was that the sudden increase in cross-border buying exposed a weakness in financial regulations. Since many of these investments were coming from funds that were controlled by the governments of foreign countries, they all operated under different disclosure rules. So in many cases, it was difficult for countries and companies to know the true intentions of their new international investors. This was of particular concern geopolitically because independent studies showed that some of the least transparent investment funds belonged to some newly wealthy countries with troubling diplomatic histories, such as China, Russia, and Saudi Arabia, while the most transparent funds belonged to more historically cooperative nations, like Norway, Singapore, and Japan.

So the IMF called on the wealthy nations of the world to come together and voluntarily establish a set of disclosure rules that would govern all international investors. As you might expect, it didn't go well. China, Russia, and Saudi Arabia enjoy keeping their investment arms opaque, so they did everything in their power to stall the proceedings. One area in particular where the talks broke down was over the definitions of "transparency" and "political motivation." As Lou Jiwei, head of the £100 billion China Investment Corporation, put it: "It seems there wasn't any agreement on that because nobody wants to accept the fact that anybody's better than themselves." In essence, China was telling the rest of the world, "Who are you to dictate to us?" So in the end, there was no global agreement on investment disclosure. The shadow market was free to continue lurking in the shadows.

This is why it's so hard to piece together what's really going on in the global economy and to galvanize worldwide solutions for financial crises. Without an undisputed economic leader, or an international financial regulatory body with real teeth, it's nearly impossible to keep up with all the different developments in wealthy foreign countries—if for no other reason than they often take place behind closed doors.

But the fact is that we can't really complain. These are, after all, the same rules that the United States created for its own financial markets. The rest of the world is just following America's lead. While China, Russia, Saudi Arabia, and countries like them obsess over keeping the prying eyes of the global financial community away from their investments, the upper echelons of America's financial system also operate under their own special set of guidelines that insure discretion and privacy above all else. It turns out that wealthy domestic investors appreciate aggressive oversight as much as wealthy foreign investors do.

For example, even the large private equity firms that have sold stock to the public, like the Blackstone Group and KKR, have managed to do so with a sleight of hand that enables them to maintain their prized secrecy. Usually when a business files for an initial public offering, also known as an IPO, its activities are governed by the SEC, which oversees all companies publicly traded in the US But in the case of a private equity firm, what the SEC gets to see depends on what the firm decides to sell to the public. In essence, the leaders of Blackstone and KKR divided their companies in half. The half that they sold in the IPO runs the business operations and collects the fees of about 2 percent on all the assets under management. But what they keep private is the half that makes the actual trades and investments and collects fees of roughly 20 percent of the profits. This allows them to have their cake and eat it too. They could raise money in the capital markets and gain the financial stability of a publicly traded stock, while at the same time keeping their trading and investment secrets safe under lock and key.

For such wealthy investors, this has been the American way for some time. In the US financial system, the inside players have always preferred to operate with as little regulatory oversight as possible. Indeed, when the US Congress started pushing for increased regulation over the hedge fund industry in 2008 and 2009, the Managed Funds Association—the primary Washington lobbying group for hedge fund managers—doled out $17 million (£10 million) in donations to politicians with influence over the financial community and spent another $15 million on lobbyists to work the Hill and push their message. Clearly, the issue of increased regulation had touched a nerve, because that was more than four times the amount the MFA had spent in previous years.

PLAYING BY THE RULES, ONE IN PARTICULAR

Over the past few decades, the primary weapon used by rich American traders and large institutions to maintain their privacy has been a relatively obscure law called Securities and Exchange Commission Rule 144A. Adopted in 1990, it governs private transactions among so-called qualified institutional buyers, which means anyone with more than $100 million (£50 million) invested in the market. Basically, Rule 144A says that these qualified buyers can conduct private transactions among themselves with few restrictions. So large companies can sell their stocks and bonds without going public, thus bypassing SEC registration requirements. Wealthy foreign entities can buy and sell securities without the US government taking a peek. And well-heeled investors and funds can swap securities among one another without the SEC looking over their shoulders.

The idea behind Rule 144A was to keep regulators out of the affairs of superrich investors. Not surprisingly, it's proven to be highly effective. And in many ways, with the growing size of the shadow market, it's also become America's dominant tool for generating capital. In each year since 2006, the amount of money raised in private Rule 144A offerings has outstripped the amount of money raised in IPOs. This helps explain why in America— with its massive mutual funds and pension funds and all of the different players that make up the shadow market floating around—only 30 percent of all traded securities are held by individual investors. Looking at the big picture, investing has become a rich man's game that only a privileged few can actually play. The reality is that there's no seat at this poker table for you and me. But there is one for each member of the shadow market. In fact, they're the guests of honor.

CHAPTER 3

The Land of Giants

O n 17th June 2009, the leaders of Brazil, Russia, India, and China, countries that may one day rule the world, or so they believe, gathered for the first time at a four-hour conference in the Ural Mountains of western Russia to declare their economic independence from the United States and the European countries that have long dominated the global financial system. Long dubbed "the BRIC countries," the four nations have co-opted the name for themselves. So this was the first ever "BRIC summit."

In a joint statement following the event, the countries spelled out their goals: "We are committed to advance the reform of international financial institutions, so as to reflect changes in the world economy." Such diplomatic patter could not disguise their galloping ambitions. After all, these four are expected to dominate the global economy in the years to come. A study by the consulting firm Ernst & Young in December 2008 showed that the BRIC countries will likely account for a whopping *40 percent* of the world's economic growth between now and 2020. The United States will likely account for 14 percent of global economic growth over the same time frame, down from as much as 22 percent in the 1990s. The report duly attributed the BRIC countries' expanding financial might to a "tectonic shift in global capital."

The BRIC nations, however, are more of a symbolic organization than a cohesive international alliance like, say, the North

Atlantic Treaty Organization, or NATO. Their political agendas are largely divergent, and their economies don't necessarily overlap. So, diplomatic experts doubt that this group can collectively forge strong positions to rally around. Instead, the overarching point of the BRIC summit was to remind the world that even though Brazil, Russia, India, and China are poised to dominate the global economy, they still have little say in global diplomacy. That's a situation they're determined to change.

"Companies and governments in the developed world have to face up to the reality that there will be a further shift in the economic balance of power in the years ahead," Mark Otty, auditing giant Ernst & Young's chairman and one of the report's authors, said when announcing the findings.

The shifting balance of power that Otty described was, of course, indivisible from the rise of the shadow market. The parts of the world that are generating the most capital, or creating the most liquidity, are changing. For generations, the United States, as the largest economy on earth, filled this role. American businesses produced products that were in high demand across the globe, and companies from all over the world clamored to gain access to the insatiable American consumer market. This enabled the US economy to generate piles of capital that American corporations and consumers could then recycle all over the planet. Today, however, the US economy and the American consumer are tapped out. So it's falling to other emerging economic powers to generate the global liquidity that used to be thrown off from the US economy. The BRIC countries are a prime example.

Jim O'Neill, the London-based economist for Goldman Sachs who coined the term *BRIC* back in 2001, thinks that the world has only started to feel the titanic economic transition that's coming from the power of these emerging nations. By his calculations, China's economy will overtake America's by 2027. What's more, within the next twenty years, he predicts, the economies of the BRIC countries will dwarf those of the powerful Group of Seven nations, or G7, a collection of countries with some of the world's most important economies: Canada, France, Germany, Italy, Japan, the UK, and the United States.

If you ask O'Neill, this trend is only speeding up. "The BRICs are ahead of the game coming out of the financial crisis," he says. "Where the BRIC countries collectively are now is where we expected them to be by 2015. The crisis has actually added momentum to the story because these countries have had to realize that they can't rely on the US so much. So generally speaking they've adjusted strongly postcrisis—though Russia less so—to make sure that their own growth performance depends on their own demand. Then, once you get growth going and people start believing that it can be done, that itself induces more animal spirits and the whole thing becomes a self-fulfilling prophecy. That's where we are now."

O'Neill argues that the rise of the BRIC nations means that the entire global diplomatic landscape needs to be realigned. And it appears that international leaders agree. For decades, the mission of solving the world's economic problems fell to the G7 and then the G8, which includes Russia. But that ended in September 2009, when the heads of the world's largest economies announced that the G20—comprised of nineteen industrial and emerging-market countries plus the European Union—would be "the premier forum" for addressing the world's economic problems. The change, which had not been expected, was a stunning acknowledgment of the shifting dynamics in the global economy. Or, as the White House said in the opening of its statement announcing the new arrangement: "Dramatic changes in the world economy have not always been reflected in the global architecture for economic cooperation." Indeed.

To appreciate how financially powerful the BRIC nations have become, consider that in July 2010, as Europe and the United States were still trying to sort out the economic ramifications of Greece's financial meltdown, an initial public offering, or IPO, by the Agricultural Bank of China raised more than £14 billion, making it the largest initial public offering in history. A similar phenomenon took place in 2009, when, in the midst of the US financial crisis, the largest IPOs in the world that year were China State Construction Engineering Corporation, which raised £4 billion, and Brazil's VisaNet, which took in £2.4 billion. IPOs are an interesting gauge of economic growth because they can help measure the financial market's demand for the businesses a country or region is generating. And based on the global appetite for initial public offerings over the past few years, economic growth has been coming from the developing economies of the BRIC nations rather than those of the Western establishment.

In addition to IPOs, the BRIC countries' stock markets also thrived during the financial collapse. Through the first half of 2009, China's Shanghai Composite index rocketed 85 percent, the Bovespa index soared 77 percent, India's Sensex index climbed 61 percent, and Russia's RTS index jumped 60 percent. Meanwhile, the Standard & Poor's 500 index in the United States was up just 8.4 percent, and Japan's Nikkei index gained only 7.5 percent. The strength of the BRIC economies and financial markets was not lost on the rest of the world. For instance, in May 2010 an investment company controlled by the government of Qatar rushed to set up two funds totaling £700 million that would invest exclusively in Brazil and Russia. Meanwhile, India launched an £7 billion infrastructure fund with roughly £3 billion to be raised from overseas investors. And oil-rich Venezuela asked India to join it in setting up a £65 billion sovereign wealth fund that would be jointly owned by the two countries.

Most important for the traditional Western powers, all of this activity was not expected to be a temporary development. Not when the World Bank was projecting that developing economies would grow 1.2 percent in 2009 and 4.4 percent in 2010, while "high-income" developed countries would contract 4.2 percent in 2009 and expand just 1.3 percent in 2010. Instead economists and diplomatic experts believe that the development of these onetime emerging-market nations into major players on the global stage is a long-term, if not permanent, trend.

SHOWING EVERYONE THE MONEY

It goes without saying that China is the most important of the four BRIC countries. Its economy has grown faster and more aggressively than any other major country in the world. From 2003 to 2008, China's gross domestic product rose nearly 11 percent per year, by far the fastest growth rate of any country in the G20. The next closest was India, at 8.4 percent. From 2010 to 2020, China's GDP is expected to grow at least 9 percent annually, followed by India at 7 percent. Plus, in China, consumer spending has traditionally accounted for just a third of the country's GDP. By comparison, consumer spending makes up roughly half of India's and Russia's GDPs and nearly three-quarters of America's. In other words, China's consumer markets have an enormous amount of room to expand in the future.

At this point, Chinese consumers don't spend nearly as much as their counterparts in Asia and the other BRIC countries, much less the United States. However, China's government economists have shown that they understand how to stimulate consumer activity when necessary. Indeed, during the financial crisis of 2009, when it seemed like the entire developed world was retrenching and spending less, countless foreign manufacturers experienced strong sales in China. The reason was that the government's massive stimulus plan encouraged consumers to spend by offering cheap credit to buy goods, reducing mortgage rates to make houses more affordable, and cutting taxes on many purchases, especially cars, trucks, and minivans.

These measures help explain why a major manufacturer of consumer products like Procter & Gamble reported that its Chinese sales grew in the first half of 2009, albeit more slowly than normal, while sales figures from all other countries dropped—in many cases precipitously. They're why Toyota's vehicle sales in China in the first half of 2009 were up 25 percent from the prior year, which offset a dramatic fall in other markets and enabled the Japanese car manufacturer's total first-half revenues to beat most auto experts' predictions. In luxury goods, Louis Vuitton reported that its sales in China remained "strong," while in America and Japan, they dropped by as much as 5 percent. Meanwhile Europe's second largest retailer, Metro AG, said that in 2008 its sales in China increased 15 percent to £600 million, while its other markets were either flat or down from a year ago.

So who was driving this boom in Chinese consumer culture? Surprisingly, it was China's young workers, who seem to be far more profligate and far less interested in saving than were their forebears. China's youth has done quite well financially, as opportunities have soared for young educated employees and students fresh out of university. Even during the worldwide economic downturn in 2009, 68 percent of China's university graduates found jobs by the time they graduated. That's six million people heading off to work in the middle of a global financial crisis.

The trend was confirmed by an April 2009 research report by McKinsey & Company, which found that on average China's wealthiest consumers were *twenty years younger* than their peers in the United States and Japan. In addition, the study found that roughly 80 percent of the wealthy consumers in China, or what the study termed the "mass affluent," were younger than forty-five, compared to 30 percent in the United States and 20 percent in Japan. The McKinsey consultants noted that companies have had to adapt their marketing messages to this shifting demographic trend.

To get precious access to China's growing wealthy class, multinational businesses have flooded the country with investments, even while scaling back their spending in the rest of the world.

Just consider this list of activity from the first six months of 2009 alone:

- Microsoft agreed to build two technology centers in the city of Huangzhou on China's east coast and make additional technological investments in the area after receiving a pledge from the Chinese government to protect Microsoft against software piracy, a rampant problem in China.
- PepsiCo opened a large factory in the city of Chongqing in southwestern China and announced plans to build another five beverage plants in other areas of the country over the next two years as part of a £600 million-plus Chinese investment plan.
- The German shipping company DHL added 10 transportation hubs in various areas throughout the country.
- Hewlett-Packard set up arrangements with China's three mobile telecommunications carriers—China Mobile Communications Corporation, China Unicom, and China Telecommunications Group—to offer cheap HP notebook computers as part of their cellular packages.
- Taiwan's AU Optronics Corp., the third largest maker of LCD screens in the world, entered into a joint venture to supply screens for the Sichuan Changhong Electric Co., a Chinese television and home appliance manufacturer.
- South Korea's Hynix Semiconductor, the world's second largest memory chip maker for computers, set up an outsourcing venture to produce chips in China.
- IMAX, the Hollywood film technology company based in Ontario that produces films to be shown on enormous multistory screens, entered into a partnership with Huayi Brothers Media Group, China's largest film studio, to release Chinese-language movies in IMAX.
- Even Citigroup, the troubled US bank that was forced to unload billions of dollars in assets to stay afloat, refused to

part with its biggest investment in China—its 20 percent stake in the Guangdong Development Bank—because it said the investment was too valuable to Citigroup's future growth plans.

"China obviously is the market everyone wants to be in," says Tao Wang, the Beijing-based head of China economic research for the Swiss multinational bank UBS. "Why? The growth story is so powerful. In China, the GDP per capita is around $6,000 [£4,000]. In the US, it's $46,000. And in other developed countries like Germany and Japan it's more than $30,000. China's growth has been incredible—when it started its reforms thirty years ago GDP per capita was around $300—so it has come a long way. But when you look ahead it still has a long way to go in terms of its stage of development."

This ongoing transformation has enabled China to create a dynamic economy where wealthy Chinese businesses and individuals are quickly catching up to their US counterparts in tangible ways. For instance, in 2000, American companies raised £42 billion from initial public offerings, while Chinese companies hauled in just £13 billion. But in 2009, US companies picked up just £9 billion from initial public offerings, while Chinese companies brought in more than £22 billion. At the end of 2000, twenty-nine of the world's fifty largest companies in terms of market capitalization were from America, and only one was from China. The largest company in the world at the time was General Electric. But by 2009, twenty-one of the world's fifty largest companies were from America, and nine were from China. And the biggest company in the world was PetroChina Company. In 2000, there were 298 billionaires in the United States and just two billionaires in China. By 2009, there were 359 billionaires in the United States and 79 billionaires in China. Are you noticing a trend?

DRIVE EAST, YOUNG MAN

Without question, the clearest way to see the impact of China's expanding consumer demand is by looking at the country's sizzling auto market. In the first quarter of 2010, in the middle of the catastrophic global financial crisis, China surpassed the United States in total vehicle sales for the first time ever, becoming the world's largest consumer car market. And it hasn't looked back since. This shift has caused car manufacturers like Daimler, General Motors, Honda, Porsche, and Toyota to completely revamp their views of the global market. "The center of gravity is moving eastward," Daimler chairman Dr. Dieter Zetsche told a crowd of reporters at the 2009 Shanghai motor show. "This has, if anything, only accelerated during the crisis."

Other car industry insiders agree with Dr. Zetsche's assessment. Automotive analysts predict that the Chinese car market will expand by around 8 percent per year from 2009 to 2015. In 2010, General Motors, working with the SAIC Motor Corporation and the Liuzhou Wuling Motors Company, sold 2.35 million vehicles in China. That same year GM sold 2.2 million vehicles in the US. China had become the largest customer of America's largest automaker. Meanwhile, Nissan, which sold about 570,000 vehicles in China in 2009, was spending £3 billion building facilities with its partner, the Dongfeng Motor Group Co., so that it could boost its production to more than 700,000 vehicles per year. And Tenneco, the giant auto parts maker from Lake Forest, Illinois, started work on its sixth Chinese plant with its partner, the Beijing Hainachuan Automotive Parts Company, which will design and build emission control systems for Hyundai and Nissan cars to be sold in China.

Of course, this increased demand for vehicles in China was not a one-way street. While foreign carmakers poured in money to entice China's consumers, Chinese car manufacturers already held enormous market share in the country. So they expanded their reach outward. China's two largest private manufacturers, Geely Automobile Holdings and the Chery Automobile Co.—both known for their tiny, cheap cars—began building more luxurious vehicles that would appeal to the global car market. Auto parts maker Wonder Auto Technology started supplying alternators and starters for North American car manufacturers.

But by far the most audacious grab was Geely's £1.25 billion bid for the Volvo Car Corporation in September 2009. Geely's most popular cars were the inexpensive Panda compact and King Kong compact. But the company, based in Wanchai, Hong Kong, had designs on reaching a wider audience. And in Volvo, it saw a worldwide upscale brand with an existing global network of showrooms that could serve as launching pads to introduce Geely's other vehicles to the world. The fact is that Geely had been sizing up Volvo for years, ever since it became clear that the Swedish carmaker didn't fit with its parent company, Ford Motor Company. So starting around 2006, Geely began preparing for a major transaction. It brought in new management talent, pumped money into research and development, upgraded its manufacturing plants, and enhanced its production operations. So when Volvo finally became available in 2009 because Ford needed to cut costs and raise cash during the financial crisis, Geely was ready to pounce. To get the financing it needed, Geely worked with Chinese state-owned investment funds, which ponied up the rest of the money that the car manufacturer didn't have on hand. In addition, Geely arranged for a £165 billion investment from Goldman Sachs to further bolster its balance sheet. With this impressive wad of cash to hand, Geely was able to make Ford the proverbial offer it couldn't refuse. And Ford didn't.

The Chinese government is also helping to push the global car market in new directions. With air pollution such a significant problem in the country, and its economic dependence on oil growing to dangerous levels, the Chinese authorities are taking extreme steps to encourage the use of more fuel-efficient vehicles and the development of cars, trucks, and minivans that run on electric engines.

Most significantly, in April 2009, Chinese authorities unveiled plans to turn their country into the world's largest producer of electric cars and minivans. To accomplish this, the government invested £880 million in corporate research grants to help spur innovation in the car industry; provided additional grants to individual companies that were working on fuel cells for electric cars and minivans; and, most important, provided up to £5,000 in direct financial subsidies to Chinese consumers who purchased one of these vehicles, which typically were much more expensive than ordinary gasoline-powered cars. The program differed from the US approach, in which the government threw $25 billion (£15 billion) at the car industry for research but provided far fewer incentives for Americans to actually go out and buy an electric vehicle.

China is also embarking on one of the most ambitious national construction projects in modern times: the building of a £600 billion nationwide high-speed rail system. When completed, it will have forty-two different train lines riding on tracks covering more than 68,000 miles. The system will feature bullet trains that can travel faster than 200 miles per hour, enabling the country to move its growing population quickly, efficiently, and without the use of aeroplanes or cars. The first leg of the system will be an 800-mile, £18 billion rail link between the economic centers of Beijing and Shanghai. At the start of 2009, more than 110,000 Chinese workers were putting together the Beijing-Shanghai route. The country expects to finish the entire project by 2020.

Beyond the national rail line, China also is embarking on a series of other costly infrastructure programs. The country plans to build more than 40,000 miles of motorways and nearly 100 new airports by 2020. At the nation's seaports, Chinese officials are planning to increase throughput (container port speak for productivity) by 85 percent between 2010 and 2020. And these examples don't take into account the incredible construction spree going on throughout the country, which is so dramatic that the skyline of the typical Chinese city now looks like a herd of cranes lifting steel beams to create a thicket of office buildings. This helps explain why in late 2009, demand for workers in China was up nearly 15 percent, while in the United States the official unemployment rate was hovering around 10 percent.

These developments mean that there will be trillions of dollars sloshing around China as the country rushes to complete its massive transportation modernization projects and upgrade its rudimentary infrastructure. Already the world's shrewdest investors are coming up with creative ways to participate in this booming market. In the autumn of 2009, the politically connected private equity firm Carlyle Group made £40 million in direct investments in three fast-growing Chinese companies, including an agriculture technology firm and a manufacturer of shipping parts. Meanwhile, Carlyle's competitor Blackstone Group, which sold a £2 billion stake to China's sovereign wealth fund, created a £442 billion investment fund that will invest in Chinese businesses and projects. It was the first Blackstone fund to hold assets solely in China's currency, renminbi, rather than in dollars.

But it's not just American investors who want a piece of the Chinese market. Kuwait launched the Kuwait China Investment Company to invest in the energy, real estate, agriculture, infrastructure, and financial services sectors throughout Asia. Qatar Holding, the investment arm of the Qatar Investment Authority, opened an office in China to oversee its Asian investments. And separately, the Qatari government made entreaties to the Chinese government to promote natural gas exports to the country.

Major corporations also have gotten into the act. In late 2009, GE entered into a fifty-fifty partnership with the Aviation Industry Corporation of China to make advanced electronic systems for a new passenger jet that's being manufactured by the Commercial Aircraft Corporation of China, or Comac, and will compete with the popular Boeing 737 and Airbus A320. Major US power suppliers such as Duke Energy, AES Corporation, and Progress Energy started teaming up with Chinese companies to gain access to the capital, technology, and equipment coming out of China's fast-developing energy sector. Disney received approval to open a £2 billion amusement theme park and vacation development in Shanghai, the first of its kind on mainland China.

What's more, the cash isn't flowing just one way. China may be attracting investments from across the globe, but it's also putting its own massive pool of capital to work around the world in more sophisticated ways than ever before as part of its "going out" strategy of international investment. The country's sovereign wealth fund, the China Investment Corporation, brought in Bill Lu, a Chinese-born investment manager, to head its hedge fund investments. Lu worked at the renowned Greenwich, Connecticut, hedge fund Tudor Investment Corporation, which is run by the billionaire investor Paul Tudor Jones II, overseeing the firm's relationship with China. He is widely considered to be the most high-profile investment hire at the CIC so far. In addition, to keep up with the global financial markets, the CIC announced plans to open up an office in London that would manage its overseas investments.

China also has started using its capital as a diplomatic tool. The country set up a fund dedicated to investing in infrastructure development in India. It offered £9 billion in credit to finance infrastructure projects in the countries of the Association of Southeast Asian Nations (ASEAN), which is comprised of Brunei, Cambodia, Indonesia, Laos, Malaysia, Myanmar, the Philippines, Singapore, Thailand, and Vietnam. It provided Argentina with access to more than £6 billion, which Argentina could use to buy Chinese imports. It loaned Brazil's national oil company £6 billion for development. It allowed Ecuador to borrow £600 million to build a hydroelectric plant. It has discussed financing infrastructure projects in Egypt. It gave struggling African nations £6 billion in "concessional loans" that come without any preconditions.

Indeed, in recent years, China has become a major financier of the African private sector and has even tried to galvanize an international "Marshall Fund" for Africa. More than thirty-five African countries have received financing from China for infrastructure projects, with the biggest recipients being Niger, Angola, Sudan, and Ethiopia. In 2006 and 2007 alone, China made £5.7 billion in financing commitments to African nations.

Africa isn't the only struggling region to receive China's attention. The country also is considering natural resources investments in Pakistan, particularly in a major coal reserve in the Thar Desert of southern Pakistan. To transport the coal, China and Pakistan are discussing a road and rail link from Pakistan's Gwadar Port on the Persian Gulf to the Xinjiang region of western China. This connection also could be used to transport oil to China from the Middle East. If the plans succeed, China is also prepared to discuss investments in Pakistan's textile, water, and manufacturing industries.

Although China is going to require a tremendous amount of energy to power its growth in the coming decades, its government is aggressively funding projects to capitalize on alternative energy sources. This is as much about China's survival as it is about contributing to the global environmental efforts. A study by the University of Pennsylvania's Wharton School of Business estimates that at its current rate of consumption, China will need £2.4 trillion in energy investments to fuel its growth through 2030. The only real way for the country to cut this figure is to reduce its consumption. As a result, the Chinese government has unveiled an array of initiatives to instill energy efficiency in the nation's culture.

In June 2009, China publicly announced that it was setting a national goal of generating 15 percent of its energy from renewable sources like solar plants, hydropower, and wind by 2020. This was notable because, at the time, just 8 percent of China's energy came from renewable sources. To make the transition, the government said it was planning to spend between £150 billion and £200 billion.

Almost overnight China started experiencing a green revolution. Major multinational manufacturing companies such as General Electric are in China right now building plants to produce wind turbines and engines to run power plants using greenhouse gases. China also is encouraging its businesses and citizens to adopt other kinds of renewable energy in their daily lives. For instance, China dramatically outpaces the United States in the use of solar power. Even the government's investment arm has gotten into the act. In November 2009, CIC put £750 million into the Chinese renewable power businesses GCL-Poly Energy Holdings, which operates energy recycling cogeneration plants, and China Longyuan Power Group, the country's fifth largest wind power company.

All of this feverish economic activity suggests the inevitable dominance of China. There are some prominent doubters, however. "I'm a bit skeptical that these new powers are going to rise unimpeded," says Simon Johnson, who teaches global economics and entrepreneurship at the M.I.T. Sloan School of Management and is a member of the Congressional Budget Office's panel of economic advisers. "In the case of China I can think of lots of things that would derail their progress, environmental problems, the cost of building out the economy, and so forth. But the key is can they innovate? Can they come up with new products that people want? Can they change technology the way the US does? That remains to be seen. Copying people and catching up is not easy and they've done an impressive job with it. But it's quite different from being on the frontier pushing innovation yourself."

Will these challenges overwhelm China's economic progress? Or will China's national wealth, powerful economy, and growing consumer markets carry the country to global leadership? These are probably the most important economic questions facing the world today, but as we are about to see, the country's leaders don't intend to leave China's future up to chance. They have power, and they've learned how to use it.

CHAPTER 4

Chinese Hardball

To get a glimpse of what Wall Street looks like half a world away from downtown Manhattan, head out to John F. Kennedy International Airport, hop on a plane, and fly about seven thousand miles to Beijing and visit Jinrongjie, or Beijing Financial Street, as it's more commonly known. Because it is here that China's awesome financial power is put to work. A zone of gleaming, modern office towers that soar over the second of the seven "ring roads" that encircle China's capital city, Beijing Financial Street stretches over thirty-five blocks and is home to more than a thousand different financial institutions as well as countless high-end hotels and chic restaurants. China's powerful central bank, the People's Bank of China, is located here. So are the country's major financial regulatory bodies (China Banking Regulatory Commission, China Securities Regulatory Commission, and China Insurance Regulatory Commission) as well as important banks and finance firms, including the Industrial and Commercial Bank of China, China Life Insurance Company, China Reinsurance (Group) Company, and China Galaxy Securities Co. Plus, it's the base for numerous major multinational financial services firms, such as Goldman Sachs, J.P. Morgan, Swiss Bank, and the Royal Bank of Canada. Each day, nearly £1 billion of capital flows through Beijing Financial Street, and 20 trillion yuan, or nearly £2 trillion, in assets are controlled here, according to figures from the Xicheng District government, which oversees the area. This amounts to 25 percent of all the financial assets in China. Roughly 90 percent of the nation's loans are held here as are 65 percent of its insurance premiums.

Beijing Financial Street wasn't always like this. A thriving ancient financial district, Jinrongjie was known as Gold and Silver Street during the Ming and Qing dynasties, from the fifteenth century to the early twentieth century. But it became a forgotten area as modern Beijing emerged. By the early 1990s, Jinrongjie was a filthy warren of back alleys and darkened courtyards. But because of its premium location in the Xicheng District—a few blocks from Zhongnanhai, the seat of the Chinese government, and next to the West Second Ring Road, a major six-lane artery that loops around Beijing—Jinrongjie was targeted for redevelopment.

Today, the imposing Zhongnanhai building complex, which is right next to the ancient Forbidden City, houses the office of Hu Jintao, the general secretary of the Communist Party, and is where the main bodies of the Communist Party all meet.

With so much political power gathered in the area, China's leaders thought it only natural to incorporate the country's economic might. So the government decided to reconfigure the area with the specific ambition of transforming it into the global business and finance center of Beijing—and eventually all of China. It accomplished this by relocating the bulk of the city's banks, insurance companies, and financial services firms to Jinrongjie from the northern district of Xidan. The project started in 1993 and took about ten years to complete. When it was done, Beijing Financial Street was born. Within a decade, it had become the country's financial nerve center. Although many Chinese people consider Shanghai's thriving ultramodern Pudong District, home to the country's financial markets, to be China's answer to Wall Street, Beijing Financial Street is the nation's financial capital.

A TRILLION HERE, A TRILLION THERE

It's no coincidence that the real base of China's financial power is adjacent to its political capital, since China's version of capitalism is much more centralized than anything seen in the West. In most Western capitalist economies, the bulk of a nation's wealth is dispersed among private companies and institutions that are owned and operated separately from the government. Companies pay a portion of their earnings to the government in the form of taxes, and they must comply with the regulations established by the government, but the companies themselves are private entities.

In China, this is not the case. The Chinese corporate culture is dominated by the government, largely because so many of the country's biggest companies are either fully or partially owned by the state. A July 2008 study by the consulting firm McKinsey & Company found that China has more than 150 companies that are owned outright by the government and that at least another 1,000 are partially state owned. Name an industry that's important to the Chinese people, and the Chinese government has a piece of the pie. In oil, it's the China National Petroleum Corporation, China National Oil Corporation, and the China Petroleum and Chemical Corporation, also known as Sinopec. In coal, it's Shenhua Group Corporation. In telecommunications, it's China Mobile and China Telecom. In pharmaceuticals, it's the North China Pharmaceutical Group Corporation. In shipping, it's the China Shipping Company or the China Ocean Shipping Company. In electric power, it's the State Grid Corporation of China. In metals, it's the Shanghai Baosteel Group Corporation and the Aluminum Corporation of China, also known as Chinalco. In chemicals, it's the China National Chemical Corporation. In motorcars, it's the Shanghai Automotive Industry Corporation. In computers, it's Lenovo, which is partially owned by the Chinese government.

Household appliances? That would be Haier, which also is partly owned by China's government.

Still, the cash generated by this vast network of state-owned enterprises is nothing compared to the seemingly limitless capital that the Chinese government has at its disposal. As of December 2010, China's central bank, the People's Bank of China, controlled roughly $2.85 trillion (£1.8 trillion) in reserves, which it manages through a state agency called the State Administration of Foreign Exchange (SAFE). This was by far the largest amount of cash ever accumulated by a single nation in the history of the world. China doesn't disclose the makeup of SAFE's foreign exchange reserves investments, but a July 2009 study by the Washington, DC-based Brookings Institution estimated that as much as 75 percent of China's reserves were held in dollar-denominated assets. Around 4o percent were in long- and short term US Treasury bonds and US agency bonds, particularly bonds issued by the Federal National Mortgage Association and the Federal Home Loan Mortgage Corporation, better known as Fannie Mae and Freddie Mac, respectively. Another 10 percent or so were directly in currencies from around the world, primarily dollars and euros. And the final 50 percent were being used to invest in state-owned companies, to recapitalize a few troubled banks, and particularly to provide funding for the country's sovereign wealth fund, the China Investment Corporation, which invests in projects around the world.

Foreign exchange reserves are important because they're a key gauge of a country's wealth and financial health. They shed light on how much money a nation has to repay its debts and how vigorously its central bank can intervene to defend its economy, fighting off inflation, defending against financial crises, and so on. And China has by far the largest financial reserves in the world. At the end of 2009, Japan, the next largest holder, had slightly more than £650 billion in reserves, according to the IMF. The entire European financial system, consisting of the European Central Bank and the sixteen countries that use the euro as currency, had just £418 billion. The US held a paltry $132 billion, the UK £42 billion.

So how did China amass such an unprecedented war chest? Harvard economist and Nobel laureate Joseph Stiglitz described China as the "valedictorian of the class of 1997." That year, much of Asia was hit by a series of economic crises that came to be dubbed the "Asian contagion." The countries that suffered the worst—particularly Indonesia, South Korea, and Thailand, the latter of which almost caused a worldwide financial crisis when its currency, the baht, collapsed—were those that didn't have enough foreign exchange reserves to protect themselves. So the obvious lesson from the "contagion" was to always have more than enough cash on hand to defend your currency and your economy. As a result, Asian nations started socking away capital, particularly US dollars. This led to a "savings glut," where increasingly wealthy countries were hoarding cash rather than circulating it back into the world economy.

The leader of the savings glut was China, which in 1996 had $107 billion (£63 billion) in foreign exchange reserves and by 2009 had increased that figure twentyfold. The Brookings study found that China accomplished this in part by continuously intervening in the currency markets to stifle any appreciation in the value of its currency, the renminbi, which, loosely translated means "the people's money" and is denominated in yuan. This intervention kept Chinese exports at artificially low prices, even as the nation's economy grew and the value of the renminbi naturally should have grown with it. To prevent this, China bought Treasury bonds, which reduced the supply of US debt and increased its value— which in turn kept the value of the dollar relatively high compared to the renminbi. From July 2008 until at least the winter of 2010, the value of the currency was 6.83 yuan to the dollar even though the United States was mired in economic turmoil and the Chinese economy continued to grow.

Chinese officials have vehemently denied that they manipulated the value of the national currency. However, the currency trading evidence gathered by the Treasury Department, the IMF, and the World Bank strongly indicates that China has been holding back the renminbi's value for years and that by 2009 it was undervalued by more than 25 percent compared to the dollar, the euro, and other global currencies. That's why US Treasury Secretary Timothy Geithner raised the issue during his confirmation hearings in January 2009. And the awesome power of China's $2 trillion in foreign exchange reserves was the reason why the Obama administration publicly backtracked from the allegations three months later.

Here's how it played out: On 23rd January 2009, Geithner, speaking during his confirmation hearings before the Senate Finance Committee, accused China of keeping the value of the renminbi artificially low to maintain cheap prices on its exports and generate trade surpluses. Naturally, China's leaders weren't pleased and quickly shot down Geithner's allegations. Then, on 13th March, Chinese premier Wen Jiabao publicly expressed concern about the security of China's investments in dollars and US Treasury bonds. "We have lent a huge amount of money to the US," Wen said during a press conference at the end of the Chinese Parliament's annual session. "Of course we are concerned about the safety of our assets. To be honest, I am definitely a little worried."

Count that as a shot aimed directly at President Barack Obama's new administration. Understanding the nature of this evolving relationship, the Obama administration quickly blinked. On 15th April, Geithner's Treasury Department issued a report to Congress saying that China was *not* manipulating its currency after all. Then, by the first week of June, Geithner was on his way to Beijing to discuss financial and economic policy with Chinese president Hu Jintao, as well as Premier Wen and Vice Premier Wang Qishan. During his trip, Geithner gently nudged China to diversify its economy away from a heavy reliance on exports. But more important, he assured everyone that the United States definitely planned to deal with its enormous deficit and was dedicated to protecting China's investments in America. And he never brought up the possibility that China might be manipulating the value of its currency to improve its exports. See how a lot of money can change things diplomatically?

In the spring of 2010, it appeared as if the United States had finally made some headway in encouraging Chinese officials to allow the value of the renminbi to rise. That March, Zhong Shan, China's vice commerce minister, visited Geithner in the United States. Although Zhong came away from the meeting reiterating that China would not be bullied into changing its policy, he also told the *Wall Street Journal* that the two countries had the "wisdom and ability to resolve existing problems."

At the heart of those existing problems was a semiannual exchange rate report due on 15th April from the US Treasury Department that was almost certainly going to label China as a currency manipulator. Although neither side would acknowledge it publicly, both Chinese and US officials felt the report's conclusions would seriously damage the emerging fiscal détente between the two nations. For its part, China was beginning to come to the conclusion that it had to allow the renminbi's value to increase, if for no other reason than to fight inflation and prevent a potential financial bubble from forming. And the United States realized that constantly trying to persuade Chinese officials to come down from their valuation stance would only trigger more obstinate behavior since China did not want to appear to be bending to America's wishes. So the Treasury Department decided to delay its exchange rate report until the two sides could sit down and have diplomatic discussions over the issue. China's president Hu Jintao personally reassured President Obama that his country was taking steps to rework the way it established the value of the renminbi.

Still, whether American and Chinese economic officials wanted to face up to it or not, the fact was that the value of China's currency had been kept artificially low for some time, which gave

China enormous economic leverage over the United States and the rest of the world. As Chinese products remained inexpensive in the global markets, the country was able to flood the planet with exported goods. In time, China was generating what economists call a "current account surplus." This is just a fancy way of saying that a country is taking in more money from exports than it's spending on imports. And in China's case, it was taking in *a lot* more money from exports than it was spending on imports.

Indeed, the Brookings Institution study found that China's current account surplus represented nearly 80 percent of the growth in the nation's foreign exchange reserves from 2000 to 2008. In particular, China's account surplus grew exponentially during the period from 2004 to 2008, when the United States was experiencing a dramatic lending bubble fed by cheap capital from abroad. Although American consumers deserve blame for their voracious appetite for debt and their eagerness to live beyond their financial means leading up to the global financial crisis of 2008–9, China's financial policies certainly were a major contributor to the expansion of the US lending bubble. It's like the relationship between a heroin addict and his dealer. The junkie alone is responsible for putting the needle into his veins. But the dealer is enabling a potentially lethal habit. In this case, America's addiction was to cold, hard cash. And China enabled the United States to continue its irresponsible ways long after it became clear that the situation could turn deadly. Ultimately this gave China the upper hand in the relationship, because the mere possibility that China could cut off America's supply of capital and start selling its dollar-based holdings was too much for the United States to bear.

"If the US was faced with a threat by the Chinese to dump US securities, it would materially influence foreign policy decision making in Washington," says the Council on Foreign Relations' Sebastian Mallaby. "We just lived through a credit crunch caused by deleveraging, where people thought they could borrow money and suddenly they couldn't and it was awful. So what happens when our largest lender says we can't borrow money anymore? The Chinese could inflict on us the conditions for a collapse if they wanted to. And that's a major strategic vulnerability for the West."

One obvious area of tension between China and the United States is China's deep interest and potential interference in America's fiscal policy. It's hardly surprising that the Chinese leadership is keeping a close eye on what's going on in America considering China owns more than $2 trillion (£1.25 trillion) of US currency and debt. Lately, Chinese officials haven't been shy about prodding their American counterparts to start seeing the world through China's eyes. In particular, Chinese officials have expressed concerns about the growing level of US debt and the unstable value of the dollar.

At the US-China Strategic and Economic Dialogue in July 2009, Qishan met with Geithner and behind closed doors delivered a stern lecture on the importance of America getting a handle on its debt and protecting the value of the dollar. Afterward, Wang walked over to a flank of reporters, where he was asked about his primary message to Geithner. Speaking through an interpreter, Wang said, "As a major reserve currency–issuing country in the world, the US should balance and properly handle the impact of the dollar's supply." Then he added that he was satisfied because Geithner had assured him that the Obama administration was putting "a lot of importance" on cutting runaway spending and reducing the budget deficit.

While the summit ended with a friendly outcome, it also signaled a major change in the diplomatic relationship between the two countries. The Obama administration had entered the talks with the goal of persuading Chinese officials to shift the focus of their country's economy away from exports and toward boosting demand within China. That's about as controversial as the Americans were prepared to get. The teams of Geithner and Peter Orszag, who heads Obama's Office of Management and Budget, barely even touched on hot-button topics like the Chinese government manipulating its currency or Chinese companies dumping products in foreign markets to boost the nation's current account surplus. Of course, it wouldn't have mattered even if they had. According to people in the meetings, the Chinese officials essentially "blew off" the topics they didn't want to discuss. Instead much of the conference was devoted to US financial officials reassuring the Chinese that America's rising tide of debt wasn't about to cascade into a tsunami.

"This wasn't what I'd call a two-way street," said one government official who attended several of the financial meetings. "It was pretty much one-way. They didn't do a lot of listening. They really just wanted to tell us what they wanted us to do. And we were there trying to reassure them."

As a result of these transformations, China is increasingly able to set the terms for the dialogue between the two countries. Just consider President Obama's first official state visit to China in November 2009. Diplomatically speaking, the trip was much more notable for what the president didn't, or couldn't, say than for what he actually did say.

Obama's primary mission was to begin the tricky talks between the world powers on a host of crucial international issues, including the environment and the global economy. However, on the thorniest economic issue between the two countries, Obama didn't publicly challenge China's leadership to stop manipulating the value of the renminbi and allow the costs of Chinese goods to rise. Instead China took steps to blunt the criticism before it even came up. First, roughly a week before Obama arrived, the World Bank's chief economist, Justin Yifu Lin—a Chinese national who received his doctorate in economics at the University of Chicago— gave a lecture at the University of Hong Kong in which he criticized plans to force China to let its currency appreciate in order to rebalance the global economy. "Currency appreciation in China won't help this imbalance and can deter the global recovery," he said.

Then, just hours before Air Force One touched down in Beijing, China's top banking regulator, Liu Mingkang, gave a blistering assessment of the US financial system. A weak dollar and low interest rates had set the stage for the enormous worldwide speculative bubble that created "unavoidable risks for the recovery of the global economy, especially emerging economies," he scolded. Now Chinese officials wanted to know how the plans for a US national health insurance program would affect America's budget deficit. The pointed questions were only natural considering that China, as America's primary banker, likely would end up financing much of the program through purchases of US government debt issued to cover the costs of the plan.

Even worse, on the trickiest diplomatic issue between China and the rest of the world, Obama was unable to get Chinese leaders to join other international powers in threatening Iran with tough sanctions if it didn't stop its nuclear weapons program. China and Iran have had deep economic ties for years based on the elemental mutual interests of money and oil. In July 2009, for example, Iran "invited" China to invest £26 billion in Iran's oil industry. Iran has the second largest crude oil reserves in the world, which makes it a highly attractive trading partner for China. However, Iran still has to import around 40 percent of the gasoline it uses because it lacks the capability to refine the oceans of oil it controls. This makes Iran particularly susceptible to economic sanctions because the global community can effectively cut off nearly half of Iran's gasoline supply. So Iran would use the Chinese investment to build refineries that could insulate the nation from those pressures. Ultimately China upped its investment to nearly £40 billion, further strengthening the bond between the two countries.

It's hardly a surprise that China would be eager to get involved in such an arrangement. Iran is China's third largest supplier of oil after Angola and Saudi Arabia, and its reliance on Iranian petroleum is only bound to increase as the oil wells it is financing start producing. In return for access to this precious resource, China has long served as Iran's shield in diplomatic matters. Time and again it has thwarted international efforts to rein in Iran, even as its uranium enrichment program has come under increasing scrutiny from nuclear specialists who are convinced that the country is trying to build an atomic weapon. In light of China's financial heft and close ties to Iran, getting the Chinese leadership on board with the proposed sanctions would be essential in order for the measures to have any teeth. But Obama couldn't get China's leaders to move on the issue, at least in public. (In private, however, it appears that the US president was able to make some headway because in June 2010 the U.N. Security Council imposed new sanctions on Iran with China's approval. Only Brazil and Turkey opposed the resolution.)

What's more, the American president appeared weak by allowing his Chinese handlers to dictate the public relations tenor of the proceedings. Obama even participated in embarrassing staged events like a "press conference" where he couldn't take questions from the press and a "town hall meeting" where the people in attendance weren't allowed to speak. Beyond that, Obama also avoided publicly chiding China for its sketchy record on human rights, a regular point of contention between the two countries. Indeed, just a year earlier, in August 2008, at the dedication ceremony for the new US embassy in Beijing, then president George W. Bush expressed his "deep concerns" about China's restrictions on religion and free speech. The Chinese government was furious and issued a terse statement maintaining that it "puts people first, and is dedicated to maintaining and promoting its citizens' basic rights and freedom."

For his part, Obama didn't even touch the contentious issue of human rights. This was particularly notable because in October 2009, just a month before his visit, the international advocacy organization Human Rights Watch reported that forty-three Chinese men and teenage boys of Uighur descent had "disappeared" following July 2009 clashes in western China between ethnic Han

Chinese nationals, who represent 90 percent of China's population, and Uighurs, who are ethnically Turkic Muslims with ties to central Asia and have lived in the region for centuries. "The cases we documented are likely just the tip of the iceberg," Brad Adams, the Asia director for Human Rights Watch, told a BBC reporter when the study was released. "Disappearing people is not the behavior of countries aspiring to global leadership."

And yet the American president remained silent.

DEATH OF THE DOLLAR?

Since China isn't looking to go to war with the United States or any other major geopolitical power, rhetoric has become the main weapon the country must use to prod other nations into doing what it wants. Well, rhetoric backed up by more than £1 trillion in assets and the fastest-growing economy on earth. The Chinese government typically has a representative lob a controversial verbal grenade over the fence in the press and then they judge how the rest of the world reacts as it explodes.

That explains why, on 24th March 2009, China very publicly floated a once-unthinkable idea: what if the major economies from around the world got together and created a single currency that would replace the dollar as the global standard? The controversial proposal was made by Zhou Xiaochuan, governor of China's central bank, as part of his call for sweeping changes in the global financial system that would give developing countries like China more sway in international economic matters. Since Chinese central bank governors don't make global financial policy proposals without prior approval from above, the economic world saw Zhou's words as coming straight from China's leadership.

In his paper, Zhou argued that the world needed to reduce its reliance on a few important currencies like the dollar, pound, and euro because it makes the financial system more volatile. He described the conundrum thusly: "Issuing countries of reserve currencies are constantly confronted with the dilemma between achieving their domestic monetary policy goals and meeting other countries' demand for reserve currencies. On one hand, the monetary authorities cannot simply focus on domestic goals without carrying out their international responsibilities; on the other hand, they cannot pursue different domestic and international objectives at the same time. They may either fail to adequately meet the demand of a growing global economy for liquidity as they try to ease inflation pressures at home, or create excess liquidity in the global markets by overly stimulating domestic demand. . . . The issuing countries of reserve currencies cannot maintain the value of the reserve currencies while providing liquidity to the world."

Zhou's solution, which was also backed by Russia, was to reform the international monetary system by creating "an international currency reserve that is disconnected from individual nations and is able to remain stable in the long run, thus removing the inherent deficiencies caused by using credit-based national currencies."

Because the dollar accounted for about 65 percent of the world's currency reserves, according to the IMF, it was obvious that Zhou's plan was targeted at the United States. Many economists assumed that China's leaders were losing patience with their financially codependent relationship with America, particularly as the value of the dollar fluctuated wildly during the crisis of 2009. This was an expression of that frustration. The proposal pointed out that the dollar's dominance as a global currency had given the United States an unfair advantage by enabling it to borrow vast sums from overseas and run titanic deficits, while transferring the risk to the holders of Treasury bonds. In simple terms, the Chinese were worried that the large amount of debt America was taking on eventually would lead to inflation in the United States, which would eat away at the dollar's value. After all, when the value of the dollar falls, the value of Beijing's dollar-based assets tumbles along with it. That's why Chinese leaders are constantly pushing US financial officials to maintain a strong dollar policy over all other considerations: they don't want to see their holdings take a hit.

To American and international economic policy makers, Zhou's proposal was an all-out broadside, though not entirely unexpected. Indeed, over the previous few months, Zhou had made statements hinting at this position. Still, it wasn't until the plan was out in black-and-white that many international economists began to consider the concept in earnest.

As Zhou's proposal started to sink in, the general consensus in the economic community was that the plan was probably a good idea for the long term but wasn't a practical solution right now. Many experts saw it as China's first trial balloon. Indeed, in January 2011, in an e-mail interview with the *Wall Street Journal*. China's president the Jintao stated, "the current international currency system is the product of the past." America's economic leaders have reluctantly come to accept this reality as well. US Treasury Secretary Geithner said it was possible, even likely, that the dollar could eventually be replaced by a multinational currency.

However, that said, economists and currency experts also recognized that it would take decades to create the kind of system China was calling for. Having the financial world tethered to the fortunes of a single country is dangerous, as we've seen with the dollar. But the fact is the dollar became the preeminent global currency after World War II.

"Over time China will establish itself as the world's reserve currency," says Kevin Chau, a respected currency strategist at the financial research firm IDEAglobal. "But it's going to take quite a bit of time. I think the *Wall Street Journal* said it will take ten years, but I would extend it to twenty years or maybe even more. It's going to happen, I'm sure of that. But there's a lot of time between now and then."

In addition to manipulating the United States, Zhou also was trying to get the rest of the world to pay attention to China as well. Since 2007, China has been increasingly asserting its power on the global stage. The Beijing Olympics were a launch pad that gave the Chinese government increased confidence about the country's improved standing around the world. Then, at the 2009 London summit of the Group of Twenty nations, also known as the G20, China came out all guns blazing. Chinese officials continued to push the idea of a global currency while also advancing a series of trade and antiprotectionism measures that would open up more markets to Chinese products. China also showed how it could combine economic negotiations and political goals by using the forum to insist that it had sovereignty over Tibet as well as to shoot down a host of environmental proposals. Furthermore, leading up to the G20 meetings, China announced that it had set up £60 billion worth of currency swaps with Argentina, Belarus, Hong Kong, Indonesia, Malaysia, and South Korea. Currency swap agreements are fixed-rate loans between governments. Geopolitically, they usually signify a strengthening financial alliance among countries. So China was showing the world how its increased financial clout was winning the country a growing number of friends. Indeed, when President Hu Jintao huddled privately with President Barack Obama during the G20 gathering, diplomats joked that it was a meeting of the "G2," recognizing that China had joined the United States as deserving a special seat at the table.

China also has been pushing its influence with organizations it once shunned, particularly the IMF, which is made up of most of the wealthiest countries in the world and seeks to provide financing for poorer developing nations and oversee the global economy by keeping tabs on its members' economic policies. Twice each year, the IMF reviews the economies of each of its members and reports on its findings. But from 2005 to 2008, China blocked the IMF from even looking at its economy because IMF executives continually accused China of manipulating its currency exchange rates. China complained that the IMF was dominated largely by the United States, its largest shareholder. So Chinese authorities concluded that the IMF was just mouthing America's political position on

China's currency. However, the IMF countered that a host of economic evidence showed that the renminbi was being vastly undervalued in the currency markets. That's where the impasse began. China's solution was to stop dealing with the IMF altogether.

But in June 2009, Chinese officials invited the IMF to analyze the country and restart the review process. The report once again found that China's currency was "misaligned," meaning that it was being kept artificially low. Chinese authorities added a line to the report stating that they "disagreed with the staff's assessment." In economic diplomacy terms, this amounted to a monumental compromise on China's part.

So what was driving Beijing's interest in rekindling its relationship with the IMF? In a word: influence. Right around the time of the global financial crisis of 2009, China launched a policy of reengaging with the world beyond its borders, particularly with organizations like the IMF and the World Bank, another international organization that helps to fight poverty by lending money to poor developing countries. China's aim was to increase its worldwide clout. For years, the IMF and World Bank had become increasingly marginalized on the global stage, in part because of their own incompetence but also because of declining contributions from member countries. President Barack Obama entered office with the goal of fortifying the IMF to help stave off any future global financial crises. He sought to raise $500 billion (£350 billion) to put the organization on solid footing. The United States, the European Union, and Japan all agreed to kick in around $100 billion each. But China balked. Its message was that it didn't want to contribute a penny unless the IMF's governance was changed to give China more say. Chinese officials were adamant that these issues had to be addressed somehow. So IMF officials pledged to begin reworking the power structure in the coming years. Only after receiving that assurance did China pony up nearly $100 billion to enable the IMF to reach its financing goal.

"The rise of China within the Bretton Woods institutions like the IMF goes back a ways," says Sebastian Mallaby, director of the Council on Foreign Relations' Center for Geoeconomic Studies. "This has been a gradual rise. Bit by bit the Chinese will be given, as the IMF calls it, more quota, meaning more share in the institution, more say on the board. This will confer power to them, which is what they're after. It happened at the World Bank too. I wrote a book about the World Bank, which was published in 2004, and towards the end of that book there's a whole description of how the Chinese board member teamed up with the Indian guy and reversed a central World Bank policy. The policy was about how much you defer to environmental campaigners when you're building infrastructure projects. The Dutch and the Swedes and various other catholic donor countries liked the policy, but China and India didn't. And China and India won. This is what their goal is with the IMF and other institutions like it, to have an increasing say in global policy."

Not that the IMF is immediately handing China the reins just because it's the richest nation in the world. IMF officials, particularly those from the European Union, have speculated that it would take several years of negotiations to completely overhaul the organization's power structure. Plus, they complain that China hasn't shown any serious willingness to openly regulate its own financial system, which is one of the IMF's fundamental principles. So it would seem that China still has a ways to go before it can have a significant say in what the IMF does or doesn't do. However, with that big bag of money just sitting off in the corner, it's only a matter of time before China buys itself a major piece of the IMF—and just about anything else it wants on the face of the earth.

A BIG FAT RABBIT

Since September 2007, when the Chinese government set up the country's first sovereign wealth fund, the China Investment

Corporation, and staked it with a £102 billion nest egg from a government bond sale, Chinese officials have debated what the country should do with the overwhelming pile of capital it was amassing. One idea from the government's economically conservative wing was to hoard the cash in Beijing by having the central bank hold it in state-owned banks and only spend it to directly support the Chinese economy or the renminbi. This proposal was *so* conservative that it could be considered analogous to Americans during the Great Depression hiding their money under their mattresses for fear of losing it. Yet in the past, this might have been China's course of action. This time, however, it was quickly dismissed by the country's leading economic thinkers. Times had changed indeed.

Today's modern China is far more eager to engage with the rest of the world, at least economically, largely because it has so much more to gain from financial globalization than it has to lose. So instead of stockpiling its treasure, China decided to put its capital to work in the global financial markets. The plan was for the country to put its money in what Chinese investment experts considered proven, substantial, profitable global assets. It seemed like a good idea at the time. Unfortunately, it didn't work out that way. The reason? The substantial global assets China decided to buy into were Western banks. In 2007. Right before the global financial crisis began. Ouch.

In addition to the major investments by China Investment Corporation in Blackstone Group and Morgan Stanley, China's state-owned securities brokerage firm CITIC Securities International Company put up £500 million for 6 percent of the Wall Street trading firm Bear Stearns. And its State Administration of Foreign Exchange poured £1.25 billion into an investment fund run by the private equity firm TPG, which TPG promptly handed over to the troubled savings and loan Washington Mutual. Two years later, Bear Stearns and Washington Mutual were gone as independent entities, both swallowed up by J.P. Morgan as part of the carnage from the financial crisis of 2009. And CIC's Blackstone and Morgan Stanley investments had each lost more than half of its value.

At a speech in Washington in February 2009, CIC chairman Lou Jiwei summed up his disappointment in the performance of his fund's investments this way: "If there is a big fat rabbit, we will shoot it. Maybe we were shot by Morgan Stanley. Who knows?"

If CIC was shot by Morgan Stanley the wound certainly wasn't fatal, and the patient made a relatively swift recovery. To China, CIC's financial hits were severe enough to attract the attention of government officials. But they were hardly financially crippling to the country. More important, they served as a necessary lesson about the ways of the investment business. While China would consider the ability to buy ownership stakes in major American financial institutions as politically advantageous at just about any price, the object of investing isn't to lose money, and certainly not a lot of money. The fact is that the US financial system was hot in 2007 leading up to the bursting of the financial bubble, and China's investments in Blackstone, Morgan Stanley, Bear Stearns, and TPG are examples of getting in at the top of the market.

Yet give Chinese investment officials credit: they definitely learned from their mistakes. After the Blackstone and Morgan Stanley investments in 2007, Lou Jiwei and the general manager of CIC's investments, Gao Xiqing, pulled back to reassess the investment market. After conducting an extensive review of their investment process, they decided that their purchases were way too focused on one industry—banking and financial services—which left the organization vulnerable when the global capital markets started to crack. As a result, Lou and Gao decided to take a hiatus from investing, revamp their operations, and generally bide their time before diving back into the markets.

By 2009, CIC was back with a vengeance—and a brand-new investing style. Using their time away from the financial markets to strategize, Lou and Gao completely reorganized the way the business ran and brought in new blood, including a new international advisory council consisting of respected academics, financial regulators, and investment professionals from around the world. CIC also actively participated in global recruiting drives for international investment talent led by the entire Chinese financial services industry, including the Bank of Shanghai, CITIC, the Shanghai Pudong Development Bank, and the Shanghai Stock Exchange. The organizations were generally looking for senior executives with risk management backgrounds and five to ten years of experience at multinational companies. As the Chinese found out, in a depressed worldwide job market, the available pool of talent for these positions was surprisingly deep. In December 2008, China's finance industry held job fairs in hotel ballrooms in New York, Chicago, and London, and thousands of professionals turned out for a chance to hand over their resumes and sit down for an interview. As of July 2009, CIC had a staff of 194, including 73 with international finance experience, 18 of whom weren't Chinese nationals.

Suddenly CIC was looking more and more like a successfully diversified major multinational investment firm rather than a fly-by-the-seat-of-the-pants operation that was built to chase after Wall Street's latest fashions. In August 2009, CIC released its first ever annual report, which showed that the fund had nearly £180 billion in capital to deploy. "CIC has already made sufficient preparations to welcome investment opportunities in 2009 and beyond," Lou stated in the report. "Our ample cash holdings will help us grasp potential investment opportunities in the future and realize satisfactory returns."

Ample cash holdings indeed. In February 2010, CIC disclosed its stock holdings in American companies as of the close of 2009 in a filing required by the SEC. Excluding its investment in Blackstone, which wasn't listed in the report, CIC held £6 billion worth of stock in US companies, which is an enormous number, to be sure. However, since it represented only 3 percent of CIC's total capital, it didn't amount to much exposure to the US market. Instead it appeared as if CIC's investment managers had avoided much of the meltdown in the American economy. At the close of 2009, the fund held relatively tiny positions in well-known large-capitalization companies like Aetna, Apple, Citigroup, Coors, Eli Lilly, Freeport-McMoRan Copper & Gold, Goodyear, Johnson & Johnson, Merck, Pfizer, UnitedHealth Group, Visa, and Wells Fargo. If the list was remarkable, it was for its *lack* of bold moves. CIC seemed to be building a diversified long-term portfolio rather than creating a saber-rattling active investment fund like many people had feared. However, that doesn't mean that CIC will remain a passive investor as it continues spreading its cash around the globe. The fact is, in 2009 being cautious was a good investment strategy in the damaged US market: safe and with a focus on long-range value. But that won't always be the case. As Chinese investors gradually become major shareholders in American companies, it's hard to imagine they'll hold their tongues. Few major investors do.

In the meantime, as CIC was deemphasizing investments in US stocks it was searching the rest of the world for valuable commodities. According to the Chinese government's official press agency, Xinhua, economists at the Asian Development Bank, which advises CIC on investment moves, found that investments in bulk commodities like oil and natural gas would help "mitigate risks in China's huge foreign exchange reserves." So in 2009, in addition to CIC's £1 billion investment on a 17 percent stake in Canada's mining company Teck Resources, the fund spent £590 million on an 11 percent stake in the Kazakhstan oil and gas company JSC KazMunaiGas Exploration Production; £190 million on a 45 percent stake in Nobel Oil Group of Russia; and £450 million on a 20 percent stake in GCL-Poly Energy Holdings, the largest maker of polysilicon in China and a significant player in the Chinese solar energy industry. In addition, CIC added to its "alternative assets" by putting £600 million into the Los Angeles private equity firm

Oaktree Capital Management to go along with its Blackstone investment and a £2 billion investment in the Manhattan private equity shop J. C. Flowers & Co. The fund also pumped a billion dollars into a variety of hedge funds through outside investment managers. And it made a direct investment of £125 million in the London hedge fund Capula Investment Management. With all of these moves, CIC posted a return of about 10 percent on its investments in 2009, up from 6.8 percent in 2008. The transformation had begun to pay dividends already.

But beyond simply revamping the country's sovereign wealth fund, Chinese authorities also took a fresh look at the way they were using their reserves. As a result, the government launched its own massive purchasing program in 2008. Using its state-owned businesses and the reserves in the SAFE, it gathered up key assets that it was sure would gain in value over time; specifically, the natural resources that China requires but doesn't control. In 2009, China spent £15 billion in oil and natural gas acquisitions and tens of billions more on other natural resources. And the splurge has continued.

China's spree has been focused on Australia's vibrant metals and minerals industry. Sinosteel Corporation bought the iron ore mining company Midwest for £650 million (A$1.3 billion). Chinalco teamed with Alcoa to buy 12 percent of Rio Tinto for £8.8 billion. China Minmetals Corporation bought Oz Minerals for £940 million. Hunan Valin Iron and Steel Group invested £500 million for a small piece of Fortescue Metals Group. Yanzhou Coal Mining Company bought Felix Resources Ltd. for £1.9 billion. China Power Investment Corporation signed a £40 billion contract with Australian mining company Resourcehouse to build an enormous network of mines in the Australian outback that over twenty years will produce 30 million tons of coal for Chinese power stations. China's Anshan Iron & Steel Group Corporation signed a £43 billion, thirty-year deal to buy iron ore from Gindalbie Metals Ltd. And Chinese officials indicated that they would be actively on the prowl for additional deals.

After bulking up its metals supply, China turned its attention to the worldwide quest for oil and natural gas. The state-owned Chinese oil company Sinopec spent £4.4 billion to buy the Swiss oilfield exploration company Addax Petroleum, which has reserves in Nigeria, Gabon, and Iraq. The China National Offshore Oil Corporation, also known as CNOOC, purchased the Norwegian oilfield services firm Awilco Offshore for £1.25 billion. CNOOC and Sinopec paid £800 million for a 20 percent stake in an Angolan oil field owned by Marathon Oil Corporation. PetroChina bought a 45 percent stake in the major oil refining firm Singapore Petroleum Company for £600 million. China National Petroleum Corporation tried to buy Vernex Energy of Calgary, Canada, which has a 50 percent interest in a Libyan oil field, before the deal was scuttled.

But it wasn't just China's oil companies doing the deal making. The government itself also got in on the act. China signed a deal to lend Russian crude oil producers Rosneft and Transneft £17.5 billion in return for 15 million tons of crude a year for twenty years out of the companies' Siberian oil field. That's 300,000 barrels a day, or roughly 4 percent of China's total demand. It agreed to spend £16 billion to build three oil refineries in Nigeria. It loaned £7 billion to the Brazilian oil producer Petrobras, which will enable the company to gain access to a highly promising but hard to reach oil field off its coast and, in turn, provide China with 160,000 barrels of crude a day. The country entered into £7.25 billion worth of cash-for-oil deals with Venezuelan oil companies, with the explicit blessing of the country's outspoken president, Hugo Chávez, which amounted to a series of down payments on cheap oil. China loaned the government of Kazakhstan £6 billion in return for about 56,000 barrels of crude a day, which is roughly half the output of the Kazakh oil company MangistauMunaiGaz. The deal also will help Kazakhstan build a pipeline from the Caspian Sea on the country's west coast to the south near Uzbekistan, which is closer to the Chinese border. And China's sovereign wealth fund invested more than £600 million on a joint venture with Canada's Penn West Energy to develop oil sands along the Peace River in Alberta.

"This is an example of what I call energy diplomacy," says Mikkal Herberg, the research director on Asian energy security at the National Bureau of Asian Research and a former director for global energy and economics at ARCO. "You have these Chinese oil companies that want to go out and explore for oil where everyone else is, that's their corporate instinct. So what they do is feed the Beijing leadership's perception that they can support China's international expansion and create new allies while at the same time providing for the country's energy security. Then Beijing willingly supplies the funding for these companies to go out and capture oil. But the truth is, in many ways Beijing wants to remain at arm's length from the regimes it does business with. Their attitude is let's access the energy resources, but let's not get dragged into the domestic politics and geopolitics of these regions. They do what they call friendship and cooperation, which basically is building soccer stadiums and things like that, and they have official state visits where they profess deep long-term relationships with their new friends. But for the most part they don't want to get involved in influencing policy in these regions. They're just trying to support their own business and economic interests. And this detached attitude often is very attractive to the countries where China's investing, because the last thing they want is outside influences telling them what to do."

Of course, energy diplomacy isn't the only thing a wealthy country can accomplish with a gigantic wad of cash. You also can use it to buy all kinds of new alliances. That helps explain why in 2009 the Chinese government started to strategically spread its wealth around. It wanted to make friends and influence nations. Beginning in its own backyard, China used its tremendous capital advantage to reach out to neighbors and mend rocky relationships. As a way of helping Southeast Asia fend off the global financial crisis, the country set up a £6 billion infrastructure fund and put together £9 billion in credits and loans. Then it spear-headed a £6 billion investment cooperation fund with the powerful regional economic organization, the Association of Southeast Asian Nations (ASEAN), whose ten member countries were also offered £9 billion in credits and loans. Finally, it gave nearly £25 million in direct aid to the deeply impoverished nations of Cambodia, Laos, and Myanmar, while also pledging 300,000 tons of rice and establishing 2,200 scholarships for students in those countries. Talk about creating goodwill.

"The game for the next thirty, forty years is going to be about resource competition," says David Rothkopf, visiting scholar at the Carnegie Endowment for International Peace and a specialist on international trade policy in the Clinton administration. "The Chinese have been very aggressive in tying up the resources they think they're going to need, whether it's agricultural resources, which by extension means water resources, or mineral resources, or energy resources; they've gone around the world and bought it. They also have leveraged their financial power by being much less politically demanding than we've been. We set all sorts of conditions for the aid that we give, but China has very few conditions. They just want access to the resources. So they don't say that you have to be democratic or that we're going to give you a hard time on human rights issues. They'd appreciate it if you didn't support the government of Tibet or Taiwan, but those two issues are so narrow that if you're in Angola, what do you care? You want the best deal. And in a world in which many countries are skeptical about the intent of the United States and big US companies, it's good to have an alternative like China."

HOW CHINA BOUGHT TAIWAN

China also made friendly overtures toward Taiwan, the tiny island nation just off its coast that since 1st October 1949, has served as a capitalist refuge following the Chinese Civil War that ushered Mao Tse-tung's Communist Party into power. The relationship between the two bitter rivals began to thaw in 2008, when Taiwan President Ma Ying-jeou took office and pledged to put aside old hardened feelings about mainland China and begin a new era of cooperation between the two countries. Since then, China and Taiwan have engaged in a series of economic deals that have closely tied the nations together. The British bank Standard Chartered calls the dramatic change in relations the "great leap across the Strait," referring to the 110-mile-wide Taiwan Strait in the South China Sea that separates the two countries. Meanwhile, the investment bank Goldman Sachs describes it as a "paradigm shift" in Southeast Asian economic dynamics.

In a surprisingly short amount of time, the bonds between the one-time rivals have become extremely deep. In May 2009, delegates from China and Taiwan signed £3.8 billion in cooperative "cross-strait" economic deals. At the same time, the Chinese government was sending its first trade delegation of forty-six companies—including Haier, Lenovo, Sinosteel, and Sichuan Changhong Electric—to Taiwan to buy several billion dollars' worth of goods from Taiwanese technology companies, like liquid crystal display panels and memory chips. This was followed by a trip to Taiwan organized by the Chinese Video Industry Association, during which Chinese companies bought £1.5 billion worth of television production equipment.

For their part, Taiwan officials said they were eagerly welcoming the influx of Chinese people and businesses to their island. In 2008 Taiwan opened its borders to Chinese tourists and shortly afterward launched flights between the mainland and the island, ending a six-decade ban on air links. Today more than six hundred thousand tourists from China annually flock to scenic Taiwan. In July 2009, Taiwan allowed Chinese companies to invest in Taiwanese businesses for the first time, although the potential investments would be limited to one hundred different sectors, including textiles, telecommunications services, motorcar manufacturing, wholesaling and retailing, hotels, and airport and seaport management. And in February 2010, Taiwan, for the first time, allowed its cutting-edge technology companies that make silicon chips and flat-panel video screens to conduct business in China.

The logic behind the loosening of trade restrictions was easy to see. China is expected to become the leading market for flat-screen televisions by 2011 or 2012, so the Taiwanese technology industry needs to have a presence there. Economic realities like these are pushing Taiwan and China closer and closer together. Despite the limitations on trade that remain between the two nations, the door to cross-strait partnerships has been kicked open. Clearly this is not your parents' geopolitical rivalry anymore.

However, diplomatic and trade ties with China often have multiple meanings. In this case, Taiwan's new closeness with the mainland could be seen as a sensible economic move for the tiny island nation. But at the same time, it was part of China's bear hug strategy—trying gradually to squeeze Taiwan into its empire.

That's why Chinese officials were so furious in January 2010 when the United States announced the sale of $6.4 billion (£4 billion) worth of military equipment to Taiwan. The deal included Blackhawk helicopters, Patriot and Harpoon missiles, mine-hunting ships, and communications technology for Taiwanese fighter jets. America had been providing arms to Taiwan since 1979, when then president Jimmy Carter's administration signed the Taiwan Relations Act to protect the island from China's encroaching influence. China never approved of this arrangement, because it viewed Taiwan as a breakaway province that would eventually return to the fold.

Now China was furious, but, oddly, not with Taiwan. Instead it was irate with the United States for meddling with its budding friendship. After the arms deals became public, the Chinese government issued a stern statement from Vice Foreign Minister He

Yafei: "This US plan will definitely further undermine China-US relations and bring about serious negative impact on exchanges and cooperation in major areas between the two countries." The statement also warned America to "fully recognize the gravity of the issue, revoke the erroneous decision on arms sales to Taiwan, and stop selling weapons to Taiwan. Otherwise, the United States must shoulder the responsibility for the grave aftermath."

Then, to more concretely express China's displeasure, Chinese officials threatened to place sanctions on the American companies involved in the arms deals. China also temporarily suspended military exchanges with the United States and cut off all meetings between US and Chinese military officials. It threatened to boycott President Obama's planned nuclear summit in the spring of 2010. China's state-owned airline, Air China, decided to give a £1 billion contract for twenty new jets to Airbus, the European aviation consortium based in France, rather than America's Boeing Company. And Chinese government officials refused to go along with diplomatic proposals backed by the United States, Europe, and Russia calling for tighter sanctions on Iran because of its expanding nuclear program.

In short, China threw up a huge diplomatic roadblock around the world to make its point. The only party spared China's wrath was Taiwan, which purchased the weapons in the first place. Why did Taiwan get off so easily? It's impossible to know for sure, because Chinese government officials never discuss such issues, but the fact is that China was busy courting Taiwan during this whole process. It didn't want to disrupt the improving relations between the two nations. Instead China continued its push for increased trade and diplomatic ties with Taiwan. After all, that's what this was all about. And ultimately the strategy paid off. In June 2010, China and Taiwan reached an agreement on a broad trade pact that reduced tariffs and opened up the financial services markets in both countries. Following the deal's signing, Taiwanese officials announced at a press conference that they were seeking an even closer economic alliance with their gigantic neighbor. Clearly, China's bear hug had worked.

China's "charm offensive" in Southeast Asia has even spread to nations that once were sworn enemies of China but have recently softened their diplomatic stances toward the country for economic reasons. In May 2009, Vietnam's government intensified its efforts to bring in investment capital from Chinese steel companies, even as the country's environmentalists and political hard-liners—who refused to forgive or forget China's invasion in 1979—aggressively fought the deals. But Vietnam had a problem: namely, a rising trade deficit with China, which stood at £7 billion in 2009. So Prime Minister Nguyen Tan Dung decided to try to correct the imbalance by providing China with the natural resources its population required. Against an overwhelming tide of criticism within the country, Vietnam National Coal-Mineral Industries Group entered into a £300 million joint venture with Chinalco to extract bauxite, a key raw material for producing aluminum, from Vietnam's mountainous Central Highlands. And the Vietnamese government indicated that more deals were in the pipeline. Vietnam's Central Highlands are of particular interest to Chinese metals manufacturers because it's believed to hold the world's third largest reserve of bauxite: 5.4 billion metric tons' worth. The Vietnamese government estimates that it will take more than £10 billion in investment capital to build the drilling and refining facilities necessary for maximizing the area's mining potential. And when you need that much cash, there are only a few places in the world you can turn to. Which explains why Vietnam's leaders are willing to defy their people's wishes and deal with the Chinese. Because they have to.

It's not just nations in China's corner of the earth that have been seduced by the country's financial might. Latin American nations have been particularly eager to get access to China's deep pockets. For example, when Argentina feared in March 2009 that its peso was losing the confidence of the currency markets, it signed a three-year £7 billion currency swap deal with China that would enable Argentina to manage the value of its currency. Argentina is an important market for China because China buys about two-thirds of Argentina's key export, soya beans. So it stepped in and provided assistance. The same thing happened in Jamaica, which was descending into economic chaos in the spring of 2009. With Jamaica's two usual financial saviors—the United States and the United Kingdom—distracted by their own issues, the island nation's leadership turned to China for assistance. China responded with £95 million in loan packages that *overnight* made it Jamaica's largest financial partner. Although the deals came with no strings attached, Jamaica is rich with mineral resources, particularly bauxite. Jamaica is the fourth largest producer of bauxite ore in the world.

"When you think about it, the number of tools governments have to influence other countries is really limited," Rothkopf says. "We're in a world in which outright warfare isn't really an option anymore because it's too costly in terms of human life and in terms of finances. So you really can't use force to make your point. And the global institutions are very weak, so using those mechanisms isn't very effective. The biggest power is the power of the checkbook. During the Cold War, the United States and Russia wrote a lot of checks to get people on one side of the ledger or the other. At the end of the Cold War we thought that we were entering a period in which the United States would be the sole superpower and have all this leverage. And it did, until it couldn't write the checks anymore."

Even established "old world" nations have been forced to acknowledge China's emerging global economic authority. Leading up to the G20 summit in 2009, China and France, which for decades had battled over the sovereignty of Tibet, agreed to restore high-level diplomatic contacts and pledged to promote a more cooperative relationship. As part of the agreement, France promised not to support Tibetan independence "in any form," the

Chinese news agency Xinhua reported. China actually pushed this agreement to completion with some old-fashioned hardball tactics. Chinese officials were livid when French president Nicolas Sarkozy met with the Dalai Lama, Tibet's exiled Buddhist leader, in 2008. So in early 2009, all of China's trade missions to Europe skipped France. This got the attention of Sarkozy and his advisers, and a few months later, France was agreeing to give up the goal of Tibetan independence.

But for the pinnacle of international diplomatic cachet, China managed to arrange a meeting with Britain's Prince of Wales in April 2009, a first on UK soil. Prince Charles traditionally hasn't been a big fan of China's leaders, most notably referring to them as "appalling old waxworks" when he met them at the handover of the former British colony Hong Kong. He's never paid a visit to mainland China. In 1999 Charles ruffled diplomatic feathers by failing to attend a state banquet in London held for then Chinese president Jiang Zemin. And in 2005 he managed to avoid President Hu Jintao on his visit to Britain, even arranging to be out of the country during Hu's state dinner. The prince has also stated his admiration for the Dalai Lama. But on 2nd April 2009, Prince Charles finally agreed to hold a private meeting with Hu Jintao in Hu's suite at the Mandarin Oriental Hotel in London. The prince's press staff described the meeting as part of a general thawing of relations between the two countries.

"The attitude frankly just about everywhere in the world is that the Chinese have got lots of money, and they represent a huge market, and they're the most dynamic part of the global economy, so we need to seize this opportunity before anyone else does," says the Council on Foreign Relations' Mallaby. "There's been a huge amount of grasping at the big opportunity represented by China. And it's perfectly natural that this should happen. If you're, say, an African country and you've been dealing with your traditional Western partners for a long time and you see this new player coming on the scene that's willing to invest lots and lots of money in your economy and will want various commodities in exchange, you get interested. It means you have another big money partner to play off of your traditional ones, which puts you in an advantageous situation. This is a transformation we're seeing play out all over the global economy."

NEGOTIATING WITH AN IRON FIST

Despite all that China has done to try to open itself up to the modern global economy, doing business in the country remains a challenge for many foreign companies because of China's notoriously byzantine corporate culture. China erects formal barriers to foreign businesses, such as its indigenous innovation policy, which encourages the growth of Chinese technology companies by giving Chinese manufacturers of computers, software, telecommunication products, and other high-tech equipment favored status in gaining government contracts. An April 2010 report by the American Chamber of Commerce in China found that more than half of the US businesses operating there believed that they would be hurt by the rules. Furthermore, the Chinese government uses a series of tax rebates and quotas to discriminate against foreign agriculture and manufactured goods, the US Trade Representative's office reported in March 2010. China's real estate industry is so highly regulated that it has become increasingly difficult for foreign investors to buy property. And the nation has a formal system of scrutinizing foreign acquisitions of every Chinese company for potential national security problems.

But beyond the difficulties that foreign corporations have in simply breaking down the door and gaining access to the Chinese market, many find that it's just as tricky to survive once they're inside because conditions are fluid and can change rapidly. In China, business regularly mingles with politics, foreign policy, and the legal system in ways that people from the West have a hard time understanding. This clash of cultures can result in real consequences for the individuals caught in the middle.

Perhaps the best example of how even wealthy multinational executives can suffer when things turn sour in China was the March 2010 prosecution of Stern Hu and three other employees of the Australian mining conglomerate Rio Tinto on bribery and corporate espionage charges. As the case starkly revealed, when it comes to conducting business in China, nothing is as simple as it seems.

Stern Hu was a man who deeply understood the ins and outs of China's intricate and mercurial corporate world. Born in 1963 in the crowded industrial seaport city of Tianjin on the bustling Bohai Gulf in northeastern China, he was given the name Hu Shi-tai by his dissident parents, who endured years in Mao Tse-tung's brutal labor camps during the Great Proletarian Cultural Revolution that lasted from 1966 to 1976. With his parents working as peasants in the countryside for much of his early childhood, Hu was raised by his grandparents and was often left alone to fend for himself, even as a very young boy. This hardened the child and left him with a relentless drive to succeed.

Fortunately, he was a natural student who excelled in school. Through education, Hu was able to overcome his Dickensian upbringing, eventually graduating from the prestigious Peking University, where he studied history and met his wife, Zhulie, and earned a master's degree from the Chinese Academy of Social Sciences. A trained violinist, Hu decided to adopt the English name Stern after seeing Isaac Stern perform in Beijing.

With his degrees in hand, Stern Hu started his career at the state-run China International Trust and Investment Bank. However, he was asked to leave the bank in 1989 after a picture of him taking part in the Tiananmen Square demonstrations appeared in an Italian magazine. So he took a job with the Australian communications technology manufacturer AWA Limited, selling traffic management systems out of the firm's Beijing office. In the early 1990s, Hu's wife and the couple's first son, Terence, moved to Manly, Australia, a gracious beach town suburb of Sydney, while Stern shuttled back and forth to Beijing. During their time in Australia, Zhulie Anglicized her name to Julie and became pregnant with the couple's second son, Charlie. After Charlie's birth, the Hu family, including Stern, became Australian citizens, surrendering their Chinese citizenship as required under China's immigration laws.

The move very well could have been controversial within China's insular business culture. But it appeared to have absolutely no impact on Hu's career. Indeed, his reputation as a savvy operator who could cut a smooth path through the complex bureaucracies of the Chinese government and corporate world only grew.

Eventually, Hu left the technology field for the lucrative Far Eastern metals industry. He was hired to be the main iron ore salesman in northern China for a division of the company that was about to become, through a series of corporate mergers, the massive Anglo-Australian mining conglomerate Rio Tinto Group. At Rio Tinto, Hu rose quickly through the corporate chain of command. In particular, he developed a knack for using his northern Chinese background to build close relationships with customers, something that often eluded foreign nationals who weren't sensitive to China's quirky social mores. In time, Rio Tinto named him the lead price negotiator for its entire multibillion-dollar Chinese iron ore business.

To apprehend just how significant the job of chief negotiator is, you have to understand the way the metals industry operates in China. Since 1996, China has been the world's largest producer of steel, which, of course, is made from iron ore. Throughout the late twentieth century, the country largely relied on its domestic iron ore deposits to satisfy demand. But over the years, that demand continued to grow exponentially, to the point that by 2008, China was consuming almost 60 percent of the planet's annual iron ore supply. And nearly all of it was being imported from abroad.

Chinese metals executives, however, weren't surprised by this development. Indeed, they could see the shift coming. By the late 1990s, Chinese steel experts already had recognized that the country was in an untenable position; there was no way that China's domestic iron ore deposits could satisfy the country's increasing demand for steel. So starting in 2001, the nation stepped up its overseas importing of iron ore. By 2003, it was the largest iron ore importer in the world. As a result, major international mining companies like Rio Tinto and BHP Billiton of Australia and Vale of Brazil suddenly started doing enormous amounts of business with large customers in China, such as Shanghai Baosteel Group Corporation, Jinan Iron and Steel Co., and LiaoNing An-Ben Iron and Steel Group—a situation that continues to this day.

The way the relationship works is that each year, the Chinese steel companies independently estimate how much steel they're expecting to produce. They then get together and, usually led by Shanghai Baosteel, negotiate with the major global mining companies to lock in a contracted price for the iron ore they're going to need over the next twelve months. The annual price talks, which almost always are shrouded in deep secrecy, usually begin in January and are wrapped up by June. Considering that Chinese steel companies buy more than four hundred million tons of iron ore each year, these contracts are worth hundreds of billions of dollars and typically amount to some of the biggest annual business deals in the world.

As Rio Tinto's chief iron ore price negotiator, Hu represented the company on the other side of the table from his Chinese counterparts. Although he still maintained a home in Sydney, he rarely returned there. Instead the Hu family spent almost all of their time in Shanghai so that Stern could stay close to his customers. Along the way, Hu developed a well-deserved reputation for squeezing every possible yuan out of China's metals industry. In 2008 he was part of the mining negotiating team that secured a 71 percent increase in the price that Chinese steel producers paid for iron ore. And that was on top of a 31 percent price hike in 2007.

In short, Hu had become a significant player in the international metals market. In many ways, he was a modern Chinese success story, despite the fact that he worked for an overseas company and had surrendered his Chinese citizenship. He was still a symbol to the world of how even the most deeply scarred children from Mao's Cultural Revolution managed to survive and thrive, eventually earning leadership positions in the global economy.

But all that changed on 5th July 2009, a hot and sticky summer Sunday night in Shanghai. Hu was still busy trying to wrap up the annual steel price negotiations for 2009 and 2010, which had missed their 30th June deadline. The Chinese steel companies were pushing for a 40 percent cut from the previous price. Hu, however, was holding out for a reduction of 30 percent to 33 percent, which was what other Asian nations had settled for. But for some reason, the Chinese had become absolutely intractable on this point. By then, the talks had gone on longer than any Hu had experienced—longer, in fact, than any iron ore price negotiations between China and Australia. So he was planning to spend the sweltering evening working in Rio Tinto's air-conditioned offices on the fifty-first floor of the Hong Kong New World Tower in Luwan, a largely commercial district in the center of the city, going over research in preparation for further talks.

Unfortunately for Hu, the negotiations would have to go on without him. That evening, Chinese authorities detained Hu and three other Rio Tinto employees—Liu Caikui, Wang Yong, and Ge Minqiang, all of whom were Chinese nationals on Hu's senior staff—and brought them to the headquarters of the Shanghai State Security Bureau. Chinese officials believed that they had stolen state secrets to get an advantage in the iron ore negotiations.

This being China, the rest of the world didn't learn about Stern Hu's detention until two days later, when Rio Tinto announced that four employees were being held in China. The initial statement indicated that Chinese officials hadn't told the company what its workers had allegedly done. Then the next day, Australia's foreign affairs minister, Stephen Smith, revealed that Chinese intelligence authorities were accusing the Rio Tinto employees of espionage, stealing state secrets, and causing economic harm to the country.

Rio Tinto executives were stunned by the news and quickly denied that their employees had done anything wrong. "We have been advised by the Australian government of this surprising allegation. We are not aware of any evidence that would support such an investigation," the company said in a statement shortly after the news broke.

But China refused to back down, insisting that Hu was the mastermind of a corporate espionage operation. Qin Gang, the spokesman for the Ministry of Foreign Affairs, stated that the government had ample evidence to back up its charges. "Chinese authorities have in fact obtained evidence which proves they stole—for a foreign country—Chinese state secrets, which hurt China's economic interests and economic security," Qin told reporters.

Over the next week, general descriptions of the kinds of evidence that Chinese investigators had uncovered started to dribble out in the local media. *China Daily,* an independent English-language Chinese newspaper that's typically known for reprinting the government's take on events, reported that government officials had reviewed Rio Tinto's computer files and discovered that they were filled with detailed information about China's steel mills, including "sales, purchasing plans, raw material stocks, and schedules of production." Other reports out of the Shanghai State Security Bureau stated that Liu Caikui had been observed courting and bribing executives from Chinese steel companies to get access to secret information. However, despite the anonymous leaks, the Chinese government refused to show anyone the actual evidence it had purportedly gathered.

In the meantime, Chinese authorities publicly reassured Rio Tinto executives, Australian officials, and the rest of the world that the case would proceed "properly, according to law." But to anyone familiar with China's legal system, this was hardly reassuring, for a number of reasons. First, state secret cases are tried behind closed doors. All evidence is confidential, and the defendants have limited access to their lawyers; it's very difficult to be proven innocent. Second, Chinese state secret laws are widely considered some of the most capriciously ambiguous rules in the world. A 2007 report by the New York–based group Human Rights in China showed how fungible China's state secret laws can be. "They're both a shield—classifying a broad range of information and keeping it from public view—and a sword—using it as a means to crack down on individuals who are critical of the government," the report concluded. Third, in Chinese state secret cases, the government has wide latitude in defining what actually constitutes a state secret. It can classify any document produced by any arm of the government or any state-run business as a secret and has the authority to reclassify information as a secret even after it's been publicly disclosed by the government or a corporation. Finally, sentences for Chinese state secret convictions are notoriously harsh, ranging from a minimum of five years in prison to the death penalty.

The heightened tenor of the case was amplified a week after the detentions, when *China Daily* published a scathing front page story filled with anonymous sources maintaining that corruption was rampant at Rio Tinto. The story opened dramatically: "Executives from all 16 Chinese steel mills participating in iron ore price talks this year have been bribed by Rio Tinto employees." It went on to cite an unnamed Chinese steel executive saying, "Rio Tinto bribed them [to get access to industry data], which has become an unwritten industry practice. If companies didn't accept, they would have cut supplies and so the whole steel industry has been bribed." Shortly after the story appeared, Chinese authorities revealed that they had widened their probe, detaining and questioning roughly a dozen different steel industry executives, including Wang Hongjiu, head of the ocean shipping department at the Chinese steel company Laigang Group, and Tan Yixin, a senior executive at Shougang Corp., one of China's largest steel manufacturers. Suddenly a thick air of paranoia descended over the Chinese steel business.

"The whole industry is in a state of shock at the moment," Paul Bartholomew, a steel analyst in Shanghai, told a reporter from the *New York Times* a few days after Hu was arrested. "There's a sense of fear. 'Don't talk to us,' or 'Who's going to get tapped on the shoulder next?'"

A week after the arrests, Rio Tinto pulled all of the company's non-Chinese staff out of China for their own protection. A few members of the sales staff stayed, but the rest gladly retreated to Australia. Still, even as an increasingly cautious atmosphere was taking hold in the Chinese steel business, a consensus was building among iron ore experts that the arrests weren't actually about Rio Tinto or Hu at all. Instead industry insiders believed that China was really playing hardball in an attempt to gain bargaining power in the bogged down steel price negotiations.

Over the past few years, officials in Beijing had grown frustrated by the high price the country was paying for iron ore. The government was determined to extract a steep discount, steeper than the price reductions that competing Japanese and Korean steel companies had negotiated. China's plan was to have its steelmakers negotiate together and create a bulk "umbrella" price from Rio Tinto, BHP Billiton, and Vale. But the problem for China, which imports more than 450 metric tons of iron ore a year, is that its steel industry is highly fragmented. The country has about eight hundred different steel companies with a combined total of more than twelve hundred steel mills. Most of these steel companies are relatively small. For instance, in 2008, China's largest steelmaker, Shanghai Baosteel, accounted for less than 5 percent of the country's steel production. So getting all of these different entities to work together can be like herding cats. As a result, as talks got under way, the Chinese negotiators grew increasingly frustrated with the Australian mining companies' ability to strike individual deals with small and medium-sized steel mills, undercutting the united front shown by the major Chinese steel manufacturers.

Australian Foreign Minister Smith all but confirmed this suspicion after a meeting about the Hu case with China's vice foreign minister, He Yafei. Coming out of the conference in Beijing, Smith told reporters that "it's quite clear that they are focusing on a criminal or judicial investigation relating to the 2009 iron ore negations." Then he added, "They are not interested in what we would regard as espionage or national security matters. These are commercial and economic matters, which, under their general definition of state secrets, is included." This Chinese steel industry experts took to mean that China was applying its state secret laws in an effort to get an upper hand in the iron ore price talks.

Beyond the price negotiations, China had other potential reasons for taking a hard-line position against Rio Tinto. In June 2009, Rio Tinto had backed out of a £12 billion (A$24 billion) deal to sell convertible bonds and stakes in some of its most important mining assets to Chinalco. The sales, part of China's ongoing accumulation of foreign resources, would have increased Chinalco's stake in Rio Tinto to nearly 20 percent. But at the last minute, Rio Tinto executives got cold feet. Instead they decided to enter into a joint venture with BHP Billiton and sell £9.4 billion worth of stock to its existing shareholders for financing. Chinalco's leaders and the Chinese leadership were irate. The Chinese Iron and Steel Association, a lobbying group for the country's steel mills, issued a statement complaining that the deal "goes in the direction of a monopoly." Chinalco's president, Xiong Weiping, said the company was even willing to make major concessions—such as cutting its overall ownership stake down to 18 percent, reducing its interest in Rio Tinto's enormous Hamersley iron ore mine in Western Australia, and improving the terms of the bond issue—to get the deal done.

"We believe these are very significant concessions and

amendments to the original transactions," Xiong said at a press conference after Rio Tinto cancelled the deal. "They should be sufficient to meet the requirements of both the shareholders and the Australian regulators."

The Australians, however, saw things somewhat differently. Australia has some of the world's largest deposits of valuable minerals and metals, such as bauxite, coal, copper, gold, iron ore, nickel, and uranium. And in 2009, as the world crumbled in a global financial crisis, China started throwing around its cash to gain access to prized natural resources. In particular, the Chinese leadership was targeting Australian mining companies.

China's first move came in March 2009 when Hunan Valin Iron and Steel Group bought nearly 18 percent of Fortescue Metals Group, Australia's fourth largest mining company, for £624 million. Then in April, China Minmetals Corporation tried to buy Oz Minerals for £1.3 billion. But the deal was blocked by Australia's foreign investments review board because the country's military leaders were concerned about the potential for China to spy on an Australian aerospace site near one of Oz's key mines. Eventually China Minmetals bought most of Oz Minerals for about £1 billion after removing the troublesome mine from the agreement. Still, the acquisition was the largest takeover ever by a Chinese company of an Australian mining firm. Finally, a few weeks after China Minmetals announced its initial offer for Oz Minerals, Chinalco made its bid for a major stake in Rio Tinto.

By the time the scope of China's potential investments in the Australian mining industry began to sink in, many Australians were openly questioning China's motives and asking how their country could get out of these deals. "It's the Communist People's Republic of China, one hundred percent Communist owned, buying up sections of the country and minerals in the ground that they will then sell to the Communist People's Republic of China," Barnaby Joyce, the politically conservative Australian politician who's the head of the country's National Party, ranted to the *New*

York Times. "We're going to live off the commission on the way through. But they'll try to make sure we get as little as possible."

These quasinationalist concerns about China buying up Australia's precious natural resources helped drive Rio Tinto executives to rethink their partnership with Chinalco. With the pressure mounting, they decided that a deal with another Anglo-Australian mining corporation, BHP Billiton, was politically safer than deepening their engagement with the Chinese. A month later, Stern Hu and his team were in a Chinese prison. To many observers of the global steel industry, these developments were too coincidental not to be related.

But beyond the Chinese steel industry, the rest of the business and diplomatic worlds were watching what was happening with Stern Hu and his Rio Tinto team, and they didn't like what they were seeing. Lawyers started advising their international clients to be wary of operating in China. Australian officials, including then prime minister Kevin Rudd, who speaks Mandarin and previously served as Australia's ambassador to Beijing, argued that the Chinese government was blatantly interfering with ordinary trade practices, and that the case should be dropped and the Rio Tinto employees released immediately. US Commerce Secretary Gary Locke visited Beijing on 16th July to press Premier Wen Jiabao to consider the global impact of Hu's detention. Locke told an interviewer from CNN International in China that for multinational companies to invest in the country, they "need to have assurances and confidence" that their employees will receive fair treatment from the government and not be harassed by state officials.

With outside pressure starting to build, the Chinese Foreign Ministry quickly swung into action, attempting to tamp down any calls to stop global investment in China. In an interview with Xinhua, the government's official press agency, spokesman Qin Gang insisted that the government would protect the rights of foreign companies. To explain his point he quoted two Chinese proverbs. The first was, "May you be prosperous." The second was, "A real gentleman only gains his wealth in the right ways." To explain what he meant by that, Qin, in an obvious reference to the Rio Tinto case, said, "The right way has two meanings: one is legally and the other is honestly. Companies should do business legally and honestly." Still, Qin said that his general message to global corporations was, "We wish all of you good fortune," adding that the government would provide an enticing environment for businesses to make their fortunes.

Despite these friendly entreaties, China couldn't ease the global pressure to resolve Stern Hu's legal situation. Suddenly the Chinese leadership was seriously concerned that the detention of Stern Hu would have a broad, expensive impact on the rest of the country's businesses by isolating China in the world of global commerce. With the case unraveling and the annual iron ore negotiations bogged down because Rio Tinto was focused solely on freeing its employees, Chinese legal authorities began to rethink the charges they'd levied against Hu and his team. By the end of July, China publicly backed away from the assertion that the four were guilty of espionage. On 20th July, Stephen Smith stated on Australian television that it appeared as if Chinese authorities were going to focus on the commercial bribery charges rather than the far more serious allegations of stealing state secrets. However, he added, there was no way to know for sure precisely how China was treating the case because the legal proceedings were all happening behind the veil of government secrecy.

By early 2010, the legal status of Hu and his three colleagues was still up in the air, so Rio Tinto decided it was time to reach out to China. Company executives recognized that a prolonged fight with Australia's biggest trading partner could be severely damaging. In 2009 alone, Rio Tinto's sales to China amounted to $10.6 billion (£6.7 billion), or roughly 24 percent of its total global revenues. But with the dispute between company and customer escalating, Rio saw that some corporate diplomacy would be needed to keep that cash flowing.

To help thaw the frosty relationship, Rio Tinto named Ian Bauert, who'd set up the company's first office in China back in the 1980s, to the newly created position of managing director for China. Bauert was placed in Shanghai and given the task of rebuilding the diplomatic bridge to Chinese officials. "This appointment recognizes the importance of China as a long-term partner with our organization and our intention to foster new and dynamic relationships as China's development continues," Doug Ritchie, the head of Rio's Energy group and the company's activities in China, said in announcing Bauert's appointment.

Although Rio Tinto didn't mention Stern Hu in its statement, his case wasn't far from the minds of the Chinese. Indeed, the Xinhua report on Bauert's appointment specifically noted the reasons for Rio Tinto's strained relations with China, stating, "Rio Tinto's business in China was hampered by the arrest of its Shanghai office staff member Stern Hu on charges of stealing state secrets and that Rio Tinto spurned a 19.5-billion-US-dollar investment from Chinalco last year."

Finally, on 10th February 2010, eight months after Hu and his three colleagues were detained, Chinese authorities formally indicted them. The charges confirmed Rio Tinto's suspicions that their purported crimes did not involve espionage or stealing state secrets. Instead they centered on corporate malfeasance, particularly bribery. Prosecutors in Shanghai accused Hu and his team of "taking advantage of their position to seek profit for others, and asking for, or illegally accepting, huge amounts of money from Chinese steel enterprises," according to Xinhua. The prosecutors also said that the actions of Hu and his team had caused "extremely serious consequence[s]" for their Chinese customers.

The trial of the Rio Tinto employees began on 22nd March 2010, nine months after they'd been detained. It lasted just shy of three full days. As is often the case in Chinese legal proceedings, the hearings on the industrial espionage charges before a three-judge panel at the Shanghai No. 1 Intermediate People's Court were held behind closed doors, completely out of sight and sound from the public, the press, and even emissaries from Rio Tinto and the Australian government. However, Chinese officials agreed to open the bribery portion of the trial to the defendants' immediate families and officials from the Australian consul's office, giving outsiders a rare glimpse at how Chinese justice operates.

On the trial's first day Hu and two of his colleagues, Liu Caikui and Ge Minqiang, opened the proceedings by dropping a bombshell. From the start they admitted that they had received several million dollars in bribes from Chinese steel mills looking to secure long-term contracts to buy Rio Tinto's iron ore. Hu told the court that he personally accepted two bribes totaling around £625,000 from two small mills eager for iron ore allocations. Wang Yong, who reported to a different manager at Rio Tinto, continued to maintain his innocence. The admissions of guilt were particularly surprising because Rio Tinto executives had consistently maintained to the public that their employees had done nothing wrong (although *The Australian* newspaper found that a secret internal investigation launched by Rio Tinto's top executives following the arrests cleared the iron ore division as a whole of wrongdoing but raised questions about Hu and certain members of his team). Now the Rio Tinto employees were changing their story and saying that they did take the money after all.

Legal analysts speculated that the guilty pleas likely were part of the defense team's larger strategy. The stark reality was that the case had become such a major international story that it was highly unlikely that China's legal officials would allow the Rio Tinto employees to escape punishment regardless of what was said in the courtroom. Why? Because to the rest of the world it would be seen as an admission of a mistake on China's part. So Hu and his colleagues likely were facing jail time no matter what. And the fact is that Chinese courts historically have been more lenient on parties that have acknowledged some form of culpability in a crime. So Hu and his colleagues were wise to admit any wrongdoing up front.

But based on their aggressive defense it's clear that the defendants saw the charges against them as far more complicated than just bribery or corporate espionage. For example, although three of the defendants admitted that they'd accepted bribes, they vigorously denied that they totaled anything like the £8.5 million the prosecution was alleging. Meanwhile, Australian officials pointed out in the press that since no one would be allowed to witness the corporate espionage portion of the trial it would be impossible to determine if true justice had been served. What's more, not a single employee of a Chinese steel mill had been charged with bribing Hu and his colleagues. Bribery obviously is one of those crimes where two parties have to be involved. Yet China's legal authorities were only prosecuting the Australians who had accepted the bribes and were ignoring the Chinese executives who did the bribing and then received preferential treatment from Rio Tinto.

The trial ended on 24th March. The expectation was that Hu and his colleagues would be sent to prison because three of the Rio Tinto employees had already pleaded guilty to bribery charges. However, since little was known about the espionage portion of the proceedings it was difficult to know just how severe the sentences would be. As it turned out, the sentences were pretty severe. On 29th March, the court handed down its decision. The three-judge panel found the defendants guilty of bribery and corporate espionage, according to Xinhua, ruling that from 2003 to 2009 "the four used improper means to acquire commercial secrets from Chinese steel companies. The information they obtained was used as a bargaining chip to jack up the price that China paid for its iron ore imports." Stern Hu was sentenced to ten years in jail and fined nearly £100,000 plus the amount of his "illegal earnings," which he'd already turned over. Ge Minqiang was sentenced to eight years; Liu Caikui was sentenced to seven years; and Wang Yong received the longest sentence, fourteen years, because the judges determined that he'd accepted the largest amount of cash bribes from Chinese steel mills, nearly £7.3 million. Hu accepted the verdict, but his co-defendants appealed the decision. On May 17, a Shanghai appeals court upheld the convictions and ordered the three to serve out their sentences.

From a geopolitical standpoint, the most interesting aspect of the verdicts was the divergent response from the Australian government and Rio Tinto. Australian politicians and public officials reacted as if they'd been kicked in the gut by the Chinese judges. While they readily acknowledged that China had plenty of evidence showing that the Rio Tinto employees accepted bribes from Chinese steel mills, they complained that the lengthy prison sentences were unduly harsh by Australian standards. But more significantly they bemoaned the fact that the nation's government had no way of knowing how fairly the espionage portion of the trial had been conducted. And they publicly warned Chinese officials that major multinational corporations looking to do business in China were watching these proceedings and didn't like what they were seeing.

"The difficulty comes with the second charge, the commercial secrets to which our officials were not given access," Australian Foreign Minister Smith said on the Australian Broadcasting Corporation current affairs program *The 7.30 Report*. "That's very regrettable and that leaves, I think, a series of unanswered questions, not just for Australia, but for the international business community."

Rio Tinto executives, on the other hand, were far more accepting of China's decision, despite the fact that they'd long maintained that their workers did nothing wrong. But rather than continuing to back its employees, Rio Tinto immediately fired them after the verdicts were announced and issued a contrite statement that ignored the potential problems with the closed espionage portion of the trial. "We have been informed of clear evidence presented in court that showed beyond doubt that the four convicted employees accepted bribes," Sam Walsh, who heads Rio Tinto's iron ore operation, said in the statement. "By doing this they engaged in deplorable behavior that is totally at odds with our strong ethical culture. In accordance with our policies we will terminate their employment." These comments so pleased Chinese officials that they were included in Xinhua's roundup report on the case.

So why would the company and the government have such different responses to the same decision? The answer can be found in the jumbled relationships created by the shadow market's emerging power.

Simply put, Australia is a resource-rich nation and China wants access to those resources. This puts Australia in a position of relative strength when talking to or about China, because in many ways China needs Australia as much as, if not more than, Australia needs China. Rio Tinto, however, is an Australian company that has China as its largest customer. This arrangement puts China in a position of relative strength when dealing with Rio Tinto. It also helps explain why Rio Tinto's CEO Tom Albanese was in China trying to mend fences in February 2010, a month before the trial had even started. "I think, most importantly, our long-term strategic interests are in line with China's long-term strategic interests," Albanese told the *Wall Street Journal* at the time. To anyone reading this statement closely, it was clear that Stern Hu and his colleagues *were not* part of Rio Tinto's long-term interests.

All of which neatly sums up how the shadow market controls the global economy. The groups with access to capital and natural resources hold the power. And everyone else is just a pawn in a much larger chess match going on over their heads.

WHO'S YOUR DADDY?

Ironically, at the same time that Stern Hu's case was playing out, separate accusations of corporate corruption were being hurled very close to China's leadership. Yet the outcome of this incident was very different than the Hu case.

In July 2009, European and African authorities revealed that they were investigating a company controlled by Hu Haifeng, one of Chinese President Hu Jintao's sons, for bribery and anticompetitive business practices. For years, Hu Haifeng was the president of the NucTech Company, a Chinese state-owned enterprise that's one of the world's leading manufacturers of X-ray scanners for airports, seaports, and container ports. Little is known about Hu's management style or ability, largely because NucTech refuses to reveal much about itself financially or otherwise, and Hu never gives interviews. But that summer, officials in Namibia started looking into allegations that NucTech had made an illegal payment to secure a £32 million contract to provide cargo scanners for the African country's airports and seaports. Namibian authorities arrested a NucTech employee and asked to interview Hu Haifeng.

Meanwhile, in the European Union, NucTech was being investigated for undercutting its competition, otherwise known as "dumping" its products, by giving customers "soft loans" to help defray the costs of its equipment. This illegal and highly anticompetitive practice is a common complaint from China's business competitors. Indeed, in late July 2009, the European Union slapped preemptive tariffs on imports of steel pipe from China to protect the region from the underpriced steel that China supposedly was dumping on the market. And in Namibia, three NucTech employees were arrested on bribery charges. A trial was expected to take place sometime in 2010.

Chinese officials immediately leapt to the defense of the president's son and denied that any allegations of wrongdoing were true. The country said it would vigorously oppose any investigations into the matter. And there was no way that Hu Haifeng would sit for an interview with any international inquisitors. But those public steps weren't the only protective moves the government took to stop the potentially embarrassing story from spreading. Almost immediately after the news surfaced, any item on the Internet that contained information about NucTech—particularly a BBC report that was getting big play throughout the world—was scrubbed by China's censors, which have broad discretion over what the Chinese people can and cannot see online. Even the basic search word *Namibia* was blocked on the country's dominant web portals, Sina and NetEase. As for Hu Haifeng himself, he was quietly promoted out of sight to a senior position at NucTech's parent company, Tsinghua Holdings Co. No charges were filed against Hu. And within weeks, the international furor and cries of Chinese corruption died down. In time, it was as if it had never happened at all.

SPY GAMES

Beyond dumping underpriced products on US markets, China has an even more pernicious method for undermining the American economy and gaining a competitive advantage globally: corporate espionage. Over the past few years, prosecutors have brought more than a dozen cases involving people of various nationalities stealing technology and defense secrets from US companies and handing them over to Chinese intelligence officials. For instance, in February 2010, Dongfan "Greg" Chung, a seventy-four-year-old former engineer at Boeing and Rockwell International and a naturalized US citizen who was born in China, was sentenced to fifteen years in prison for keeping in his home hundreds of thousands of pages of trade secrets from the US aerospace industry that he intended to give to the Chinese government. For its part, China denied it was involved in any corporate spying. "The allegations about a Chinese person stealing trade secrets in the US for China is purely fabricated out of ulterior motives," the Chinese Ministry of Foreign Affairs said in a brief statement issued after Chung was convicted. The Chinese government offered no response to his sentencing, even though in light of his advanced age and poor physical health, it's likely that Chung will die in prison.

Chung was the first person convicted under a 1996 US law that made stealing corporate secrets for a foreign government a federal crime. But he was hardly the first person US officials have caught handing over secrets to China. The US-China Economic and Security Review Commission concluded in a 2007 report to Congress that "China is supplementing the technologies that its defense industry obtains through commercial transfers and direct production partnerships with an aggressive and large-scale industrial espionage campaign. Chinese espionage activities in the United States are so extensive that they comprise the single greatest risk to the security of American technologies."

In fact, Chung's capture derived from another corporate espionage case, this one against Chi Mak, a so-called "sleeper" spy who worked for the US defense contractor L-3 Power Paragon. In March 2008, the sixty-five-year-old Mak was sentenced to twenty-four years and five months in prison after being found guilty of trying to provide China with US Navy technology. Mak's coconspirators included his wife, his brother, his sister-in-law, and his nephew. Mak's brother received a ten-year sentence, and his wife got three years and will be deported on her release. Mak's nephew and sister-in-law were sentenced to the time they'd already served in prison and were deported back to China.

And in yet another incident, Gregg Bergersen, a former Pentagon weapons analyst who also worked as a private-sector defense contractor, was convicted of providing military secrets to China. Investigators discovered that Bergersen was passing information to a Chinese spy, Tai Shen Kuo, a naturalized US citizen who was born in Taiwan. Bergersen believed that the information he gave Kuo was going to Taiwan, an American ally, rather than to China. In the end, Kuo was sentenced to fifteen years in prison for his role in the plot, Bergersen was sentenced to just under five years, and a third co-conspirator, Yu Xin Kang, was sentenced to eighteen months.

Another case involved Li Fangwei, who was indicted in 2009 by then Manhattan District Attorney Robert Morgenthau for using US banks to make financial transactions to help Iran develop its nuclear weapons program. The trouble was that Li was living in China at the time. Since China and the United States had no extradition treaty and Li insisted that he was innocent, there was no way the Chinese government was about to hand over one of its citizens to American authorities to be tried in a US court. So the case stalled.

Furthermore, researchers at the University of Toronto uncovered a vast "cyberspying" scheme they called GhostNet, which originated almost exclusively from China and hacked into government and private office computers in more than one hundred countries around the world. The researchers could not definitively conclude that the Chinese government was involved, and Chinese officials vigorously denied that they played any role in the GhostNet system. However, one of the main targets of the cyber infiltration was the Dalai Lama, China's Tibetan rival, whose exile centers in Dharamsala, India, Brussels, London, and New York were all hacked. Then, in April 2010, the *Financial Times* reported that the Indian government had banned the purchase of telecommunications equipment made in China because of national security concerns.

What's important to recognize here is that these incidents aren't happening in isolation. Authoritarian strategies such as relentless corporate espionage, cyberspying, and strong-arm business tactics are just symbols of the economic challenge that China's emergence as the most powerful force in the shadow market poses for the international community. With an autocratic government backed by an economy powered by capitalist might, China's success flies in the face of everything we thought we knew about the way the world works. For generations, political economists convinced us that we could increase the number of democratic governments across the globe simply by encouraging the spread of free-market capitalism to closed economies. But China's evolution into a robust machine of capitalism that also features a strong autocratic government has turned this economic article of faith on its head, although the Chinese people have enjoyed increased personal freedom as the country has grown more prosperous.

"I think it's too early to tell if China has created new rules," UBS economist Tao Wang says. "It's true that as people get richer and have property rights and wealth to protect, the demand for participation increases. In the case of China, if you look at the top of the government hierarchy it appears as if there has been no progress toward a quote-unquote Western-style democracy, which means an elected government. We aren't moving toward that. But I've worked in the Middle East and Southeast Asia, and I've found that there are many different kinds of elected democracies. So if you look at the grassroots level in China and how a person lives his life, how households have the freedom to choose where they want to live and how they want to work, there has been a tremendous change. It's a different world compared to when I was younger. So in a true sense I think democracy has progressed. But in the simple narrow definition of an elected government, it hasn't."

Regardless of the progress made by the Chinese people, it's clear that the United States and China have a very different view of the link between government and business. And considering all the questions about shady Chinese companies and business practices, it's notable that US officials have been reluctant to take a more aggressive stance. Case in point: in late July 2009, while the Stern Hu case was playing out and the allegations of Chinese corporate espionage were increasing, China and America held summit talks in Washington. On the opening day of the conference, President Barack Obama offered the assembled officials some welcoming remarks. Toward the end of his speech, Obama directly addressed the complicated and evolving relationship between the two countries.

"Let's be honest," he said. "We know that some are wary of

the future. Some in China think that America will try to contain China's ambitions; some in America think there is something to fear in a rising China. I take a different view. And I believe President Hu takes a different view as well. I believe in a future where China is a strong, prosperous, and successful member of the community of nations; a future where our nations are partners out of necessity, but also out of opportunity."

Given everything going on in China at the time, Obama's deeply conciliatory tone was strikingly counter to the way that previous administrations have spoken to their Chinese counterparts. His key message was a plea for cooperation "out of necessity" and "opportunity." Clearly the diplomatic conversation between the United States and China has changed.

SEARCH THIS!

That said, America has started to push back against some of China's hard-line stances. It's just not the US government doing the pushing, but the private sector, which has grown weary of the country's restrictions on foreign investments, its steep export tariffs, its policies that require all public agencies to buy only products made in China, and its overall attitude toward government intervention in economic matters.

A good example is Google's battle with China over censorship. In December 2009, China unveiled a sweeping new Internet policy aimed at controlling the content Chinese people could see online. Government officials insisted that the program was designed to protect the nation's children from being exposed to pornography, to protect China's 380 million Internet users from falling prey to financial scams, and to protect foreign creative interests from having their movies, television programs, and music pirated online. However, human rights groups complained that the real motive behind the move was to tighten the government's grip on any potential political opposition. Earlier in the year, Chinese authorities blocked social networking websites like Facebook, Twitter, and YouTube, as well as thousands of other sites that the government found troubling. Under the new program, more than 700 additional websites would be shut down, including the country's largest file-sharing website, BT China.

The situation came to a head in January 2010, when Google announced that it was considering pulling out of China because of government censorship and interference in its business. In a statement posted on Google's blog, the company's chief legal counsel, David Drummond, said that Google had "detected a highly sophisticated and targeted attack on our corporate infrastructure originating from China that resulted in the theft of intellectual property from Google. However, it soon became clear that what at first appeared to be solely a security incident—albeit a significant one—was something quite different."

Drummond then explained that Google engineers had discovered attacks on at least twenty other companies from a variety of sectors. The main goal of the attack on Google appeared to be accessing the email accounts of human rights activists in China. But the company also found that the email accounts of dozens of advocates for human rights in China who were based around the world had been infiltrated as well. In light of these findings and the other steps China had taken over the past year to curb free speech on the Internet, Drummond said Google had decided that "we should review the feasibility of our operations in China." Google's assertion about China's involvement in the attacks was later backed up by technology security specialist Joe Stewart of SecureWorks in Atlanta, Georgia, who found "digital fingerprints" of Chinese hackers in the invasive Trojan horse software known as malware that was used to infiltrate Google's computers.

While few of the other companies alluded to in Drummond's statement were eager to publicly acknowledge that their computer systems had been invaded, the well-known names mentioned in the press included Yahoo, the Dow Chemical Company, defense contractor Northrop Grumman Corporation, software developer Adobe Systems, computer networking equipment manufacturer Juniper Networks, and ironically, the Symantec Corporation, the largest maker of computer security software in the world. In addition, two foreign journalists in Beijing had their Google email accounts changed to forward messages to outside addresses. The Google email accounts of Chinese and Tibetan activists on US college campuses were attacked using phishing programs and spyware. The Los Angeles law firm Gipson, Hoffman & Pancione, which brought a $2.2 billion (£1.5 billion) copyright infringement suit against the Chinese government and several of the country's software developers, said its computers were hacked. And the human rights groups Chinese Human Rights Defenders, Civil Rights and Livelihood Watch, and Independent Chinese PEN Center, as well as the Chinese news websites Canyu and New Century News, were all targeted in cyber attacks.

Although many people in the intelligence community had long assumed that China was involved in some variety of cyberspying, Google's bold statement shocked the world. Suddenly someone was standing up to China. While Google's Chinese business was relatively small—in 2009 its revenues were just $300 million (£200 million) out of a global total of $22 billion—its share of the Chinese search market was growing. In the fourth quarter of 2009 roughly 36 percent of the Internet searches in China were done on Google, compared to just 13 percent when the company started in 2006. Google was making inroads, and, considering the hundreds of millions of Chinese who use the Internet each day, the company had high hopes for its business in China. Now it all appeared to be unraveling because of a clash of cultures that stretched nearly six thousand miles from Silicon Valley to Beijing.

With the evidence against China piling up and the geopolitical implications of the cyber attack increasingly apparent, it became incumbent on the US government to wade into the dispute. Yet the

Obama administration was reluctant to aggravate its most important financial "partner." So it had to handle the situation delicately. The strategy it came up with was to keep President Obama mum on the subject and leave the tough talk to Secretary of State Hillary Clinton.

On 21st January 2010, in a speech at the Newseum museum of news in Washington, DC, Clinton tackled the problem of government censorship of Internet content head on, saying, "Some countries have erected electronic barriers that prevent their people from accessing portions of the world's networks. They've expunged words, names, and phrases from search engine results. They have violated the privacy rights of citizens who engage in nonviolent political speech. . . . We look to the Chinese authorities to conduct a thorough review of the cyber intrusions that led Google to make its announcement. And we also look for that investigation and its results to be transparent."

As one would expect, Chinese officials responded ferociously to Google's accusations and Clinton's condemnation. While some Chinese citizens left bundles of flowers outside of Google's Beijing offices in a show of solidarity, the government fired verbal missiles at the company and the American government. "Foreign companies in China should respect the laws and regulations, respect the public interest of Chinese people and China's culture and customs and shoulder due social responsibilities," Foreign Ministry spokesperson Ma Zhaoxu said at a press briefing. "There is no exception for Google."

Two days later, after Clinton's broadside, Ma gave an interview to Xinhua and said, "The US side had criticized China's policies on Internet administration, alluding that China restricts Internet freedom. We firmly oppose such words and deeds, which were against the facts and would harm the China-US relations."

The Chinese government then leapt into full damage control mode to ensure that what it considered to be a minor dispute didn't turn into a global conflagration. It cracked down on the Chinese media's reporting on Google's accusations, heavily censoring the news and cutting out words like *free speech* and *surveillance* from individual stories. Then it flooded the state-run airwaves and newspapers with dozens of commentaries condemning the positions taken by Google and the United States. The opinion pieces, said to be orchestrated by the Communist Party's Propaganda Department, echoed the hard line taken by the Foreign Ministry's Ma.

Even Yahoo got publicly slapped around by its Chinese partner after offering its backing to Google. Yahoo owns a $1 billion (£600 million), 40 percent stake in Alibaba Group, a Shanghai holding company that controls China's largest online retailer and its biggest electronic marketing firm. But after Yahoo said in a statement that it stood "aligned" with Google in its response to the cyber attacks, Alibaba issued a blistering statement of its own saying that "Alibaba Group has communicated to Yahoo that Yahoo's statement that it is 'aligned' with the position Google took last week was reckless given the lack of facts in evidence. Alibaba doesn't share this view."

As the standoff continued, Google's leaders started making some conciliatory remarks about their desire to continue doing business in China. Speaking at the World Economic Forum in Davos, Switzerland, Google Chairman and CEO Eric Schmidt said that his company wants to be in China, but "we just don't like censorship. We hope that will change and we can apply some pressure to make things better for the Chinese people." Then, a few weeks later, Google cofounder Sergey Brin was speaking at the high-powered TED (Technology Entertainment and Design) Conference in Long Beach, California, and said, "I want to find a way to work within the Chinese system to bring information to the people. Perhaps it won't succeed immediately, but maybe in a year or two."

In the end, Google's solution was to move its search service to Hong Kong and try to offer unfiltered searches for Chinese citizens from its offshore outpost. But Chinese officials in Beijing hardly viewed this as an acceptable compromise. So China's censors continued to interfere with searches on Google for controversial terms like "Falun Gong" and "Tiananmen Square." What's more, technology experts on Wall Street could see how much financial risk Google had taken by starting this fight. Many were left wondering if, when it was all over, the battle will have been worth it. Google took an admirable moral stand, but at the same time made an enemy of the Chinese government. That's not the same thing as making an enemy of the US government or any other Western government, because the Chinese government has far more weapons at its disposal to hurt its enemies.

By June 2010, it was clear that Google had figured out that it needed China—the world's largest Internet market with more than 400 million users—more than China needed it. The company sheepishly announced that it was abandoning its Hong Kong plan because the Chinese government told Google that it was "unacceptable" and that if it continued doing what it was doing China would not renew Google's license to operate in the country. What Google proposed to do to comply with the wishes of Chinese regulators was unclear. But suddenly its admirable ethical stand seemed somewhat shaky. After all, in the face of losing access to China's gigantic market Google did what any other corporation would do—it capitulated.

So Google may have won the initial public relations battle with its righteous stance against censorship and cyber espionage. But the company forgot that it was fighting China. Google was never going to win the war. Can anyone?

CHAPTER 5

Too Small to Fail

The concept behind the emergence of the shadow market—that governments can build mammoth financial war chests and dominate the capital markets—began about fifty years ago with the dissolution of the British Empire. For centuries, the Crown had conquered countries with an eye toward exploiting their natural resources and creating wealth back in London. But after World War II, Britain needed money to rebuild itself and no longer could afford to maintain a far-flung empire. Because the UK controlled a series of quasi-independent microstates capable of generating enough wealth to literally pay for their own independence, parliament decided to focus on these smaller colonies.

In the late 1940s, UK economists identified the Kiribati Islands, a small archipelago in the South Pacific with plentiful phosphate mines and a minuscule population, as an ideal candidate for the first sovereign wealth fund because the territory could easily generate enough cash to finance its peaceful secession. However, those plans were scotched when the emir of Kuwait caught wind of the idea and pushed to have his country go first. Since Kuwait was a small Arabian nation that produced a lot of oil, the economists saw immediately that it had an even greater potential to generate cash than Kiribati. So the British government decided to bend to the emir's wishes.

In February 1953, the Kuwait Investment Board began operation in London and became the world's first sovereign wealth fund. Designed to manage Kuwait's national wealth, the institution was funded exclusively with profits generated by the nation's oil revenues. Over the next few years, it would accumulate enough capital to enable the country to create a national government from scratch. By 1961, Kuwait had its own leadership in place and was able to declare independence from Britain.

Overnight, Kuwait was one of the richest countries on earth as measured on a per capita basis. It had a constant stream of cash that was more than capable of supporting its citizens. Under the emir's specific instructions, the proceeds from the Kuwait Investment Board would be used exclusively for the benefit of the Kuwaiti people. And the organization would purposely invest in extremely safe securities to keep the nest egg secure rather than seeking higher returns in the risky financial markets. For decades, that's precisely the way the country's investments were managed.

Viewed from a distance, it could appear as if Kuwait was going through a phenomenon similar to what China would experience a few decades later: generating far more capital than it could spend. Indeed, the geopolitical power locked up within all of that liquidity is the reason both counties have ascended to global prominence. However, the Chinese and Kuwaiti economies could not have been more different. China's economic strength was primarily the result of its massive population serving industries that manufactured products at prices cheaper than those made by companies in other countries. But the economic strength of Kuwait, and most other Arabian oil states, for that matter—was based solely on the colossal value of the subterranean oil reserves under its control and the relatively inexpensive needs of its tiny population. This dichotomy has had an enormous impact on the ways that the two nations have behaved economically. China decided to invest its money to acquire the natural resources it needed. Kuwait, meanwhile, tried to use the capital generated from oil profits to diversify its economy away from oil so that the country's success would no longer be tied to a single natural resource.

"From a fundamental point of view the economies of pretty much all of the Persian Gulf countries are vulnerable to oil shocks," says Farouk Soussa, the chief Middle East economist at Citigroup. "Because the non-oil economy is largely driven by government expenditures, and government expenditures depend on government revenues, of which 90 percent come from oil. So when you have a sharp fall in oil prices government revenues fall significantly, and traditionally that has meant they've had to tighten budgets and government expenditure comes down, which has a big knock-on effect on the economy. So they're trying to break that vicious cycle. One way to do this is to diversify their economies away from this government expenditure-led model and away from the oil sector. So across the board, Gulf countries are trying to get private sector non-oil economies up and running."

JUMPING OUT OF A SAND TRAP

Kuwait entered the modern investment era on 10th December 2003. That was the day its government named Bader M. Al Sa'ad to take over the Kuwait Investment Authority, the modernized organization that replaced the Kuwait Investment Board. This was no idle move. Al Sa'ad was a well-known Kuwaiti banker who'd long argued that the emirate was missing out on opportunities to amass serious wealth because of its overly conservative investment policies. Now he was being asked to put his bold ideas to work for his country. Sovereign wealth funds would never be the same again. Indeed, in many ways, the modern era of aggressive investing through SWFs can be traced to the day that Al Sa'ad took over the Kuwait Investment Authority.

Two years prior to getting the job at the Kuwait Investment Authority, known as the KIA, he commissioned a study to find out how the fund's investments had performed compared to other top investment vehicles. And what he discovered was deeply troubling. Initially the KIA made some shrewd investments, like buying major positions in Daimler-Benz and British Petroleum in the 1960s and 1970s. But by the late 1990s, after the first Gulf War and a dramatic fall in oil prices, the KIA was in a deep malaise. Its investments had become so conservative that Kuwaitis were losing money by missing out on market rates of return. In fact, in 2001 and 2002, even with the bulk of its capital in highly safe investments, the fund lost money. Two losing years in a row was unacceptable to Al Sa'ad. So he decided to dramatically alter the KIA's investment style.

At the time of Al Sa'ad's appointment, the KIA managed roughly roughly £75 billion, which made it a substantial institutional investor. So Al Sa'ad wanted the KIA to behave like one. He studied the investment policies of the Yale University and Harvard University endowments, both of which were considered pioneers in institutional investing because of their lengthy track records of managing money for high long-term returns without taking on too much risk. What he found was that both endowments largely avoided the volatility of the 1990s Internet bubble by putting their capital into an array of alternative investment classes such as property, emerging-market financing, hedge funds, and private equity funds. This concept was eye opening to Al Sa'ad. Suddenly he saw that there were ways to capture the returns the market provides while also protecting your flank. This was how he wanted to structure his fund.

In particular, Al Sa'ad focused on David Swenson, the head of the Yale endowment, who's considered one of the savviest institutional investors in the world. When he finally felt confident that he knew enough to give it a shot, Al Sa'ad took a portion of the KIA portfolio and invested it based on Swenson's guidelines. For example, Yale had 28 percent of its money in hedge funds, 17 percent in private equity funds, 20 percent in property, and the rest in various stocks and bonds. By comparison, Kuwait had 2 percent in real estate, 1 percent in private equity, and the vast majority in safe, low-yielding US Treasury bonds. No wonder the performance of Kuwait's sovereign wealth fund was falling short. It wasn't even in the game.

Al Sa'ad shifted the mix, and the results were staggering. Almost overnight, the portion of the KIA that was modeled after the Yale endowment was returning around 15 percent compared to around 3 percent before. From that point on, Al Sa'ad decided that the KIA had to operate more like sophisticated university endowments, which traditionally have been run as hybrids of hedge funds and private equity funds, taking some aspects of both strategies while still maintaining a relatively conservative bias. He brought in the financial consultants Mercer Investment Consulting, who helped him transform the KIA into a fund that owned higher-risk, higher-reward assets without exceeding the overall risk threshold that Al Sa'ad had established. In 2005 the fund returned 11 percent, and in 2006 it returned more than 13 percent. Clearly change agreed with the KIA.

Still, generating returns wasn't the KIA's only objective. It was also tasked with developing the domestic Kuwaiti economy by stimulating the private sector. Looking into the future, Al Sa'ad saw Kuwait as a global financial center and a gateway to investing in the Arab world. So he gave the Kuwaiti financial services industry a massive boost by spreading around seed money. His plan was that the KIA would match any amount of capital raised by an investment house for an investment fund. This, in essence, made the KIA a partner in every new asset management business in Kuwait, which was highly attractive to foreign investors because the Kuwait Investment Authority was considered a "brand name" in global finance. Within a year, the KIA handed out £500 million to twenty-three new investment funds, and capital started pouring into the country. Before Al Sa'ad started his program in 2004, there were fewer than five investment houses in Kuwait. Five years later, there were around fifty, with hundreds of billions of dollars in assets under management. And, as the icing on the cake, the KIA had earned a roughly 43 percent return on its seed investments.

But not all of Al Sa'ad's moves worked out as planned. At the end of 2008, the KIA managed roughly roughly £155 billion, about twice, nearly twice the amount in the fund when he'd taken over. Yet almost all of those assets were sitting in cash. Why? Because the fund had been burned by its major investments in the troubled US financial services firms Citigroup and Merrill Lynch and lost £20 billion in nine months. Meanwhile, the Kuwait economy was crumbling as well. The country's stock exchange lost 38 percent of its value in a single year. The Global Investment House, one of Kuwait's best-known financial services firms, defaulted on £2 billion in debt and was declared insolvent. The bond-rating agency Moody's downgraded several Kuwaiti banks. And one of the country's largest lenders, the Gulf Bank, required a £1 billion injection from the KIA just to stave off bankruptcy. The KIA also kicked in several billion dollars to the Kuwaiti bourse to keep it in the black. As a result, with 2008 drawing to a close and the entire global financial world melting down all around him, Al Sa'ad decided to sell off his international stocks and shift the bulk of the KIA's money into short-term liquid investments until the storm blew over.

What caused Kuwait to boom and bust like that? The simple answer is that the country still faces one challenge that it can't overcome: its economy remains inextricably tied to the price of oil. A 2009 study by the debt ratings agency Standard & Poor's found that Kuwait was the leading Persian Gulf State on its Oil Price Vulnerability Index, meaning the nation is more dependent on oil revenues than any of its neighbors. So as the price of oil soared to nearly one hundred dollars a barrel in the summer of 2008, the country got fat and rich. The government launched public works programs based on the assumption that the high oil prices would continue. Banks loaned money freely as if there were an unending pile of capital on which to draw. And businesses, primarily in the financial sector, expanded their operations, thinking that the economy would be able to keep up with their ambitions. But when the price of oil contracted in late 2008 and 2009, dropping to below forty dollars a barrel, most of Kuwait's economy was left vulnerable to the vagaries of the commodities market. Since the other significant part of Kuwait's economy is dominated by the finance industry, the global economic meltdown provided a brutal double whammy.

At the dawn of 2009, with oil selling for around fifty dollars a barrel, Al Sa'ad set a new goal for KIA. He wanted to use the fund to help Kuwait's economy branch out from the influence of oil and the financial services industry. In a televised interview on the TV network Al Arabiya, Al Sa'ad said that he saw opportunities in international real estate and some undervalued multinational businesses, though, in typical fashion, he declined to name his specific targets. But he emphasized that the key to Kuwait's future success was developing businesses within the country with expertise in areas other than financial services, such as technology and specialized manufacturing. In the meantime, Kuwait's government was stepping up its global diplomacy efforts, improving trade ties with economically important countries like India, Russia, and China. However, as Al Sa'ad said, the most important thing for Kuwait to do is to think like the savviest investors in the world and diversify. If it doesn't, the country will forever be susceptible to ruinous financial shocks, and all that oil won't be able to insulate it from economic hardship.

A WELL-OILED MACHINE

If you want to see a diversified Persian Gulf State for yourself, go to Abu Dhabi, which according to the S&P Oil Price Vulnerability Index is the Middle Eastern oil state that's best insulated from the natural swings in commodity prices. Abu Dhabi is the largest of the seven emirates that comprise the federation of the United Arab Emirates, which also includes Ajman, Dubai, Fujairah, Ras al-Khaimah, Sharjah, and Umm al-Qaiwain. The UAE sits next to Saudi Arabia on an oil-rich shelf in the Persian Gulf and has the world's fifth largest store of proven oil reserves, estimated at around 97 billion barrels. Abu Dhabi controls the wells that produce about 90 percent of that oil, or roughly 2.23 million barrels a day. Naturally, Abu Dhabi's government revenues and gross domestic product are highly reliant on the production of petroleum. In 2009 its oil revenues were approximately £27 billion, which was more than 60 percent of its GDP. Abu Dhabi is so rich that its opulent Emirates Palace Hotel has an ATM that issues gold instead of cash.

But what sets Abu Dhabi apart from the other fabulously wealthy Arabian oil states is the way it has treated its bounty of capital, estimated at more than £450 billion, according to figures compiled by the research and consulting firm the Sovercign Wealth Fund Institute. Instead of investing haphazardly based on Wall Street fashions, Abu Dhabi has put its budget surpluses into a diverse array of businesses and asset classes, primarily through its main investment vehicles: the Abu Dhabi Investment Authority, the International Petroleum Investment Company, and the Mubadala Development Company. For example, Mubadala and the Abu Dhabi government jointly own half of the Abu Dhabi Ship Building Company, the only builder of specialized naval warships in the Persian Gulf. The fast-growing company, which booked £198 million in revenues in 2009, up nearly 40 percent from 2008, constructs, repairs, and refits naval ships for the Abu Dhabi government and other UAE states. But Abu Dhabi Ship Building's potential for expansion is even greater in overseas markets, so it has also forged partnerships with foreign businesses such as the French shipbuilder CMN, the Turkish shipbuilder Yonca-Onuk, and South Korea's STX Offshore & Shipbuilding Company and the Korea Shipbuilders' Association. For Abu Dhabi, varied holdings like this, coupled with a diverse investment portfolio, provide an extensive financial safety buffer in case the price of oil plummets.

"Abu Dhabi has a tremendous revenue stream from abroad," says Citigroup's Soussa, who helped develop the Oil Price Vulnerability Index when he was an economist at S&P. "That means that even in the event that oil prices were to plummet they still have the cushion of assets that they can liquidate and use to fund government expenditures. They're very secretive about their investments, but they tend to be a mix of bonds, equity, private equity, and real estate. We don't know what the mix is, but we do know that after 2008 and the collapse of Lehman Brothers they went into more liquid stuff to try to maintain their value. Basically they're in a very strong position to ride out any crisis."

It wasn't always this way. The Abu Dhabi Investment Authority, or ADIA, was founded in 1976, a time when just 20 percent of the nation's population could read. ADIA's investments were handled by Abu Dhabi's patriarch, Sheik Zayed Al Nahyan, who, despite his lack of formal training, managed to produce impressive returns of roughly 10 percent a year. His investment style was fairly conservative, primarily based around taking large ownership stakes in major international companies such as General Motors and Procter & Gamble. But by the time Sheik Zayed died in 2004, his preferred method of investing had grown stale in an increasingly sophisticated global financial world. And since the sheik's death, the country's financial leadership, led by Sheik Zayed's sons Crown Prince Mohammed bin Zayed Al Nahyan and ADIA chief Sheik Ahmed bin Zayed Al Nahyan, has grown far more aggressive with the nation's capital.

Here is the Abu Dhabi government's activity in 2009 alone:

- Announced plans to start four private equity funds designed to buy businesses throughout Africa and the Middle East, and to spend £17.5 billion financing fifty-two development projects in Egypt.
- Signed a series of partnership deals with its cozy partner, the US conglomerate General Electric. By the middle of

2009, the emirate's Mubadala sovereign wealth fund had accumulated nearly sixty-six million GE shares, making it one of the company's ten largest shareholders. Under one of the GE agreements, Abu Dhabi will build a maintenance network for General Electric Aviation, the world's largest maker of jet engines; in another, it will partner with GE to provide debt and equity financial services in Saudi Arabia.

- Entered into a joint venture to provide maintenance, repair, and overhaul services for Rolls-Royce aircraft engines.
- Signed a deal with Occidental Petroleum Corporation to develop natural gas fields in the Sultanate of Oman.
- Created a £725 million joint infrastructure fund with UBS Global Asset Management to invest in Persian Gulf infrastructure projects.
- Entered into a £1.5 billion-plus joint venture with the UK oil and gas services company Petrofac to build a natural gas liquids supply train.
- Completed a £550 million power plant in Algeria.
- Invested £1.1 billion to develop property in Malaysia.
- Signed a development and production sharing contract with Bahrain's National Oil and Gas Authority to develop an oil and natural gas field off the Bahrain coast.
- Paid £10 billion for a 38 percent stake in Cepsa, Spain's second largest oil producer.
- Reached agreement on a deal with Sikorsky Aerospace Services to build the most advanced aircraft maintenance center in the Middle East.
- Bought 50 percent of the Los Angeles–based hospitality development firm Kor Hotel Group for an undisclosed sum.
- Acquired 9 percent of the German carmaker Daimler for £1.8 billion.

- Pocketed a profit of £1.5 billion by selling its 14 percent stake in the British bank Barclays.
- The country's Mubadala sovereign wealth fund reached an agreement with both ConocoPhillips and Kazakhstan's national oil and gas company, KazMunaiGas, to develop an oil field controlled by Kazakhstan. Mubadala also entered into a multimillion-dollar joint venture with the silicon chip maker Advanced Micro Devices (AMD), which made Abu Dhabi the leading shareholder in the number two chip maker in the world.

Whew! That's a lot of activity. However, investors need to be careful about thinking that they'll get rich by simply mimicking ADIA's moves. Because based on its track record it's doubtful that all of these deals will turn out to be home runs. In March 2010, ADIA reported that over the preceding twenty years the return on its investments was 6.5 percent a year. The figure was respectable but hardly inspiring, reflecting the fund's traditionally conservative approach that didn't focus on growth as much as other similar institutions. For example, Singapore's sovereign wealth fund Temasek Holdings returned 13 percent a year and Harvard University's endowment fund returned almost 12 percent a year over the same time frame. So ADIA wasn't necessarily considered a bellwether for the global financial markets like legendary investors such as Warren Buffett.

That said, things could be different this time around. Abu Dhabi officials have been made well aware of the nation's lack of domestic investing prowess. So the emirate's sovereign wealth funds have been aggressively buying up global investing talent like Manchester City shopping for players from foreign clubs. And the result is much more sophisticated financial operations. For instance, Mubadala and ADIA employ more than seventeen hundred foreign nationals in their investment operations compared to fewer than twenty in Kuwait. And some of Abu Dhabi's recent hires have been big names in the finance field. In 2009, the ADIA brought in Bill Schwab—the former top property investing executive at J.P. Morgan and Deutsche Bank and the former chief lending officer at Goldman Sachs—to head its global property investment operations. It named Anders Lundqvist, the former head of asset management for the Swedish carmaker Volvo, to be its chief investment officer. And it hired Thierry Gimonnet, a well-connected Goldman Sachs investment banker, to be its new head of finance.

With all the capital flowing through the emirate, Abu Dhabi's leaders have also launched a multibillion-dollar project to make the state a regional center for culture, education, and medicine. The government has brought in Middle Eastern branches of the Louvre and Guggenheim museums. It has established a satellite campus for New York University. And it even opened an outpost of the prestigious Cleveland Clinic medical center.

The Abu Dhabi government is also throwing a lot of money at the development of sustainable energy and carbon-neutral technology. The emirate is spending £10 billion to construct Masdar City, a zero-carbon, zero-waste area on the edge of Abu Dhabi that will house forty thousand people and provide commercial space for another fifty thousand workers. It is the largest government investment of its kind in the world. Along the way, Abu Dhabi is also creating the Masdar Institute of Science and Technology in collaboration with the Massachusetts Institute of Technology, which will give scientists the facilities they need to develop green projects. So who was the first major tenant to sign on to the Masdar City project? Why, General Electric, of course, which has committed to put its new "ecomagination center" in the development.

But perhaps most important, Abu Dhabi's abundance of cash has served as a magnet for Western nations desperate for capital investment, opening up diplomatic doors that had long been shut. The United States clearly counts Abu Dhabi as a close friend, as witnessed by the vast number of deals between the emirate and

American companies. But diplomats from France and the UK have gone even further by openly courting Abu Dhabi investments. French President Nicolas Sarkozy negotiated a joint venture agreement between Mubadala and France's sovereign wealth fund, the Fonds Stratégique d'Investissement, to work on investment opportunities. France also opened up a small military base in the emirate that will house up to five hundred troops as part of Western efforts to contain Abu Dhabi's belligerent neighbor, Iran. The UK was even more transparent about its ambitions to get a piece of Abu Dhabi's nest egg. In April 2009, then British business secretary Peter Mandelson met with representatives from ADIA and came out of the meeting effusive in his support for Abu Dhabi's investments in the country.

"We welcome sovereign wealth fund investments, unlike some other countries that are hesitant, and we strongly encourage investments from the UAE and others into Britain," Mandelson said at an impromptu press conference. "We need liquidity in the system, we need funds to flow, we need credit to flow. So if investments from Abu Dhabi or anyone else will do that, we're interested."

Still, for all of its worldwide wheeling and dealing, and all of its international construction projects, Abu Dhabi has probably attracted the most media attention because of its eye for buying legendary trophy properties throughout the world. If you live in a major global city with a significant piece of architecture up for sale, there's a good chance that property specialists from Abu Dhabi are sizing it up right now. For example, in July 2008, the ADIA spent £400 million to buy 90 percent of the Chrysler Building, the iconic Art Deco landmark in Midtown Manhattan. The deal drew headlines around the world. Suddenly a monument to American capitalism was owned by a foreign government. However, the rest of the world might as well get used to Abu Dhabi buying up major properties across the globe, because this is just the beginning. Sheik Ahmed said recently that his fund sees plenty of opportunities in the worldwide property market.

MONEY MIRAGE

Simply having access to an enormous pile of cash is not all a nation needs to insulate itself from economic disaster. In the financial world, bad investments have consequences for the rich and poor. The difference, however, is in the degrees of consequence. For instance, in late 2009, when financially hobbled Dubai had to be bailed out by Abu Dhabi, its neighbor to the south and fellow member of the United Arab Emirates, it was still able to be ruthless with its lenders and investors, even though it was the one in trouble. The reason? Because the multinational banks that helped finance Dubai's boom wanted to continue doing business with the UAE. That's the power of wealth. It gives those that have it room to protect their own interests even in the midst of a full-fledged economic crisis.

In late November 2009, the government of Dubai announced that the conglomerate Dubai World was in desperate trouble. Over the previous decade, Dubai's leaders had used Dubai World as the emirate's primary investment vehicle. It collected prestige holdings around the world such as the MGM Mirage hotel in Las Vegas, the luxury department store Barneys New York, the QE2 luxury ocean liner, the Cirque du Soleil circus troupe, and the Hilton London Metropole hotel, as well as sizable stakes in the London Stock Exchange and major banks like HSBC, Standard Chartered, and Deutsche Bank. It was also responsible for bankrolling Dubai's physical transformation into a major global financial center and tourist destination. Flush with cash, Dubai World's property division, Nakheel World, built some of the most opulent and glitzy hotels and resorts on the planet and constructed a dazzling cluster of hundreds of islands in the shimmering blue water off the Dubai coast in the Persian Gulf.

These extravagant plans were backed by Dubai's government because the emirate wasn't blessed with remotely the same amount of oil reserves as Abu Dhabi. Indeed, the United Arab Emirates expects Dubai's oil reserves to be completely depleted within the next twenty years. So the nation's leaders could see that they had to find other ways of bringing in revenues. With Dubai's distinctly ambitious architecture and over-the-top real estate developments, they seemingly had their answer as the emirate became a symbol of the new, open, tourist-friendly Middle East.

But when the global economic crisis spread from West to East, Dubai wasn't spared. In particular, its property market tanked. By the summer of 2009, Dubai apartments and offices were selling for half of what they'd been worth just a year earlier. For Dubai World, this was a disaster. Suddenly the firm found itself way over-leveraged, with less capital coming in as real estate prices plummeted. With 2009 drawing to a close, the company owed about £50 billion in total debt and was looking at billions more coming due in the next few months. After a quick glance at the books, Dubai World executives determined that very soon the company would be unable to meet its financial obligations. So the government asked the company's lenders to give it a six-month stay on £40 billion in debt payments. This, Dubai's leaders said, would enable the government to reorganize Dubai World before it collapsed under the weight of its liabilities.

The news shocked investors around the world. Stock markets from London to Hong Kong fell in unison as traders tried to determine if Dubai's troubles were about to trigger another global financial crisis. Of particular concern was what Dubai's collapse would mean to the UK, since its banks had loaned more than £30 billion to borrowers in the UAE, making Britain the UAE's largest creditor by a wide margin. In the financial markets, the amount of money that Dubai had to pay to insure its debt against default skyrocketed, putting the former economic powerhouse in league with countries like Pakistan and Latvia, which traditionally were considered much higher risk investments. Panic was setting in.

So the UAE central bank stepped in to calm the investment community. It pledged to keep all of the banks operating in Dubai afloat by creating a special liquidity fund for local and foreign banks that faced steep losses on their loans. "The UAE banking system is more sound and liquid than a year ago," the central bank proclaimed. The highly public move was aimed at allaying fears in the financial markets that Dubai World's troubles were about to bring down Dubai as a whole. Then Dubai World issued a statement saying that it was looking to delay payments on £16 billion of its debt, which was significantly less than the £36 billion figure Dubai's government had originally floated. If just 25 percent of Dubai World's creditors accepted these terms, the company would avoid default.

Dubai World's statement was targeted particularly at the concerns of the company's investors and lenders, stating, "It is envisaged the restructuring process will be carried out in an equitable way for the overall benefit of all stakeholders." Within hours of Dubai World's unveiling its new debt restructuring plan, Moody's Investors Service unofficially blessed the idea, saying that with the program in place, the UAE's high credit rating would remain unchanged. The market had spoken. It liked this new arrangement.

But as soon as the UAE's leaders sensed that the pressure was lessening, they started behaving in a far less cordial manner. Why? Because deep down they knew that the rest of the world wanted to—or needed to—do business with the UAE because of its vast oil reserves. So while Dubai may have been in seemingly dire trouble for the moment, once the situation was settled, it would be back to business as usual.

This attitude shift first became apparent when the head of Dubai's Department of Finance, Abdulrahman al-Saleh, went on state-run television and said that the Dubai government *would not* guarantee Dubai World's debt. His argument was that Dubai World should be judged as a company that borrowed money from different banks. In his view, the problem was that the banks did not properly assess the risk of each project. Of course, Dubai World's lenders saw it very differently. Their point was that Dubai

World had always been perceived as a sovereign entity with the implicit backing of its government. That's how the bond market had been pricing Dubai World's debt, as if it had been issued by a government agency rather than by an independent corporation. This point, however, was lost on Dubai's rulers.

The company's lenders and investors felt even more squeamish when they learned that the UAE was balking at the size of a Dubai bailout package and that Abu Dhabi was reluctant to even get involved in helping out its neighbor in need. Sensing that they had lost control of the proceedings, a few hostile hedge funds that owned pieces of Dubai World banded together and started pressing the government to sell off its assets and pay them their money right away. They even threatened to sue in London and in local courts to force the company to do something to mollify its financial backers.

Eventually Abu Dhabi helped settle things down by saying that it would give Dubai £6 billion to ease the financial pressure. But even that pledge was not what it seemed, as behind closed doors, Abu Dhabi quietly reduced the offer to around £3 billion. More to the point, however, Dubai World's leaders weren't intimidated by the threats anyway. They knew that it was just empty posturing. The best outcome for investors and lenders was to work with Dubai, not against it. Everyone could see that. So Dubai World didn't even respond directly to the irate hedge fund managers— although al-Saleh did acknowledge that the company *might* have to sell some assets to raise cash, a move that was endorsed by Moody's. But Dubai World warned any potential vulture investors that it would not be bullied into dumping its prized possessions at fire-sale prices. In May 2010, Dubai World reached an agreement with its lenders to restructure more than £15 billion in debt. Under the terms of the deal, the group of banks would get back £3 billion within five years at an annual interest rate of 1 percent and £7 billion back within eight years at a floating interest rate of around 2 percent. The rest of the debt would be converted to equity that gave the banks a stake in Dubai World. In all, it was a very attractive package for a financial entity that not too long ago was on the brink of failure. But once again, that's the power of the shadow market.

Meanwhile, financial experts focused on figuring out which country would become the next Dubai. Plenty of small nations had boomed in recent years because of an overabundance of capital and reckless lending practices, particularly in Europe. It could be Ireland. Or one of the Baltic states, like Estonia or Lithuania. Maybe even Greece. No one in the finance world knew for sure where or when the next crisis would originate. But many feared that another one was coming.

NATIONAL SECURITY

For all the financial frustrations surrounding the rise of economic power of wealthy oil states in the Persian Gulf, it's the geopolitical implications that are truly frightening. When it comes to Middle Eastern oil money, investments can often have two contexts: financial and political. The fact is that these sovereign wealth funds and government-sponsored investment vehicles are tightly overseen by their country's leaders, and while they usually aren't subject to the kind of meddling that's assumed to be happening in Russia and China, they can have agendas beyond profit making. The oil states in the Mideast are so close geographically and culturally that politics and economics have become intertwined in their centuries-old relationships. Over time, these deep ties have brought a measure of unity to a disparate collection of ancient desert tribes. For the United States and other Western nations, however, these ties can mean potentially deadly conflicts. How so? Think about key pieces of our national security system being turned over to companies owned by countries with allies that have geopolitical agendas vastly different from our own. After all, that's precisely what happened nearly four years ago in the now notorious "Dubai ports deal," which took place before Dubai nearly imploded.

For years, container ports in New York, Philadelphia, Baltimore, Miami, and New Orleans had been operated by a British conglomerate called the Peninsular & Oriental Steam Navigation Company. But in February 2006, P&O was sold for £3.9 billion to DP World, a subsidiary of Dubai World. Because DP World was a major multinational controlled by a friendly government with holdings all over the world, the US Treasury Department's Committee on Foreign Investment saw no problem with the deal and quickly approved it in December 2005, two months before the takeover was complete.

However, when the news broke that an Arabian company was going to be running several major US ports, Capitol Hill erupted over the potential security concerns. Although the Dubai government was considered an American ally, and DP World was a totally legitimate global conglomerate that did business with US companies overseas, the political symbolism was brutal—particularly since two of the nineteen hijackers in the 9/11 World Trade Center attacks were from the United Arab Emirates. In addition, the UAE government also was very close to Saudi Arabia, the home of another fifteen hijackers. On the surface, this plan seemed like an especially bad idea in light of the natural sensitivity Americans felt about their national safety after being attacked by terrorists from the Middle East. Still, the US government ultimately agreed to the deal despite the protests of numerous lawmakers.

That changed, however, as the media's coverage of the arrangement turned increasingly incredulous. In the end, pressure from within the United States overwhelmed the deal despite its active backing by then president George W. Bush and his administration. To settle the controversy and get the deal done, DP World was forced to unload all of the US ports owned by Peninsular & Oriental. But it was allowed to keep P&O's international holdings.

Problem solved, right? Not exactly. By altering the terms of the Dubai ports deal, the United States might have kept itself safe—or not. But the larger point is that this issue isn't likely to go away any time soon. There are plenty of Middle Eastern countries with vast oil wealth that have belligerent attitudes toward America. And they've been building their own sovereign wealth funds, which will invest in projects right alongside countries from the Persian Gulf that have more collegial relationships with the West, like Kuwait, Abu Dhabi, and Dubai. But because these investment funds are reluctant to divulge much about their inner dealings, it's likely that someday soon US companies won't even know which countries own pieces of the businesses they're dealing with. What's worse, even if they did know, they wouldn't be in a position to turn down the investments. America needs Persian Gulf investment dollars. So when there's a major business deal at stake, it's far less likely that the United States will allow thorny issues like potential national security concerns to interfere with the demands of commerce. That's what is so scary.

For instance, take a look at a recent agreement between America and the United Arab Emirates that received far less attention than the Dubai ports deal. In May 2009, President Barack Obama offered his formal blessing to a deal that would allow US companies to share nuclear technology with the UAE, which wants to build a series of nuclear reactors that will provide electric power throughout the region. To get the deal done, the UAE agreed to allow extensive inspections by the UN, to buy nuclear fuel from major international suppliers, and to not enrich uranium or reprocess plutonium, which the United States and the UAE said would prevent nuclear materials from ending up in the wrong hands. Obama administration officials promoted the agreement, which was actually initiated in 2008 at the end of the Bush administration, as "peaceful" and part of the government's effort to control the development of nuclear power throughout the world.

The plan faced a bit of opposition in Congress, where some representatives believed there was a tremendous risk in providing nuclear technology to countries that are allied with nations that have deeply troublesome diplomatic records. "The UAE's long history as a conduit for Iran's nuclear weapons program, its failure to fully implement effective export controls, and the danger of expanding nuclear facilities and expertise in the Middle East make this agreement a dangerous precedent," Republican Ileana Ros-Lehtinen, the vice chairwoman of the House Foreign Affairs Committee, said at the time.

Oddly, public opposition wasn't nearly as fierce as you'd expect, particularly considering the outcry against the Dubai ports deal. Even Ros-Lehtinen acknowledged that the pact was likely to breeze through Congress. And she was right. On 18th December 2009, the United States and the UAE finalized the agreement.

The weak opposition had little to do with national security. Rather, it was about economics. The contracts to build the nuclear facilities were worth £25 billion, and General Electric and Westinghouse were considered the leading candidates to get the jobs. Here's what a study by the US Commerce Department concluded about the deals: "Even though the plants would be located in the UAE, those contracts would create jobs in the US The nuclear power plants that Westinghouse is building in China and that GE is building in Taiwan have helped create and support more than 10,000 US jobs over a period of years. Moreover, the jobs themselves are high-quality, skilled craft, and engineering positions."

In the end, GE lost out on the contract to a bid from a South Korean consortium that included Westinghouse. But the fact remains that in an economy starved for cash, no business is in a position to turn down a £25 billion deal. That's why GE and Westinghouse joined with nuclear energy advocates in quietly lobbying Washington to support the pact with the UAE. Money talks. The UAE was the third largest oil exporter in the Organization of Petroleum Exporting Countries, OPEC. And the governments of the Persian Gulf collectively controlled more than £250 billion in US assets, making them America's second largest creditors after China. So when the Obama administration considered everything, from an economic standpoint it found itself in an extremely vulnerable negotiating position. There was no way to stop these deals.

Sure, supporters argued that the agreements involved countries that traditionally have had friendly diplomatic relations with the United States. But that looked past the larger issues. The problem here wasn't about how the government of the United Arab Emirates felt about America. The problem was that some of its close friends and neighbors didn't feel the same way—most notably Iran, which United Nations weapons inspectors have said is actively developing an illegal nuclear weapons program. The UAE and Iran have deep cultural ties, particularly because nearly a quarter of Dubai's population is of Iranian descent, and there are more than ten thousand Iranian businessmen working in the country. Considering how slippery information can be in the Middle East, would anyone be surprised if Iran was able to get its hands on the UAE's new nuclear technology? Probably not. What's more, assuming that oil prices remain at reasonably high levels over the next few years, Iran and other troublesome oil states are going to get wealthier and look to invest their capital globally alongside their Middle Eastern brethren. So the potential security threats to the West will only become more urgent as time goes on. But there isn't much we can do about it now. We've let the investment genie out of the bottle in the Persian Gulf. There's no way we can shove it back in.

MORE FOOD FOR THOUGHT

Until now, we have considered the nations and SWFs of the shadow market as entities that interact with the US, the UK, Europe, and the broader markets. But this is an incomplete picture, for they also compete with one another in developing world locations for resources. This battle will have both local and international repercussions and is marked by staggering complexity and unpredictability—even the potential for war.

Since 2008, when booming commodity prices resulted in an international "food shock," the world has been going through an all-out landgrab. Vast territories of the planet are quietly being acquired by foreign governments to protect their food supplies and outsource their food production. In the West, where food is relatively plentiful and obesity is the most troubling societal health problem, it's difficult to imagine that other parts of the world are deeply concerned about food crises. But they are. As a result, many countries that rely on imports to feed their people—the Persian Gulf States, for instance, import more than 60 percent of their food supply—are becoming increasingly concerned about the risks of rising food prices. The solution? Wealthy shadow market countries have begun trolling for arable farmland that they can buy or lease to produce the food their populations will require. It's a new form of economic imperialism. And it hasn't gone unnoticed by international diplomatic observers.

"You have to look at what's happening domestically in these countries to see the potential problems," says Joachim von Braun, an agricultural economist at the University of Bonn and former head of the International Food Policy Research Institute in Washington. "In many of the countries where farmland is being sold you have a feudal system of land ownership, and as a result at the foundation of these investments in the target country often is the illegitimate acquisition of land by local elites. Since agriculture is local, China, Korea, the Gulf States, and other wealthy countries typically are buying land from some government figure or large landowner who acquired land through military force or linkages. This is particularly true in places like the Sudan and Pakistan, where small farmers regularly have their land taken from them and given to generals. These are the so-called willing sellers. And the number of eager buyers is only increasing."

Indeed, if you track the deals, the trend is unmistakable. Over the past five years, Bahrain, China, Egypt, India, Japan, Jordan, Kuwait, Libya, Malaysia, Qatar, Saudi Arabia, South Korea, and the United Arab Emirates have all spent billions of dollars buying or leasing enormous tracts of farmland throughout the world, from Brazil and Argentina in South America to Uganda and Tanzania in Africa. These new agricultural colonialists are snapping up territories so large that they, in essence, are creating independent food-producing states within foreign countries.

Saudi Arabia, for example, a desert nation with vast oil wealth but little arable farmland, has farming partnerships in Brazil, Egypt, Ethiopia, Indonesia, Kazakhstan, Pakistan, the Philippines, Senegal, Sudan, Turkey, Thailand, Uganda, and the Ukraine. In July 2008, the Saudi bin Laden Group, a government-connected construction conglomerate owned by the family of Al Qaeda terrorist leader Osama bin Laden, announced that it was spending £2.2 billion to create a farm roughly the size of Northern Ireland out of dense forest land on the Indonesian island of New Guinea. The massive farm will grow rice, sugarcane, and soya beans, among other crops that the Saudis covet. Then, in May 2009, Saudi investors paid about £65 million for a wheat and barley farm in war-ravaged Ethiopia, where the kingdom already owns hundreds of thousands of acres of farmland. Meanwhile, South Korea is harvesting wheat on a 2,600-square-mile farm in the Sudan. The food from this farm is being produced by a partnership of companies from Korea, Sudan, and the Arabian Peninsula. South Korea also has farming partnerships in Argentina, Cambodia, Indonesia, Laos, Mongolia, and Russia.

Such arrangements help establish economic alliances that may not be clear on the surface, at least to the rest of the world. Take, for example, China's farming partnership with Russia. China and Russia typically are considered cordial neighbors and trading partners. But their relationship is far more intricate than that. In simple terms, the countries share farmland and produce food together. For example, in May 2008, the Chinese government revealed that it had contributed £11 million to develop nearly 200,000 acres of farmland in Russia to grow rice, soya beans, and other vegetable crops. Under the terms of the agreement, the bulk of the food will be exported back to China, with the rest remaining in Russia.

So what's the big deal? Just one partnership between neighbors, right? Well, if you dig a little deeper, you'll find that over the past few years, the countries have made more than a dozen similar arrangements, some of which are far larger in scale. For instance, since at least 2004, a company from the Heilongjiang Province in the northeastern corner of China has been growing rice on a 162-square-mile plantation in Russia's nearby Far East provinces.

These farmland-sharing arrangements work for both countries, giving Russia needed capital and enabling China to diversify its food production. Obviously, they aren't the kinds of sexy international deals that wind up on the front page of the *Wall Street Journal*. But combined they create important alliances that could have significant diplomatic effects in a world that runs on money. It's precisely what we saw in the Pentagon's economic war games, where global alliances were established that the United States couldn't recognize until it was too late. And we're talking not just about China's relationship with Russia. China also has farming partnerships in Australia, Brazil, Cameroon, Cuba, Kazakhstan, Laos, Mexico, Mozambique, Myanmar, the Philippines, Tanzania, Uganda, and Zimbabwe.

Of course, China isn't alone in this global landgrab. Just about every wealthy country on earth is trying to insulate itself against a potential future food shock. So they're all out scouring the planet for large farming plots. "Agriculture is becoming a major strategic asset," says Carl Atkin, the head of research of Bidwells Agribusiness in the United Kingdom, which has helped broker some large land deals. "The food price spike in 2007 and 2008 brought this to a lot of people's attention, but there's a structural change going on in agricultural commodity prices. The outlook for agriculture prices over the next ten years is significantly higher than it was for the previous few decades—obviously not to the level of '07, but much higher than it has been. What's driving this? Well, the demand side has been discussed to death, from population to diet to biofuels. But it also involves factors like the availability of land supply, water's role as a strategic resource, and the impact of climate change on agriculture production in various parts of the world. So it's really quite complicated."

From an investing point of view, what has been most impressive about the shadow market's version of neocolonialism has been its ability to get into places that typically have been hostile to Western governments and businesses. How has it accomplished this? By using a bottom-line approach to directly tap into an emerging country's desire for money. For the most part, Western nations' interactions with Africa and other troubled parts of the world have been based on failed carrot-and-stick strategies where countries receive aid in return for behaving a certain way. But the shadow market doesn't let behavior get in the way of its commerce. For example, a May 2010 story in *The Atlantic* magazine explained how China handles its investments in Africa: "China could not be more different from the West. It has focused on trade and commercially justified investment, rather than aid grants and heavily subsidized loans. It has declined to tell African governments how they should run their countries, or to make its investments contingent on government reform. And it has moved quickly and decisively, especially in comparison to many Western establishments." The rest of the shadow market generally acts the same way. Don't ask questions, just make deals. With that kind of approach, is it any wonder that the shadow market has been welcomed into potentially profitable parts of the world that shun the West?

Obviously this isn't the first time wealthy countries have purchased overseas land for agriculture purposes. In the 1980s, Japan bought a half million acres of American ranch land in California, Montana, Colorado, and Florida to raise grass-fed cattle for tender Kobe-style beef. But what makes this current trend distinct is that exceedingly wealthy countries are cutting deals with exceedingly poor agrarian countries, many of which are ruled by corrupt dictatorships. A September 2010 World Bank study revealed that 70 percent of all international land deals took place in Africa, where disclosure regulations are essentially nonexistent. The possibility of easy exploitation is alarming to diplomats and food aid experts. They fear that desperately impoverished countries like Ethiopia and the Sudan, where people are starving from food shortages, will ultimately have their crops loaded onto planes and shipped all over the world, while the nation's people continue to suffer. That's why the International Food Policy Research Institute (IFPRI), a think tank dedicated to finding solutions for hunger and poverty, is calling for increased transparency and an international code of conduct for agriculture land deals.

"If large-scale land acquisitions cause land expropriation and unsustainable use, foreign investments in agricultural land can become politically unacceptable," the IFPRI wrote in an April 2009 report. "It is therefore in the long-run interest of investors, host governments, and the local people involved to ensure that these arrangements are properly negotiated, practices are sustainable, and benefits are shared."

Some poorer countries are beginning to fight back against these deals. For example, the Korean industrial giant Daewoo International Corporation had planned to produce corn and palm oil on a 5,000-square-mile tract of farm land on Madagascar. But instead it wound up triggering a bloody civil war on the Indian Ocean island.

In January 2009, the Madagascar government agreed to lease the enormous parcel—roughly half the arable land on the tropical island—to Daewoo for ninety-nine years. Madagascar president Marc Ravalomanana said that his goal was to attract more international investors and show that his country was open for business. But to the seething Malagasy people, the Daewoo deal became an infuriating symbol of years of poverty and government corruption. "They sold the country's territory to foreign companies!" opposition leader Andry Rajoelina bellowed at a French radio reporter during one of the riots. "We demand a transitional government."

By March 2009, Rajoelina's forces had overthrown Ravalomanana and seized control of the government. One of Rajoelina's first acts as the new president was to cancel the Daewoo deal.

Still, this is only one violent response to a flurry of activity that shows few signs of slowing. Global money managers are setting up agricultural hedge funds to invest in farm land, and wealthy foreign governments are snapping up fertile territory with abandon. The primary targets include Brazil, Georgia, Kazakhstan, Malawi, Nigeria, Paraguay, Russia, Senegal, Ukraine, Uzbekistan, and even Australia. On average, the investors are looking at timelines of roughly ten years for the deals to start paying off. Ultimately, they're expecting returns of as much as 400 percent on their cheapest purchases, particularly in Africa. So agricultural investing is definitely expected to be a profitable enterprise. Yet the world has little idea what these deals will mean to the poorest members of the global population.

"The tricky issue with international agriculture regulations is that these two resources, land and water, in many poor countries are not properly regulated and property rights are not clearly defined," agriculture economist von Braun says. "The international community has to act before it loses control. It must quickly delineate property rights at the communal and individual level, which isn't difficult today with satellite imagery and mapping tools. And it must regulate the investor side of these transactions with clearly defined codes of conduct. We have that for the mining industry, and agriculture should be no different. If we don't do these things the opportunities for exploitation will only increase."

But where is the leadership that von Braun wants going to come from? The United States? Good luck. That's simply not the way the world of finance works. As a result, the global landgrab can continue largely unabated. The shadow market's tentacles will extend even farther. And there's really nothing America can do or say about it.

CHAPTER 6

Rogue Oil

As we've seen in China's actions against Rio Tinto and Google, authoritarian regimes can interpret economic laws to pressure independent international companies doing business within their borders. Still, if the interference stopped there, it wouldn't be such a problem for the rest of the world. Unfortunately, it often doesn't. Some governments, especially those sitting on vast reserves of oil, have used the power of their wealth to influence the legal systems in *other* countries over which they have no control. As the following example shows, this strategy may be outrageous, yet it is all too predictable as the nations of the shadow market gain increasing geopolitical authority.

EXPLODING JUSTICE

Abdel Basset Ali al-Megrahi feared that he'd never see his homeland of Libya again. His fifty-seven-year-old body was stricken with incurable prostate cancer that had metastasized to his other organs. Looking in the mirror each morning, he'd become an almost unrecognizable version of his former self. His once bulky frame was so frail that he could no longer walk or even support himself without a cane. The defiant glimmer in his deep-set dark eyes was gone. His speaking voice was so soft that it often barely registered above a whisper. And most of his days were spent in a medicated haze from the cocktail of sedatives he had to take just to numb his pain.

A Scottish doctor tending to Megrahi gave him no more than three months to live. He was rotting away in HM Prison Greenock, situated approximately twenty-five miles west of Glasgow. All for a horrific crime he swore he didn't commit. To the numerous British citizens and government officials who believed that Megrahi might be innocent, the dying prisoner deserved their government's compassion. They wanted to see him safely returned home to Tripoli, where he could at least live out his final days with his family and friends. This, they said, was the only fair way to handle a deeply regrettable situation. This, to them, would be justice.

The Scottish government agreed, and on 20th August 2009, Megrahi was freed on "compassionate grounds," allowing him to return to Libya, presumably to die in peace. On his way out of Scotland on a private jet operated by the Libyan airline Afriqiyah, Megrahi defiantly proclaimed that justice had at long last been served. "I say in the clearest possible terms, which I hope every person in every land will hear: all of this I have had to endure for something that I did not do. The remaining days of my life are being lived under the shadow of the wrongness of my conviction."

A heartwarming story of fairness and morality winning the day? Not so fast. To many others in the UK and the United States, Megrahi was a beast, a living embodiment of evil. He was, they said, the terrorist and Libyan intelligence agent responsible for the bombing of Pan Am flight 103, which exploded in midair over the village of Lockerbie in southern Scotland on 21st December 1988. The plane, a Boeing 747, was traveling from London to New York and was carrying a number of American university students heading back home for Christmas. A total of 270 people died in the attack, including 11 Scottish citizens on the ground who were bombarded with fiery debris. At the time, it was the deadliest assault on American civilians ever and the most violent terrorist attack in British history.

What possible legal outcome could be considered justice for a man behind such a heinous crime? Life in prison? Death behind bars? Clearly, that's what the grieving families and friends of the victims of Pan Am flight 103 had in mind in January 2001 when Megrahi was convicted on 270 counts of murder by a panel of three Scottish judges following a grueling eight-month trial at a special neutral court set up at a former NATO military base in the Netherlands. Many of those still grieving for the victims found comfort in the fact that Megrahi would never again see the light of day as a free man.

So it was hardly surprising that his release from prison after serving just seven years of a supposed life sentence set off an inferno of criticism, both in the UK and the United States. Many families and friends who didn't accept Megrahi's protestations of innocence were irate. Robert Mueller, the director of the US Federal Bureau of Investigation, gave voice to their sense of indignation in a scathing public letter to Scottish Justice Minister Kenny MacAskill.

"Your action in releasing Megrahi is as inexplicable as it is detrimental to the cause of justice," Mueller wrote. "Indeed your action makes a mockery of the rule of law. Your action gives comfort to terrorists around the world who now believe that regardless of the quality of the investigation, the conviction by jury after the defendant is given all due process, and sentence appropriate to the crime, the terrorist will be freed by one man's exercise of 'compassion.' Your action rewards a terrorist even though he never admitted to his role in this act of mass murder and even though neither he nor the government of Libya ever disclosed the names and roles of others who were responsible."

But Scottish officials looked past this anger and insisted that Megrahi deserved their country's compassion because he was a dying man imprisoned in a foreign land. However, public doubts about this explanation persisted. In truth, the story behind Megrahi's release is far more nuanced than the official version. And, perhaps not surprisingly, it appears that the machinations of the shadow market, more than the power of grace, were really at work.

TO CATCH A TERRORIST

For years, Libya's volatile leader, Colonel Mu'ammar al-Gadhafi, and his surrogates had been pressing the British government for Megrahi's release, bringing it up at every diplomatic opportunity. Not only were they acting out of loyalty to their countryman, who was a cousin of one of Gadhafi's closest aides, Said Rashid Kisha (better known in intelligence circles as simply Said Rashid), but they also believed that Scotland's case against Megrahi was flimsy. To the Libyans, Megrahi was convicted not on the strength of the evidence but rather to mollify the Britons and Americans who were still bitter about the attack and wanted to imprison someone—anyone—to avenge the deaths.

Before he was implicated in the Lockerbie bombing, Megrahi was the head of security for Libyan Arab Airlines, the country's national freight and passenger air carrier. He was also the director of Libya's Center for Strategic Studies in Tripoli. However, the FBI maintained that his position at the center was actually a cover for his "real" job as an agent in Libya's secret service—the Jamahiriya Security Organization, or JSO—an accusation that Megrahi denied repeatedly.

Shortly after flight 103 exploded, British and American investigators concluded that the attack was probably an example of state-sponsored terrorism by Libya. Although Gadhafi denied the allegations, the detectives believed that the incident was most likely retribution for a US airstrike on Tripoli and Libya's second largest city, Benghazi, in April 1986. That deadly attack killed forty

Libyan civilians—including Gadhafi's four-year-old adopted daughter, Hanna—injured hundreds more, and destroyed the Libyan leader's home. At the time, the shelling was considered America's retaliation for the bombing of a Berlin nightclub frequented by US soldiers. The act killed three people, including two GIs, and was believed to have been carried out by Libyan intelligence agents.

Investigators were able to connect Megrahi to flight 103 through a couple of personal links and a handful of physical evidence. The first link was his cousin Rashid, who was a top JSO agent at the time. In fact, many intelligence officials believe that he may have been the true mastermind behind the Lockerbie attack. Back in 1991, US State Department spokesman Richard Boucher described Rashid as "the leading architect and implementer of Libya's terrorist policies and a powerful member of Libya's inner circle." Assuming that Rashid was involved, there's little doubt that he would have wanted someone he trusted completely, like a close relative, to carry out the treacherous mission.

The other link was through Libyan Arab Airlines' office in Malta, an archipelago of small islands about sixty miles south of Sicily in the Mediterranean Sea. Historically it has had friendly relations with Libya, meaning that Libyan nationals could move freely in Malta without being tracked by the government or European security agents. FBI detectives maintained that this freedom ultimately enabled Megrahi to travel throughout Europe using several different fake passports. In particular, he was able to go to Zurich, Switzerland, where he supposedly picked up the timing mechanism for the bomb that would be placed on flight 103. In addition, with the help of the Libyan Arab Airlines' station manager at Luqa Airport in Malta, Al Amin Khalifa Fhimah, Megrahi was able to accumulate and store the plastic explosive material used to build the bomb.

The investigators concluded that the plan to blow up flight 103 was simple: put a bomb with a timer in a suitcase, somehow get the suitcase onto the plane, and wait for it to explode. To disguise the explosive device, investigators said, Megrahi and Fhimah built it inside a Toshiba radio cassette player. Megrahi also bought some clothes and an umbrella from a shop near his Malta hotel and packed them in a brown Samsonite suitcase along with the radio. The two then illegally snagged Air Malta luggage tags and put them on the bag, which they used to route it as unaccompanied luggage on a flight from Malta to Frankfurt, Germany. From there, the bomb-rigged luggage was transferred to a Pan Am plane traveling to London. Eventually it made its way onto flight 103 bound for New York. Investigators established the suitcase's likely path by working backwards. They discovered the Frankfurt link because the suitcase exploded in a cargo bay containing only luggage from a Frankfurt feeder flight. They then concluded that the suitcase came from Malta because Pan Am's baggage tracking system showed that an unaccompanied suitcase from Malta had been placed on the Frankfurt flight.

After flight 103 exploded over Lockerbie, intelligence agents from Scotland and the United States scoured a debris field totaling roughly 850 square miles. They came up with a few key pieces of incriminating material: a brown Samsonite suitcase that had contained the bomb, charred fragments from a Toshiba radio cassette player that appeared to house the bomb, remnants of an umbrella and clothing—specifically two pairs of pants and a baby jumper—that were packed in the suitcase containing the bomb, and a tiny green shard of plastic.

Scientists determined that the green piece of plastic was part of the bomb's timing device, which investigators traced to a Swiss electronics company called Meister et Bollier, or MEBO, that was based in Zurich. It was a straightforward digital mechanism set to go off at a specific time. One of MEBO's owners, Edwin Bollier, told investigators that his company had produced several prototypes of the timer for a Libyan intelligence official. Meanwhile, investigators examined the charred scraps of cloth and umbrella.

They tracked all of the items to the same small store in Malta called Mary's House, which was not far from Megrahi's hotel. In a police lineup, the owner of Mary's House, a man named Tony Gauci, identified Megrahi as the person who purchased the items. Combined with the testimony of a key CIA intelligence source, the investigators decided that they had their men. On 15th November 1991, nearly three years after the Lockerbie bombing, US and UK authorities indicted Megrahi and Fhimah on charges of murdering the passengers of Pan Am flight 103 and the eleven Scottish citizens who died on the ground.

Megrahi and Fhimah were living in Libya when the indictments were made. Naturally, the Gadhafi regime was decidedly hostile to the entire investigation and had no intention of handing over its citizens to be tried for terrorism in a Western court. In response, the United Nations slapped significant sanctions on the country in 1992, cutting it off from the rest of the world economically and politically. Over time, the choke hold worked, and in 1999 Gadhafi agreed to extradite the two Libyans to the Netherlands for trial at a special court governed by Scottish law. That same day, the UN lifted its sanctions on Libya.

At trial, the physical evidence against Megrahi and Fhimah was largely overshadowed by the astounding testimony of the government's star witness, Abdul Majid Giaka, otherwise known by his CIA code name, "Puzzle Piece." Giaka was a CIA double agent who said that he'd been recruited into Libya's intelligence agency and then switched his allegiance to America because he was uncomfortable with Libya's involvement in terrorism and the assassination of dissidents. The CIA paid him $1,000 a month to gather information on Libya's intelligence operations. The agency even helped him avoid being inducted into the Libyan army by having him undergo a medical procedure that would make it seem like he'd aggravated an old injury and was unfit to serve militarily.

Giaka was the man who first identified Megrahi and Fhimah as the Lockerbie bombers. He was the deputy station manager at the

Libyan Arab Airlines Malta office, where he worked for Fhimah. In the summer of 1986, he told the court, Said Rashid visited the office and asked Giaka to look into ways to get an unaccompanied suitcase on a British aeroplane. A little while later, Giaka said, he went to the airport in Malta with Megrahi and Fhimah, where he watched Fhimah take a Samsonite suitcase off the luggage carousel and leave without passing through customs. He assumed this was a trial run for some operation. Giaka also discovered that a drawer in his desk was filled with two bricks of yellow crystalline plastic explosives. When he asked Fhimah about the bricks, Fhimah told him that Megrahi had acquired them and to keep it a secret. Finally, Giaka said that on the morning of the bombing, he saw Megrahi and Fhimah load a brown Samsonite suitcase onto Air Malta flight KM180 bound for Frankfurt.

When Giaka finished testifying, it seemed like the prosecution had clinched its case. Yet the government's argument still hinged on the words of a single CIA source and a shopkeeper in Malta. In response, the defense went about obliterating Giaka's standing as a credible witness. The lawyers for Megrahi and Fhimah showed how he had never actually penetrated the Libyan intelligence community beyond the surface, working for the JSO only as a car mechanic and file clerk. They offered evidence, including CIA evaluation reports, proving that within the agency Giaka was considered an unreliable source who regularly exaggerated accounts to earn his $1,000 a month. Finally, the defense hammered away at the fact that Giaka had been working for the CIA for years after the Lockerbie bombing had occurred and yet for some reason waited until July 1991 to tell the agency about his remarkable eyewitness account. Why had he waited so long to come forward? More important, if he actually had so much important information at his fingertips, why hadn't he tried to do anything in advance to prevent the attack? These questions lingered in the court as the defense pounded away at Giaka.

As for Tony Gauci, there also were inconsistencies in his

testimony. For instance, at one point during the investigation, he actually picked a different man than Megrahi out of a cluster of police photographs. Plus, he testified in court that it was raining on the night when Megrahi bought the items, but historical weather reports indicated that it had been a dry evening. If Gauci couldn't recall details like whether it was rainy or clear, how could he remember a customer from an innocuous sale that happened so long ago? That's what the defense lawyers wanted to know as they rested their case and the panel of three Scottish judges retired to render a verdict.

Ultimately, the judges agreed with the prosecution, at least in part, and found that there was enough evidence to convict Megrahi on 270 counts of murder. However, the court did not find sufficient evidence to convict Fhimah. So, on 31st January 2001, Megrahi was sentenced to life in a Scottish prison. Fhimah, meanwhile, was allowed to return to Libya.

The judges released Fhimah, but they didn't necessarily believe that Megrahi acted alone. Although they stopped short of describing the incident as outright state-sponsored terrorism, in their decision the judges specifically noted that the scheme was likely overseen by Libya. "The clear inference which we draw from this evidence is that the conception, planning, and execution of the plot which led to the planting of the explosive device was of Libyan origin," the panel wrote in its judgment.

Gadhafi and his lieutenants were outraged by the verdict. They believed that Megrahi was innocent and that the ruling had been "influenced by the US government, by pressures from the US government," as Gadhafi stated at a press conference to celebrate Fhimah's homecoming. Megrahi's lawyers immediately appealed the ruling. At the appeal hearing a year later, his defense team introduced fresh findings that it maintained brought into question the prosecution's overriding theory and cast reasonable doubt on the conviction. A new key defense witness, a retired security guard at London Heathrow Airport, told the court that there had been a break-in at the airport in the early morning hours of 21st December 1988, the day of the bombing. Someone had used bolt cutters to snap a padlock securing the doors where airlines stored their baggage containers and stored loose luggage that already had been tagged and ticketed for departure. The defense attorneys proposed to the court that this break-in could have allowed someone to place a bomb-rigged bag in the area and have it eventually loaded onto a flight taking off from Heathrow without having it enter the country from Germany or Malta. If nothing else, they said, this possible scenario offered a compelling alternate theory to the one presented by the prosecution.

Despite the new evidence, the judges rejected Megrahi's appeal. So on 15th March 2002, the convicted murderer was transported by helicopter from the Netherlands to Barlinnie, a prison in the northeastern Glasgow suburb of Riddrie, to begin serving out his sentence. In February 2005, he was transferred to Greenock, where he was housed until his release in August 2009.

BUYING PEACE

After the trial and Megrahi's conviction, Libya was left with few friends geopolitically and even fewer options economically. For more than a decade, the country had been strangled under a worldwide trade embargo ordered by the UN. All assets owned or controlled by the Libyan government that were held by banks and financial institutions around the world were frozen. All UN member nations were barred from providing any equipment or materials to help Libya refine and transport oil and natural gas, meaning that there was no money coming in from Western oil and gas companies such as British Petroleum, Royal Dutch Shell, Exxon Mobil Corporation, and Occidental Petroleum Corporation. These corporate titans would eagerly pursue lucrative contracts to work in Libya if they were allowed to. But they weren't.

And since oil and natural gas accounted for roughly 70 percent of Libya's gross national product, this was an enormous blow to its economy.

In addition, Libya's people and businesses faced extreme restrictions on travel and shipping, primarily because the country's airlines were effectively shut down under UN orders. Libyan Arab Airlines offices in airports around the world were closed, and every UN member nation was instructed to prohibit any aircraft that departed from Libya from landing—or even passing through its airspace. Plus, companies in UN countries were forbidden to do any business with Libya that might potentially help the country build aeroplanes or improve its air transportation infrastructure.

The rules were stifling. Under Gadhafi's direction Libya had, in effect, become the leading pariah nation on earth. Now its economy was dying because so few companies or countries were willing, or allowed, to do business with it. Gadhafi and his lieutenants realized that they had to do something to relieve the stranglehold. Their nation had been given a precious gift: control over more than forty billion barrels of proven crude oil reserves, the largest total in Africa and the ninth largest in the world. But the country was starving while its nest egg remained buried underground, just waiting to be extracted, refined, and sold.

Gadhafi and his aides could see that if Libya was going to thrive in the modern world, the country would have to initiate the process of reconciliation with the West. And they knew that the way to start was with a real offering of peace to the still-grieving families of the Lockerbie bombing victims. The fact was that most Libyans believed Megrahi was innocent; Gadhafi and his advisers stated it publicly all the time. But shortly after turning over Megrahi and Fhimah to Scottish authorities in 1999, Libyan government officials quietly began working diplomatic back channels to find out precisely what the country would have to do to get back in the world's good graces. The answer from the UN, the UK, and the United States was unambiguous: accept responsibility for what you've done and pay financial restitution to the families of the victims of the attack on Pan Am flight 103. And that's exactly what Libya did.

Libya's formal reintroduction to the global community began on 15th August 2003, with a contrite letter to the UN Security Council in which Libya acknowledged that it "accepts responsibility for the actions of its officials." Since Megrahi was believed to be a member of the JSO, this sentence was seen as Libya's way of acknowledging its role in the bombing. It wasn't an outright apology, but it was a step in that direction. Libya also set up a £1.7 billion escrow fund for the families of the Lockerbie bombing victims. And it pledged to not only "cooperate in the international fight against terrorism but also to take practical measures to ensure that such cooperation is effective." Gadhafi then publicly renounced Libya's programs to develop nuclear weapons, ordered the destruction of its remaining munitions supplies used to create weapons of mass destruction, and granted full access to the International Atomic Energy Agency to inspect the nation's nuclear and military facilities.

These steps seemed to satisfy the international community, and in December 2003, the UN lifted its sanctions. However, as the world would later find out, when it comes to dealing with Libya, there are apologies, and there are "apologies." A year later, British prime minister Tony Blair visited Tripoli, the first time a British prime minister had done so since Winston Churchill in 1943. Leading up to Blair's arrival, Shukri Ghanem, the Libyan prime minister and second most powerful person in the government behind Gadhafi, gave an interview to BBC Radio 4's *Today*. During the ten-minute conversation, Ghanem, an economist with a doctorate from the prestigious Fletcher School of Law and Diplomacy at Tufts University, calmly and clearly explained the logical rationale behind the decision to offer restitution to the families of the Lockerbie bombing victims.

"After a while, and after the sanctions, and after the problems we are facing because of the sanctions, the loss of money, we thought that it was easier for us to buy peace," Ghanem said. "And this is why we agreed to the compensation. Therefore, we said, let us buy peace, let us put the whole case behind us, and let us look forward."

More than a little taken aback, BBC Radio 4 reporter Mike Thomson asked, "So payment of compensation didn't mean any acceptance of guilt?"

"I agree with that," Ghanem replied. "And this is why I said we bought peace."

There's nothing like blunt candor to blow a hole through the façade of global diplomacy. Frankly, many people around the world suspected that Ghanem was simply giving voice to a naked geopolitical reality. But it still was shocking to hear it put so plainly and in such a blithe manner. That's why so many Americans and British citizens were aghast.

NUDGE-NUDGE, WINK-WINK

The only way to understand Megrahi's eventual release and the nearly miraculous evolution of Libya's geopolitical standing from pariah to power is through the lens of the shadow market. Libya mattered to the West because of its tantalizingly deep pools of crude oil and natural gas, which after more than a decade of crippling sanctions had been vastly underexplored. So gaining access to them afforded American and British energy companies an invaluable opportunity to get in at the start of a real oil and gas gusher. To be blunt about it, this was the only reason that the United States remotely cared about its relationship with Libya. If not for its oil and natural gas reserves, Libya would just be another poor African nation with a volatile leadership and a historically hostile attitude toward America. But a potentially wealthy

African nation that controlled tens of billions of barrels of crude oil and more than fifty trillion cubic feet of natural gas, all of it sitting there just waiting to be exploited? Well, that was a country the West had to care about. Deeply.

Unfortunately for American energy concerns, their UK rivals figured this out first. On 25th March 2004, the day that Blair finally made his historic visit to Gadhafi's Bedouin tent on the outskirts of Tripoli, the Anglo-Dutch oil giant Royal Dutch Shell signed an historic exploration deal with Libya that would provide the company with access to potentially more than £500 million worth of natural gas. It was the first time in more than thirty years that Shell would be doing business with Libya. Although the new "long-term strategic partnership" was inked during Blair's visit, since then, the former prime minister has consistently insisted that the two were unrelated and that the purpose of his trip was not to seal the deal for Shell. Still, the symbolism was lost on no one.

Although the deal was not a secret, the high-level negotiations between the UK and Libya were. Documents obtained by the London humanitarian and environmental activist group PLAT-FORM showed that between 2004 and 2008, Shell executives met with British foreign ministers and senior officials at least eleven times to discuss ways for the UK government to further the company's energy interests in Libya.

But that wasn't all. Less than two weeks after Blair's celebrated visit to Libya, a much more discreet delegation of British business leaders also went to Tripoli, this time at the invitation of Saif al-Islam al-Gadhafi, the urbane son of the Libyan leader. The earnestly serious younger Gadhafi, who is the second oldest of the Libyan leader's seven sons, studied international diplomacy at the London School of Economics, has an MBA from IMADEC University in Vienna, Austria, and runs a series of enterprises, including an architecture firm in Tripoli, a television news company, and Libya's official state charity. He is also generally considered to be Libya's heir apparent. The group he assembled included Lord

Charles Guthrie of Craigiebank, an antiterrorism consultant and the former British defence chief; Sir John Bond, the chairman of HSBC, Britain's largest bank; the esteemed architect Lord Norman Robert Foster of Thames Bank; and the financier Lord Jacob Rothschild and his youngest son, Nathaniel.

The reason Saif Gadhafi brought these men to his country was to discuss ways of improving commercial ties between their nations. Obviously, the meeting was successful. In the end, HSBC ended up managing billions of dollars for Libya's fledgling £35 billion sovereign wealth fund, the Libyan Investment Authority (LIA), which the country established in 2006 to manage its burgeoning oil wealth. Lord Rothschild, in turn, signed on as a key investment adviser to LIA. And Lord Foster's architecture and planning company, Foster & Partners, signed contracts to design and build two large developments in Libya.

Over time, relations between the two nations strengthened to the point where Libya felt comfortable revisiting its thorniest conflict with the West: Lockerbie. In their meetings with British representatives, Libyan officials would repeatedly state that the Gadhafi government wanted to see Megrahi released and returned to his homeland. In time, Libya's constant complaints started finding sympathetic ears within the British and Scottish governments. In 2005 Libya used its political pressure to get Megrahi transferred out of solitary confinement at Barlinnie and into somewhat more comfortable conditions at Greenock. But it wasn't until the spring of 2007, during Blair's five-day farewell tour of Africa, that the issue came to a head.

On 29th May 2007, Blair and Gadhafi met in the colonel's hometown: the seaside city of Sirte on Libya's rocky northeastern Mediterranean coast. For the British and Libyan leaders, the highlight of the day was supposed to be the signing of a massive exploration and production agreement between Libya and British Petroleum. The territory that BP was acquiring would be its largest development commitment in the world. Under the terms of the deal, BP received the right to drill seventeen wells in offshore and onshore territory controlled by Libya. In return, the company would spend a minimum of £450 million on the project's exploration phase and make significant additional expenditures when the wells started producing. But beyond the contract's impressive size, what was truly significant about the occasion was that BP was returning to Libya for the first time in thirty years. Here was yet another public symbol of how Libya was emerging from global isolation and was no longer perceived internationally as a rogue state.

"A few years back, Britain and Libya could never have had this relationship," Blair said at a press conference announcing the BP deal. "This is a change of benefit to Libya and Britain and the wider region."

However, away from all the pomp and fanfare, Blair and Gadhafi gathered together privately for four hours to sign what turned out to be a much more significant agreement. In this "memorandum of understanding," the UK and Libya pledged "judicial cooperation" between the two nations. Unlike previous diplomatic deals between the Libyan and British governments, this one received practically no fanfare. Instead it was kept under wraps for more than a week until someone in the British government leaked it to the press.

When the news of what came to be known as the "deal in the desert" became public, many of the Lockerbie bombing families erupted angrily. Logically, they assumed that the "judicial cooperation" Libya sought was the release of Megrahi. But UK officials denied this. Libyan officials, on the other hand, understood the terms very differently. They believed that the deal in the desert was the "nudge-nudge, wink-wink" start of a process that would eventually lead to Megrahi's freedom. That Megrahi's name wasn't specifically mentioned in the bargaining process was simply a matter of politics, a way for Britain and Libya to get around the thorny public challenges surrounding this controversial issue. But according to Libya's way of thinking, when the deal was signed, everyone in the room knew who, and what, was *really* under discussion: namely, that the British government would eventually sign a prisoner transfer agreement, or PTA, with Libya, releasing Megrahi into its custody. A PTA is a fairly standard diplomatic treaty that enables a prisoner being held in a foreign country to be transferred to authorities in his homeland so he can serve out his sentence there. The Libyans believed that this memorandum of understanding was the first step toward the two countries signing a formal PTA.

Saif Gadhafi made this clear in a lengthy interview with the Scottish newspaper the *Herald,* offering a detailed description of the talks: "For the last seven to eight years, we have been trying very hard to transfer Mr. Megrahi to Libya to serve his sentence here, and we have tried many times in the past to sign the PTA without mentioning Mr. Megrahi. But it was obvious we were targeting Mr. Megrahi, and the PTA was on the table all the time. It was part of the bargaining deal with the UK. When Tony Blair came here, we signed the agreement. It is not a secret. But I want to be very clear to your readers that we didn't mention Mr. Megrahi. People should not get angry, because we were talking about commerce or oil. We signed an oil deal at the same time. The commerce and politics and deals were all with the PTA."

After the BP deal and the memorandum of understanding of judicial cooperation were signed, the British government didn't seem to be urgently pressing ahead with a prisoner transfer agreement fast enough for Libya. Before long, Gadhafi was getting impatient, believing that Downing Street was dragging its feet. So, to get Britain's attention, Libya used the power wielded by shadow market nations to hit the country where it was sure to hurt: in the corporate wallet. Just a few months after inking the massive deal with BP, Libyan officials started quietly telling BP executives that they were considering pulling out. To keep the deal alive, they wanted the execs to pressure the British government to sign a PTA and secure Megrahi's release from Scotland.

BP obliged, taking the case directly to Jack Straw, then the justice secretary, on at least two occasions.

"BP did bring to the attention of the government in late 2007 our concerns about the slow progress in concluding a PTA with Libya," the company said in a statement. "Like many others, we were aware that delay might have negative consequences for UK commercial interests, including ratification of BP's exploration agreement. We did not press for any particular kind of PTA, we were just hoping for an end to the delays concluding it."

The urgency to sign a PTA and release Megrahi was apparent in a letter Straw sent on to his counterpart in Scotland, Kenny MacAskill, the country's cabinet secretary for justice. Considering the sensitivity of the Lockerbie bombing case, Scottish officials had been strongly urging British negotiators to make sure that any agreement to transfer prisoners between the UK and Libya contained a special clause *specifically excluding* Megrahi from the deal. This way there could be no question about his legal status. But Straw told MacAskill that he'd been unsuccessful in accomplishing this task: "The wider negotiations with the Libyans are reaching a critical stage, and in view of the overwhelming interests for the United Kingdom, I have agreed that in this instance the PTA should be in the standard form and not mention any individual." In other words, UK officials had tried to keep the Megrahi case separate from the prisoner transfer agreement. But Libya balked, and Britain caved in, because its business ties with the oil-rich nation superseded the squishy principles of justice.

In December 2007, Libya and the UK at last came to terms on the broad strokes of their much-discussed PTA, though the final pact wouldn't be signed for another seventeen months. And then, on 23rd December, the Libyan government gave its definitive approval to the BP contract. To the weary British officials, Libya's decision to sign off on the deal was an early Christmas gift, the rewarding culmination of months of arduously delicate diplomacy. To the Libyans, however, the oil contract and the promise of a PTA signified something far more important: the start of their real fight to free their countryman from his Scottish prison cell.

THE INTEREST IS EXTREMELY MUTUAL

Regardless of how the Libyans or British chose to perceive their agreements, to the rest of the world, the message was clear: a close friendship was blossoming between Libya and the UK. For Britain, Libya's allure as a diplomatic and trading partner was obvious. The country was swimming in untapped reserves of oil and natural gas *and* was flush with cash to invest in the British economy. For Libya, however, the appeal of the UK was more personal. Much of it rested on the tight bonds that were being forged between Mu'ammar Gadhafi and his son Saif and the British leadership. For instance, from 2007 through 2009, Prince Andrew met with the Gadhafis several times during his visits to Libya and other parts of the Mediterranean. By all accounts, the prince and the younger Gadhafi in particular formed a close friendship over their mutual interests in sports and business. The royal family even hosted Saif as a guest at Buckingham Palace and Windsor Castle. Clearly, the Libyan leadership was being courted by the traditionally chilly British aristocracy. It couldn't help but be flattered.

Over the years this charm offensive was successful in creating new markets for UK businesses. By 2009, more than 150 British companies had expanded their operations to Libya, like the retailer Marks & Spencer, which opened a store not far from the Libyan outpost of the Office of the British Council, and the pest control outfit Rentokil, which received a £24 million contract from the Libyan government to handle rat infestations in several cities. Plus, the improved relations helped bring hundreds of millions of dollars in needed investment capital from Libya's £35 billion sovereign wealth fund, the Libyan Investment Authority, into Britain.

The LIA was actively looking for investment opportunities because roughly 75 percent of its assets were sitting in cash and not earning a penny. So when the London property market crashed in the global economic downturn, the LIA's managers targeted it as a prime investment opportunity. Starting in late 2008, over a matter of months, the LIA bought the Portman House, a sleek modern commercial property on Oxford Street, London's shopping mecca, for around £155 million. It spent another £120 million for an opulent historic office building in the City of London that had previously been the headquarters of the august Lloyds Bank and sits opposite the Bank of England. The LIA itself set up a London office to oversee the fund's growing international investments. And Saif Gadhafi dropped £10 million on a mansion in the leafy, exclusive enclave of Hampstead in north London and relocated his fledgling Arab news channel to England.

But even as Libya's leaders embraced their new British partners, they never forgot about Megrahi. In September 2008, their mission to bring him home became significantly more urgent. After Megrahi complained of being in pain, Scottish doctors discovered that he was suffering from advanced prostate cancer that had spread throughout his body. The disease was incurable. Megrahi was a dying man. And so, in the blink of an eye, the tenor of the Libyan's requests to British officials changed. The conversations between diplomats from Libya and the UK stopped being theoretical kabuki dances. Instead the Libyans were now making direct demands, coupled with veiled threats, that Megrahi be freed as soon as possible.

For instance, according to notes from a meeting between Libyan and Scottish officials on 12th March 2009, Libya's minister for Europe, Abdulati Alobidi, stated in no uncertain terms that "the death of Mr. Megrahi in a Scottish prison would have catastrophic consequences for the relationship between Libya and the UK." There it was in black-and-white. If Scotland didn't free Megrahi before he died of cancer, Libya would stop doing business with

Britain. What's more, this wasn't the first time that Alobidi had made this threat; he'd said precisely the same thing a month earlier to Bill Rammell, then Britain's minister of state for foreign and commonwealth affairs. According to Alobidi, Rammell assured him that "neither the prime minister [Gordon Brown] nor the foreign secretary would want Mr. Megrahi to pass away in prison."

Gordon Brown's thinking on Megrahi's release, at least as Rammell expressed it to Alobidi, deeply concerned many of the families of the victims of the Lockerbie bombing. After all, wasn't the possibility that Megrahi might die in prison the entire point of his life sentence? The judges' ruling had stipulated that he serve a minimum of twenty-seven years, and yet Megrahi had done only seven. Did Brown think this sentence was unjust for his conviction on 270 counts of murder? Or was Brown placating a valuable economic partner?

On 5th May 2009, Britain and Libya ratified the prisoner transfer agreement between the two nations. On 6th May, Libya formally applied for the transfer of Megrahi from Scotland to Libya. With the application filed, Libyan officials stepped up their lobbying effort to release him right away. And as if Libya's cajoling wasn't enough, it also tapped its wealthy allies to start pushing for Megrahi's freedom—in particular the oil-rich Arabian nation of Qatar.

For more than a year, Scotland had been courting Qatar for possible investments in the country. On 11th June 2009, a month after Libya applied for Megrahi's release, Scotland's leader, Alex Salmond, met with Qatar's minister of state for international cooperation, Dr. Khalid bin Mohamed al-Attiyah. Salmond's notes from the meeting show that early on al-Attiyah stated that "there were a number of business opportunities they would like to explore here in Scotland." Then, later in the conversation, al-Attiyah mentioned that Qatar's emir, Sheik Hamad bin Khalifa Al Thani, had instructed him to bring up the Megrahi case. He said that Qatar "wanted to find the best way solution [*sic*] for Mr. al-Megrahi, and they were concerned for Mr. al-Megrahi's health." The Scottish leader responded that "this was a judicial matter, and politics should not and will not be part of any consideration." He then closed the meeting by suggesting that Qatar's leadership make a formal written appeal for Megrahi's freedom to Kenny MacAskill, Scotland's justice secretary. A month later, on 17th July, al-Attiyah sent a letter to MacAskill on behalf of Qatar and the entire Arab League in which he officially requested that Scotland release Megrahi on compassionate grounds, adding that in light of Megrahi's rapidly failing health, the case should be handled as "a matter of the utmost urgency."

Qatar's decision to intercede was significant because of its extensive involvement in the UK economy. In just a few years, Qatari investment vehicles had bought 15 percent of the London Stock Exchange, pumped more than £2 billion into a bailout of Barclays Bank, and acquired a 30 percent stake in the foundering British commercial properties company Songbird Estates, which controls more than half of London's Canary Wharf business district development. Qatar even spent £430 million to finance the construction of the Renzo Piano–designed Shard skyscraper next to London Bridge station, which is scheduled to be completed in 2012. Indeed, Salmond himself was asking Qatar for a cash infusion into the Scottish economy. All of these investment ties meant that when discussing the Megrahi case, Qatar had an enormous weapon with which to threaten UK officials.

Meanwhile, Megrahi's physical condition was worsening. By the middle of the summer, his doctors were giving him no more than a few months to live. His second appeal was still working its way through the Scottish court system, with little chance of a speedy resolution. The way things stood, it appeared likely that Megrahi would die in Greenock.

In July, Mu'ammar Gadhafi met with Gordon Brown at the G8 summit in L'Aquila, Italy, and personally pressed him on Megrahi's release. But according to public records of the meeting, Brown reiterated that it was a matter for Scottish, not UK, authorities, and that there was little Downing Street could do to force Scotland's hand. At around the same time, Lord David Trefgarne, chairman of the Libyan British Business Council, sent a letter to MacAskill informing the Scottish justice minister: "The Libyan authorities have made it clear that should [Megrahi] die in prison in Scotland, there will be serious implications for UK-Libyan relations." Then, a few weeks after that, Saif Gadhafi met with Peter Mandelson while the two were guests at the Rothschild family's estate on the Greek island of Corfu, and again pushed for Megrahi's freedom.

Following these meetings, Megrahi received a key piece of advice that caused him to change his legal strategy. Specifically, someone in the UK or Scottish government informed either Megrahi or his Libyan supporters that Scotland was much more likely to free him quickly on compassionate grounds than based on the outcome of a legal appeal. Under Scottish law, authorities can consider a compassionate release when a prisoner is suffering from a terminal illness and death is not far off. The law doesn't set a firm time limit, but typically, Scottish justice ministers start weighing a release on compassionate grounds when doctors say a prisoner has three months or less to live. In addition, when it comes to a compassionate release there are no restrictions on the crimes prisoners have been convicted of or the lengths of their sentences. From 2000 to 2009, Scotland freed twenty-three of the thirty terminally ill prisoners who'd applied for freedom on compassionate grounds.

Armed with this new information, Megrahi shifted his tactics and formally applied to MacAskill for a release on compassionate grounds. MacAskill received the application on 24th July and a few weeks later, on 6th August, personally visited Megrahi at Greenock prison. During the meeting, Megrahi was given an opportunity to make a direct appeal for the compassion of the Scottish government. On 14th August 2009, Megrahi dropped his legal appeal. Although it wasn't required, Megrahi believed that it would speed up the decision. He was right. Just six days later, on the 20th of August, MacAskill announced that Megrahi would be released on compassionate grounds and allowed to return home. In a speech, the justice minister explained the logic behind freeing a convicted terrorist and murderer thusly:

> Scotland will forever remember the crime that has been perpetrated against our people and those from many other lands. The pain and suffering will remain forever. Some hurt can never heal. Some scars can never fade. Those who have been bereaved cannot be expected to forget, let alone forgive. Their pain runs deep and the wounds remain.
>
> However, Mr. al-Megrahi now faces a sentence imposed by a higher power. It is one that no court, in any jurisdiction, in any land, could revoke or overrule. It is terminal, final, and irrevocable. He is going to die.
>
> In Scotland, we are a people who pride ourselves on our humanity. It is viewed as a defining characteristic of Scotland and the Scottish people. The perpetration of an atrocity and outrage cannot and should not be a basis for losing sight of who we are, the values we seek to uphold, and the faith and beliefs by which we seek to live.
>
> Mr. al-Megrahi did not show his victims any comfort or compassion. They were not allowed to return to the bosom of their families to see out their lives, let alone their dying days. No compassion was shown by him to them.
>
> But that alone is not a reason for us to deny compassion to him and his family in his final days.

Those are certainly noble sentiments. And few people would argue that there was any practical reason, beyond symbolism, for holding Megrahi. He was simply too weak to be a threat to the rest of the world anymore. As MacAskill pointed out, he was a man who soon would be facing a completely different kind of judgment. Still, for all the high-minded rhetoric, skeptics wondered how compassionate Scotland really was. Their main question was: Would MacAskill have freed Megrahi if he'd been a citizen of a country with less vital economic interests in the UK? What if the man convicted of the Lockerbie bombing wasn't from Libya, one of the most prosperous nations in Africa, but instead was from a devastatingly poor African state like Burundi or Zimbabwe? Wasn't this really just about oil, money, and geopolitical power?

After deciding to free Megrahi, the Scottish and UK governments had hoped that he would return home quietly and the issue would die down. They certainly didn't want the episode to become a worldwide spectacle. Megrahi's plane touched down at Tripoli's Ma'atiqa International Airport on the evening of 21st August 2009, and with television cameras beaming the images across the globe, he was welcomed like a long lost hero by hundreds of family members, friends, and supporters who'd gathered on the tarmac awaiting his arrival. Some wore T-shirts emblazoned with his face. Others threw flower petals to greet him. And many waved Libyan and Scottish flags to the beat of the blaring celebratory music. When Megrahi, after some delay, finally emerged from the plane's doorway and stood on the top step of the passenger stairs, people erupted in cheers, and the energetic throng surged forward. Then, with flashbulbs clicking wildly, Saif Gadhafi, who had accompanied Megrahi from Scotland back to Tripoli, stepped forward, stood next to the former prisoner, clasped Megrahi's hand in his own, and raised their clenched fists over their heads in a symbol of triumph. The crowd roared. Their fellow countryman finally was home.

To British authorities, this was precisely the scene that they'd wanted to avoid. Already the decision to release Megrahi was being condemned loudly, especially by the United States. Before MacAskill made his decision, Secretary of State Hillary Clinton and Attorney General Eric Holder personally called him and strongly urged him to keep Megrahi in prison for the duration of his sentence. But with Megrahi released, it was clear that MacAskill had completely disregarded their entreaties. As pictures of the reverie in Tripoli circulated the world, anger rose in the West. In the United States, President Barack Obama described the wild scene in Libya as "highly objectionable." The White House press secretary, Robert Gibbs, went further, calling it "outrageous and disgusting."

To make matters even worse for US-UK relations, Libya's statements following Megrahi's release continually linked the British government to the deal. For example, after Megrahi returned to Libya, Mu'ammar Gadhafi held a televised meeting with the former prisoner where he publicly thanked "my friend Brown, the prime minister of Britain, his government, the Queen of Britain, Elizabeth, and Prince Andrew, who all contributed to encouraging the Scottish government to take this historic and courageous decision, despite the obstacles." And Saif Gadhafi issued an official statement that said in part, "I would also like to personally thank our friends in the British government who played an important role in reaching this day, and I can assure them that the Libyan people will never forget the courageous stand of the British and Scottish governments. I can also assure them that the friendship between our people will continue to be strengthened and that this past chapter is now firmly behind us."

Comments like these stoked speculation that prior to Megrahi's release the UK and Libya had cemented a secret deal to swap the prisoner for valuable oil contracts. Gordon Brown's deputies and ministers immediately fanned out to deny the existence of any quid pro quo agreements with Libya and to insist that the decision to free Megrahi was made by Scottish authorities alone. The only reason that Britain's leadership was engaging in diplomacy with Libya, they said, was to coax the former rogue state into the modern global economy and convert it into an ally in the global fight against Islamic terrorism.

Libyan officials backed up Brown's version of events and confirmed that there was no explicit agreement between Britain and their country to secure Megrahi's release in return for oil and natural gas contracts. However, they went much further in acknowledging that commerce and economic relations—the two key ingredients in the power cocktail of the shadow market—had played a major role in gaining his freedom. After Megrahi was freed, Saif Gadhafi explained to Libya's national television station that the country was able to win Megrahi's freedom by relentlessly putting his case on the negotiating table "in all commercial contracts for gas and oil with Britain." And other Libyan officials elaborated on the economic meaning of Megrahi's release.

"We have a lot of things in the pipeline between Libya and the UK," Deputy Foreign Minister Mohammad Sayalah told the BBC. "There is very good room for developing cooperation with the UK. So if this political problem is an obstruction, at least we moved it away. And this will open a good avenue for developing the relations."

Finally, after the news broke that BP had intervened to push for Megrahi's freedom, the British government was forced to concede that business interests, specifically oil contracts, had in fact, played a major role in Megrahi's release. Jack Straw acknowledged that trade was "a very big part" of his decision not to exclude Megrahi from the prisoner transfer agreement between Britain and Libya. And Lord Trefgarne noted that negotiations on oil contracts had largely been stalled while the details of Megrahi's fate were being worked out. "Perhaps now, with what I would assume to be the final resolution of the Lockerbie affair as far as the Libyans are concerned, maybe they will move forward a little more swiftly," he said.

Thus had the role of the shadow market been exposed.

Unfortunately for the British government, with all the negative publicity, the Lockerbie affair just continued to live on. Nine months after Megrahi's release he was still alive, in defiance of his doctor's dire predictions. What made his turnaround particularly galling to the families of the Lockerbie bombing victims was that the *Sunday Telegraph* reported that Megrahi's doctors had been paid a consulting fee by the Libyan government, although at least one of the doctors insisted that he was not pressured to offer a particular opinion. Meanwhile, Megrahi became determined to clear his name. From his new luxury duplex villa outside Tripoli, he set up a website and posted every shred of evidence his legal team had gathered. Of course, whether the court would have found the evidence to be exculpatory was unknowable because Megrahi withdrew his appeal before the court could rule. This was infuriating to government officials from Scotland and the UK as well as the families and friends of the victims. If Megrahi had truly wanted to be proven innocent he could have continued his appeal from Libya. But he chose not to. Yet he was free to launch an attack on the prosecution from his home without answering questions himself.

By July 2010, Megrahi was still alive, having become the longest surviving prisoner ever released by the Scottish government on compassionate grounds. Regardless of what he thought of his trial and imprisonment, he had to know that he was a very lucky man, and not only for having outlived his dire prognosis. Without the power of the shadow market he likely would have been a forgotten prisoner who simply rotted away in a Scottish jail. That is the usual scenario for someone in his position. But the shadow market changed all that. For the citizens of those lucky countries with the cash to make it happen, anything's possible. Even resurrection.

BRINGING THE CRAZY

The United Kingdom isn't the only Western country with economic ties to Libya that has been forced to deal with its fickle style of diplomacy in order to remain on good business terms with the oil-rich African nation. In August 2009, Swiss President Hans-Rudolf Merz was forced to publicly apologize to Libya over the arrest of Motassim Bilal Gadhafi, the Libyan leader's fifth oldest son, and his wife, Aline. The couple had been held overnight by police in Geneva after being accused of beating their servants with belts and coat hangers. But they were released after the servants dropped the charges and received some form of remuneration.

This was not the first time that Gadhafi, who goes by the name Hannibal, had run afoul of foreign authorities. In 2001 he brawled with police officers in Rome who were guarding his hotel room. In 2004 he was stopped in Paris for driving ninety miles an hour on the wrong side of the Champs-Élysées, and his bodyguards attacked the police officers who pulled over the car. In 2005 he was arrested in Paris and accused of beating up a woman who'd rejected his romantic advances. He later whipped out a semiautomatic pistol in the lobby of the Hotel InterContinental in Paris and trashed his hotel room while security guards tried to restrain him.

So it was hardly surprising that Hannibal Gadhafi was in trouble with the law again. Nonetheless, his father responded pretty much as you might expect. He shut down commercial and diplomatic relations with Switzerland. He tossed Swiss diplomats out of his country. He froze Swiss businesses operating in Libya. He withdrew Libya's assets from Swiss banks. He disrupted oil deliveries to Switzerland. And he arrested two Swiss nationals who were working in Libya. One was Max Goeldi, who headed the Tripoli office of the giant Swedish-Swiss engineering firm ABB, and the other was Rachid Hamdani, who worked for a small construction outfit that did business in Libya.

Gadhafi's message wasn't subtle. To set things right, Merz travelled to Libya to offer a personal apology for his country's treatment of the ruler's son and daughter-in-law. "We are apologizing for what happened to Hannibal Gadhafi, and the two sides agreed to form a committee to discuss the matter," Merz told a gathering of reporters in Tripoli. The Swiss media was appalled, calling it "humiliating," a "farce," a "surrender," and a measure of Switzerland's "powerlessness." But none of that mattered to Merz. Instead he was focused on normalizing economic relations with Libya.

And it worked. Following Switzerland's public groveling, the two countries returned their respective consular staffs and restored trade ties. Merz also received an assurance that the Swiss hostages, Goeldi and Hamdani, would be freed. In February 2010, Hamdani, who had Tunisian dual citizenship, was released and driven by Swiss officials to neighboring Tunisia. Goeldi, however, remained in Libyan custody. He was one last bargaining card for Gadhafi to play.

And just in case the rest of the world was under the impression that Libya had quietly joined the modern global community, Gadhafi managed to dispel those notions once and for all in September 2009 at the sixty-fourth session of the UN General Assembly. For Libya's leader, it was his first address in front of the body during his forty years in power. So to honor the occasion he gave an all-star lunatic performance that was notable even by Gadhafi's own eccentric standards.

Allowed just fifteen minutes to speak, Gadhafi launched into a wild ninety-six-minute screed so full of bizarre non sequiturs that to describe it as rambling would be polite. He tore a copy of the UN charter and tossed it on the floor, swearing that his country would never abide by it, though it would, for some reason, accept the preamble. He suggested that the UN Security Council be renamed "the UN Terror Council." He called for investigations into a variety of past conflicts including the Korean War, the Vietnam War, the 1956 international conflict over the Suez Canal, and both Iraq wars, as well as the deaths of Dr. Martin Luther King and John F. Kennedy. He mused about whether swine 'flu had been created in a laboratory as a corporate or military weapon. When UN delegates eventually started leaving the floor, Gadhafi harangued those remaining for falling asleep. He also suggested that the UN should be moved to Libya so he wouldn't be sleep deprived. After ninety minutes his translator literally collapsed from exhaustion and had to be replaced by an Arabic-speaking UN employee. Gadhafi was not to be denied. Not on this day.

So there it was for the whole world to see. Libya might have changed, as indicated by its renunciation of terrorism and the ceasing of its nuclear activities. But its leader certainly hadn't. Indeed, by all appearances, Gadhafi was as blustery and erratic as ever. However, because of his country's deep reserves of oil and natural gas, not to mention its standing as the wealthiest nation in Africa, Libya had gone from being an international pariah to a global diplomatic force. No longer could it be ignored or economically isolated in a box. It was simply too valuable, which really is the key point that international investors have to keep in mind today. In the global financial community, it's difficult to pick sides based on what's perceived as right or wrong. The way to win is to make money, pure and simple. So if Libya is becoming a more open and valuable market, then it's wise to be there, whether that means putting money into developing Libyan companies or into multinational corporations that are aggressively bidding for Libya's business, like BP. When playing by the rules of the shadow market, a political conscience may be a luxury that investors no longer can afford.

BLOOD IS THICKER THAN MONEY

The truth is, for all of Gadhafi's wackiness, he's really just a symptom of a much larger issue for the Western countries that once dominated the world economically. The uncontrollable power of oil wealth is shifting geopolitical power across the world in ways we're only beginning to understand. According to the US Energy Information Administration, the ten largest proven reserves of crude oil on earth belong to (in order): Saudi Arabia, Canada, Iran, Iraq, Kuwait, the United Arab Emirates, Venezuela, Russia, Libya, and Nigeria. The countries in OPEC, the international cartel that largely sets the worldwide price of oil, are Algeria, Angola, Ecuador, Iran, Iraq, Kuwait, Libya, Nigeria, Qatar, Saudi Arabia, the United Arab Emirates, and Venezuela.

Looking at those two lists, how many of these countries have healthy international relations with the West? And how many of them are, or have ties to, nations that Western foreign policy experts find diplomatically troubling at the very least? Obviously, Iran is provocative because of its authoritarian Islamist regime, its links to state-sponsored terrorism, and its nuclear ambitions. And Venezuela's leader, Hugo Chávez, who in September 2006 used his address to the UN General Assembly to call then president George W. Bush "the devil," seems to enjoy riling up America with his inflammatory rhetoric. Diplomatically, Iran and Venezuela may be pariah states to the United States. But in the shadow market they aren't isolated countries. We've already seen how close relations are between China and Iran. Then, in April 2010, China agreed to give Venezuela £13 billion in loans for public works projects such as power plants and highways. Venezuela would pay back the money to China not in cash but in crude oil. The deal helped bolster the Chávez government, which was running into trouble from opposition within the country.

What's more, China even has financial relationships with groups that are considered direct enemies of the West, such as with Al Qaeda and the Taliban. In 2007 and 2008 British and American officials started warning China that Chinese weapons were regularly showing up in the hands of resistance fighters in Iraq and Afghanistan. The last straw came in early 2008 when American troops in Iraq found stores of Chinese-made missiles among Iraqi militants and Afghan police seized Chinese-made land mines and rocket-propelled grenades from Taliban forces near the border with Iran. After that, in May 2008, US Deputy Secretary of State

John Negroponte traveled to Beijing to deliver America's message in person: "Stop sending weapons to our enemies!" Whether Chinese officials listened remains open to debate, however, as China's weapons stayed in the hands of the West's enemies, aimed squarely at US, UK, and UN forces.

But what about the oil-rich countries with which we're supposedly friendly? Well, the sad fact is that in many cases, they too have issues that are hiding in plain sight. Because when it comes to dealing with Middle Eastern petroleum states, blood is often thicker than oil—or money.

Look at Qatar. The tiny country, which is roughly the size of Los Angeles, is an extremely prosperous nation that's also rich in contradictions. Jutting out of the northeastern edge of the Arabian Peninsula in the shape of a small, sandy thumb surrounded by the turquoise waters of the Persian Gulf, Qatar is a gleaming, modern Islamic state, a forest of towering skyscrapers and luxurious high-end shopping malls rising out of the desert. It controls the third largest reservoir of natural gas on earth and is the biggest exporter of liquefied natural gas in the world. Its per capita GDP is £54,000, which is the highest in the world, according to the IMF. And it has a £40 billion sovereign wealth fund, the Qatar Investment Authority, which runs a series of state-owned businesses, like the Qatari Diar real estate investment firm. Among the fund's high-profile holdings is Harrods department store in London, which it bought in May 2010 for £1.5 billion.

Geographically, Qatar sits directly next to Saudi Arabia, the leadership of which is diplomatically friendly to the West. But directly across the Persian Gulf lies Iran, which historically has been one of Qatar's strongest allies because roughly 30 percent of the Qatari population is of Persian descent. Iran, of course, couldn't be more belligerent to the West in general, and America in particular. This tension lies at the heart of Qatar's delicate geopolitical position as an honest broker between intractable parties.

Qatar hosts the largest American military base in the Mideast,

Al Udeid Air Base, which serves as a forward headquarters for US Central Command, which is responsible for military operations in the Middle East. Yet its government also supports a more populist view of Arab politics. For instance, its leadership accepts the policies of Islamist paramilitary organizations like Hezbollah in Lebanon and Hamas in the West Bank and Gaza Strip as legitimate responses to Israel's aggression against the Palestinian people. It has publicly denounced Iran's controversial nuclear enrichment program. But it has also defended Iran's right to develop peaceful nuclear technology and has rejected UN Security Council resolutions condemning Iran's nuclear program. For more than a decade, it had economic ties and trade relations with Israel, though that ended with the Israeli incursion into Gaza in 2008. But before that, Israeli officials were regularly invited to meetings and gatherings in the country. Yet, at the same time, Qatar is also the Arabian nation with the closest diplomatic ties to Israel's neighbor and nemesis Syria, which also has strained relations with numerous key Middle Eastern nations, such as Saudi Arabia and Egypt, because of its perceived meddling in Lebanon's politics.

Qatar's government believes that its geopolitical standing straddling two worlds and numerous ideologies makes it an ideal broker for peace in the Mideast. It played this role in May 2008, when it helped mediate a series of feuds between warring factions in Lebanon. Qatar also is the headquarters of the Arab television news network Al Jazeera, which since its launch in 1996 has infuriated Western and Middle Eastern governments alike by representing the news from the Arab point of view but still offering some Western perspective. The country has even organized televised debates on highly charged topics within the Islamic community, like bridging the divide between Sunni and Shia Muslims.

The problem with this balance, however, is that it can prevent the rest of the world from applying economic diplomacy to isolate problematic nations if they have strong trade relationships with Qatar. Like Iran, with which Qatar has very powerful cultural and economic bonds. The countries have "defense ties" where they collaborate on the security of the Persian Gulf. They're part of a "gas troika" with Russia, in which the three nations cooperate on extracting their gas reserves; combined, that amounts to roughly half the natural gas on the planet. And Qatari businesses in telecommunications, banking, and steel have all started investing in Iran.

Or take Syria. Qatar has set up the Syrian-Qatari Holding Company to finance infrastructure projects all over Syria. It invested in the construction of power stations across the nation. It financed the deployment of modern irrigation technology to bolster Syria's farms. It set up production plants to make phosphate-based fertilizers from the country's piles and piles of desert phosphate rocks. It developed a state-of-the-art medical complex with a hospital, treatment clinics, diagnostic services, even a nursing school. And it paid to increase Syria's dairy farm capacity and production.

In all, Qatar has made substantial investments in making sure that controversial countries like Iran and Syria have the resources to keep their economies moving. Yet because of its deep supplies of oil and capital, it is globally perceived to be part of the solution, not the problem. In today's world, cash and natural resources can buy a lot of good will.

Qatar is hardly the only small, rich Middle Eastern state that's friendly with the West but still maintains troubling alliances. Just look at Dubai, which, like Qatar, has close economic ties to pariah-state allies like Iran. Indeed, it has become the main conduit for much of Iran's international trade and investment. Dubai is Iran's largest trading partner, with roughly £9 billion in cross-border commerce each year. Plus, as of September 2009, Iranians had made a total of about £200 billion worth of investments in Dubai. Indeed, the US retail banking behemoth Bank of America dropped Dubai's state-owned Dragon Oil as a client because of its involvement with Iran. However, few other companies or countries are eager to confront Dubai officials because of the emirate's position of power within the oil-slicked UAE.

And Iran is just the tip of the sand dune when it comes to Dubai's problematic entanglements. Dubai traditionally has been considered the preferred money transfer center for many of the world's Islamist terrorism organizations, including Al Qaeda. The UAE government has repeatedly denied this charge, but evidence shows otherwise. After the bombing of the World Trade Center and the Pentagon, investigators for the National Commission on Terrorist Attacks upon the United States—better known as the 9/11 Commission—found that one of Osama bin Laden's finance aides used Dubai banks to wire a total of about $120,000 (£80,000) to Al Qaeda operatives in the United States. Authorities also believe that money from Dubai banks was used in the bombings of American embassies in Kenya and Tanzania in 1998.* Because of its lax financial regulations, Dubai has emerged as the ideal middleman for cash and distributing it across the globe. A typical route would start in Karachi, Pakistan, move on to Dubai, and from there spread out to other parts of the world. That's the way bin Laden did it, according to the 9/11 Commission.

After the 9/11 terrorist attacks, foreign governments started clamping down on clandestine financial networks like hawala. Dubai and the rest of the United Arab Emirates jumped on board, eager to eliminate the country's reputation as a financial center for

---

* The main way to get cash out of Dubai is something called *hawala,* an informal network of secret money-transfer agents all over the world that circumvents the global banking system. The 9/11 Commission report concluded that "Al Qaeda moved much of its money by hawala before 9/11." It's an ancient financial system that predates traditional banking and works very much like wiring money through Western Union. A person in Country A gives money to a local *hawaladar*—an unofficial banker that handles hawala transactions. The hawaladar then contacts a hawaladar in Country B and tells him to deliver the cash to a person in Country B. The hawaladars take a fee for the service, which is less than what a bank would charge, and privately settle up their financial obligations to each other.

terrorists. In 2008 the UAE even hosted a conference of ministers from the Mideast and North Africa to discuss combating terrorist financing. However, a report prepared by the IMF and several other Arab countries found that the UAE still hadn't put in place regulatory measures to meet even the minimum standards for battling the financial activities that support international terrorism. Instead Dubai remained a terrorist financing playground.

The world received a further reminder of Dubai's role as a terrorist haven in May 2010, when Faisal Shahzad, a naturalized US citizen from Pakistan, was arrested on charges of unsuccessfully trying to blow up Times Square in New York City with a sports utility vehicle packed with explosives. Two days after the bomb was discovered, agents from the US Department of Homeland Security pulled Shahzad off an Emirates airlines flight heading to Dubai. From there, Shahzad was planning to travel to Islamabad, Pakistan. Shahzad had recently been placed on the US government's no fly list because of his suspected terrorist ties, and US government officials criticized Emirates airlines for allowing Shahzad on the flight. In addition, investigators believe Shahzad had links to a Pakastani Taliban group, meaning yet another terrorist group viewed Dubai as a safe zone. Had Shahzad reached the emirate there's little doubt that he would have made it to his final destination.

The key point in all of this is that the economics and geopolitics of Middle Eastern oil are tricky, whether a Western country is dealing with an erratic dictator like Mu'ammar Gadhafi or more seemingly welcoming nations like Qatar and Dubai. The fact is that Qatar may actually be an honest diplomatic arbiter that successfully straddles the economic cultures of the West and the Middle East. And Dubai may be an essential gateway financial hub to the Persian Gulf. But with their feet in two completely different worlds—just like their neighbors Abu Dhabi and Kuwait— these microscopic countries have become power brokers more than honest brokers, capable of helping their closest friends while keeping potential enemies (or, more important, the enemies of their friends) at bay. This presents a deadly conundrum for the needy nations of the West. For each barrel of oil they buy from Middle Eastern suppliers and each deal they make with Middle Eastern investors, they are indirectly bolstering the economies of treacherous nations like Iran and Syria and helping to support institutions that illegally transfer funds for the very terrorists who want to kill Western citizens. That's the power of the shadow market.

CHAPTER 7

Beware the Do-Gooders

Yngve Slyngstad goes to work each morning with a single primary objective: do the right thing. Admittedly, it's not a particularly original sentiment. Plenty of people around the world try to live by some form of this credo. But it does set him apart from most of his colleagues. Because Slyngstad is the CEO of Norges Bank Investment Management, the investment arm of Norway's central bank. This means he's in charge of one of the largest stockpiles of investment capital on earth: Norway's £300 billion sovereign wealth fund, the Government Pension Fund Global, otherwise known in the financial community as the Petroleum Fund, or *Oljefondet* in Norwegian. The massive fund, which is the second largest SWF in the world after the Abu Dhabi Investment Authority, is such a significant force in the international financial markets that it alone owns 1 percent of all the shares of stock available for sale on the planet. Typically, the goal of financial institutions of that size and scope is to rake in as much cash as possible, as quickly as possible, by any means necessary. So it's surprising that "doing the right thing" is even on the list of daily priorities for Slyngstad and his team. But that's what makes the Petroleum Fund unique.

"For a sovereign wealth fund to be successful it has to have legitimacy at home," says Dag Dyrdal, the head of strategic relations at NBIM. "It has to be aligned with the broad standards of the country's population. That has very much been the think-ing with the fund from the outset, our 'bigger purpose.' It's what the country wants. We focus on traditional corporate governance areas, transparency, shareholders rights, and board accountability. We also look at issues like child labor, water management, and cli-mate change, when it comes to our investments. But you have to realize that it is our belief that if we succeed, this will improve the fund's performance over time. This is very important to under-stand. We *are* a financial investor."

The way that Norway has structured its Petroleum Fund all but insures that this big pot of money will have a higher meaning than most other investment vehicles. When it comes to ethics, the fund is beyond reproach. It's broadly based on the so-called Santiago Principles, which offer a framework that guides sovereign wealth funds toward investment practices that are fair and encourage a free flow of trade. The fund also focuses on the responsible invest-ing principles that finance professionals call ESG, which stands for environmental, social, and corporate governance issues. It even has its own ethical guidelines built into its charter that require the fund to openly disclose all of its dealings and to dump any invest-ments in companies that don't meet its virtuous standards. Finally, the fund's managers have to answer to a Council on Ethics, which consists of specialists in economics, the law, human rights, and health and safety, who evaluate whether its investments meet the country's stringent moral benchmarks.

In many ways, this makes Norway the most curious player in the shadow market. The Petroleum Fund is a test case for whether a nation can spend its capital in a manner that coaxes the rest of the world toward more principled behavior. To do this Norway has had to employ many of the strategies used by the other wealthy nations of the shadow market, such as bringing global politics into its investing strategy. In particular, the country has used the fund to wade into some complex geopolitical disputes, such as the Israeli-Palestinian conflict.

In September 2009, the Petroleum Fund sold its £3.7 million stake in the Israeli company Elbit Systems, which supplies surveillance equipment for the barrier separating the West Bank from the rest of Israel, to express Norway's disapproval of Israel's policies toward the Palestinians. In a statement announcing the fund's decision, Norway's finance minister, Kristin Halvorsen, who had previously called for an outright boycott of all Israeli businesses, said, "We do not wish to fund companies that so directly contribute to violations of international humanitarian law."

In other words, like any other member of the shadow market, Norway was using the power of its capital to make a political point. In a November 2009 report about the Petroleum Fund's stance on global governance, Larry Catá Backer, founding director of the Consortium for Peace and Ethics and a law professor at Pennsylvania State University, concluded that "Norway is consciously pursuing state policy indirectly through its funds. Investment is clearly meant to project Norway's political power by other means, and to move policy in particular directions."

So what's the difference between Norway's investment strategy and China's or Libya's? Only that Norway's aggressiveness is often applauded by humanitarian groups and corporate governance advocates around the world. Other than that, it's still using the outsized power of its wealth to influence geopolitical behavior. This is what makes Norway an influential part of the shadow market. And the country is starting to become equally tough in the private sector, prodding the companies that it invests in to behave in ways that Norway considers to be more ethical and in line with good corporate governance.

All of this constitutes a noble effort, to be sure, and one that could provide a model for individuals and institutions who want their investment portfolios to more accurately reflect their geopolitical views. But the bottom line is, beyond the admirable intentions, the Petroleum Fund experiment will be deemed a success only if the investing strategy makes money. If not, Norway is just fooling itself. What's more, it runs the risk of squandering its "bigger purpose" for future generations by trying in vain to make the world a better place.

BLUE-EYED ARABS

Norway's economic ascension through oil wealth started in 1962, when America's Phillips Petroleum applied for the exclusive rights to explore for oil and gas in the North Sea off the Norwegian coast. In return, the company offered to perform a million-dollar seismic study of Norway's entire territory. Phillips had targeted the area because energy companies had already found a large natural gas field to the south, in offshore territory belonging to the Netherlands. Since then, Britain and Denmark had divvied up their patches of ocean for exploration. But Norway was largely unspoken for, in large part because few scientists believed that oil and gas reserves extended that far north. Phillips, however, was willing to take a shot. So the company decided to get in early and seek exclusive rights to Norway's sea territory. Unfortunately for Phillips, the Norwegians refused and instead issued a few licenses to a series of drilling consortiums, which included Phillips.

For years, the oil companies banged away but came up dry, finding only traces of the potential mother lode lying beneath the sea floor. All told, they drilled roughly thirty wells, each of which was barren. In addition, the North Sea's frigid temperatures, one-hundred-mile-per-hour winds, and wildly undulating ninety-foot swells were proving to be an extra challenge for the workers, who were accustomed to more hospitable conditions. Ships broke free of their moorings during icy storms and nearly capsized. More than twenty roughnecks died from drownings and other accidents in the treacherous conditions. As a result, by the summer of 1969, Phillips was ready to give up and pull out. However, the company still was paying for the lease on its rig, the Ocean Viking. So rather than waste the money it had already spent, Phillips decided to drill one last well in a slice of continental shelf off of Norway's southern coast, roughly halfway to Great Britain. And wouldn't you know it, on its desperate last shot Phillips finally hit pay dirt. To the company's shock, it discovered what it believed to be a vast reservoir of oil unlike anything it had seen before. Back at Phillips headquarters in Oklahoma, company executives were literally dancing around the office over the news.

Norway, however, was more skeptical. Up to that point, many of the wells in its sector had generated lots of initial excitement but ultimately proved to be disappointments, yielding relatively skimpy resources that weren't remotely commercially developable. But Phillips insisted that the field it had discovered was different. And on Christmas Eve 1969, Norwegian authorities confirmed the company's suspicions. Phillips had indeed located the first commercial oil field in Norway's offshore territory. The area, which they called Ekofisk, contained more than three million barrels of oil—a relatively paltry amount compared to the major Middle Eastern oil fields, but a significant find for anywhere else in the world.

Naturally, the discovery of Ekofisk set off a frantic race among oil companies and investors to exploit the natural resources buried beneath the North Sea. All of a sudden, northern Europe had become the hot spot to drill for oil. More than 350 different companies and consortiums were set up to finance North Sea exploration projects. And the quaint eighth-century port city of Stavanger on the southern Norway coast was inundated with thousands of foreign oil workers, mostly from America and France.

The conditions at sea remained perilous, however, making the cost of this kind of complicated offshore drilling roughly twenty times more expensive than simply extracting oil from the deserts of the Arabian Peninsula. But when you accounted for the savings on taxes and shipping costs (tankers from the Middle East had to travel more than ten thousand miles around the horn of Africa to reach Europe or the United States), North Sea crude still was a cheaper alternative for Western nations than Middle Eastern oil. So the major US and European oil companies kept on drilling. In 1971 partners Shell and Esso, the oil company that eventually renamed itself Exxon, found the Brent field in British waters. Brent had just shy of two billion barrels of oil and deep stores of liquid and natural gas. But more important, geologists noticed that it sat along a structural trend in the sea floor that extended into Norwegian territory. The oil executives figured that if they just followed the line, they'd eventually uncover a massive supply of energy resources. And sure enough, they were right.

In 1974 Mobil Oil came up with the biggest oil discovery in the history of the North Sea. The field was named Statfjord, and it contained more than 3.5 billion barrels. Suddenly, with the Statfjord and Ekofisk fields online and in operation, tiny Norway, which had fewer than four million citizens at the time, was a global oil power. The finding was so significant that today the Statfjord field and its seven-hundred-foot-high offshore drilling platforms are recognized by the Norwegian government as an official cultural heritage site because they symbolize the evolution of modern Norway.

With gigantic sums of money suddenly pouring in, Norway realized that it had to reassess its oil policy. The country had traditionally maintained a largely socialist balance in its society, and its citizens wanted to keep it that way. But government officials feared that an influx of oil wealth would destroy this important aspect of Norwegian culture. So the government decided to change the way it granted drilling licenses for its territories. First, in 1972, it created a state-owned oil company called Den Norske Stats Oljeselskap, or Statoil, and gave it an extremely powerful mandate. As of 1973, all new drilling contracts had to include Statoil as a 50 percent partner. As part of the deal, the foreign companies applying for licenses would have to cover all of Statoil's exploration costs, and Statoil reserved the right to increase its stake to as much as

85 percent depending on each project's success or failure. Next Norway introduced a special new oil tax that drillers would have to pay. Finally, the government created the Norwegian Petroleum Directorate, which ran the country's exploration operations, decided what companies could work together, and determined the areas that could be drilled and how many wells could be placed on them. In essence, Norway was no longer treating the foreign oil companies as partners. Instead they were contractors. It was a complete about-face from where the relationship had started.

Since all this change was playing out against the backdrop of the oil shocks and embargoes of the early 1970s, most foreign oil companies swallowed Norway's new rules just to get access to the country's North Sea crude and natural gas. But that doesn't mean they liked it. Indeed, many Europeans and oil executives who were put off by Norway's new imperious attitude toward its oil and gas holdings started to refer to Norwegians as "blue-eyed Arabs of the North"—a not-so-veiled reference to the racist slur "Never trust an Arab," which was an oft-heard expression in Britain after World War II.

Norway, however, was too busy counting its kroner to care much about the insults. Like its neighbors in the UK and the Netherlands, Norway appreciated the sudden influx of cash. However, unlike the British and Dutch, the Norwegians didn't get so caught up in their oil wealth that they cratered their economy in a phenomenon known as "Dutch disease": the problematic side effects of a sudden increase in a nation's income. The term is based on the economic crisis that occurred in Holland during the 1960s after natural gas was discovered in the nation's waters and a flood of money led to an equally rapid rise in the value of the Dutch gulden. As a result, the price of the Netherlands' other exports became phenomenally expensive in the global market, and the country's industrial sector crumbled. A similar thing happened in Britain in the late 1970s and early 1980s, when oil wealth led to a surge in the value of the pound and soaring inflation across the

UK. To keep up, British workers demanded higher wages, and soon the country's exports were overpriced. It was only a matter of time before its economy crashed too, which is precisely what happened. In 1979 Great Britain elected Margaret Thatcher's Conservative Party government which quickly installed a fiscal austerity program to fight inflation. It raised interest rates, cut spending to reduce the national budget deficit, and reduced the money supply. Although the policies were designed to save the British economy for the long run, the short-term effect was devastating economic stagnation. Consumers stopped spending and businesses stopped investing. Exports suffered because the value of the pound was rising so fast. By 1981 the UK's GDP fell 2.2 percent. And three million Britons were unemployed.

Seeing all of this, the Norwegians were clever enough to realize that their oil wealth would turn out to be ephemeral if they spent it frivolously. Oil and natural gas were not renewable resources, they were resources that a country had to deplete in order to gain capital. This was an immutable law of physics. No matter where you were, whether it was the North Sea or the Persian Gulf, it you were taking oil and natural gas from the ground, it would eventually be gone. The only question was, would your money be gone too?

Norway received its wake-up call in 1986, when the economy overheated and spurred inflation. Then oil prices collapsed, and the value of the krone came plummeting down with them. The government was forced to run up budget deficits to cover its expenses. The destabilization was jarring to a country whose citizens were accustomed to a relatively placid economy that didn't feature wild swings in currency values. So Norway decided to do something about it. First government officials tried to put a conservative ceiling on annual oil and gas production in an attempt to control its level of exports. But that didn't work because it ran counter to the way the oil and gas markets typically operated, where fluctuations in price drove demand, which in turn drove production.

As a result, Norway had a very hard time regulating its output on its own, because its oil and gas production was affected by much larger international market forces that were controlled in large part by the OPEC cartel. Fighting this dynamic was fruitless.

So Norwegian finance officials decided to turn around the equation. Rather than trying to control the country's oil production, they would instead control the cash flow it generated from the oil and gas industry. In order to do this, Norway would establish a publicly owned investment fund that would manage its oil and gas revenues and preserve them for future generations. Norway was bringing in around £185 million a week in revenues from the oil and natural gas industries. By pumping the budgetary surplus generated by that capital infusion into a petroleum fund, the country could effectively separate how much oil and gas money it spent from the amount of oil and gas being extracted from the North Sea floor each day. The concept seemed plausible enough. In 1990 Norway launched its Government Petroleum Fund. To start, it was given a relatively modest stake of £250 million, which came in the form of a cash transfer from the Ministry of Finance. Little did the Norwegians know that within just twenty years it would become one of the mightiest investment vehicles on earth.

CASH WITH A CONSCIENCE

Initially the Government Petroleum Fund was set up to invest very conservatively. The main idea, according to Svein Gjedrem, the current head of Norges Bank, who was deeply involved in the fund's formation back in 1990, was to make it an instrument that, through long-term savings, could pay for Norway's future social security and health care requirements for its aging population. As a result, the fund's rules were set up to make sure that it didn't lose money rather than trying to make as much as it could. The fund wasn't allowed to invest in stocks or non-government issued bonds. It had to stay away from emerging markets. And it couldn't invest in Norway at all. The reason for this was that Norwegian finance ministers wanted to completely separate the country's natural-resources wealth from the rest of the economy, using the fund purely as an investment vehicle. By investing only abroad, the government was, in effect, attempting to shield Norway from the day-to-day vagaries of the oil and natural gas markets. The capital the country generated from oil and natural gas was removed from the economy before anyone could notice it was there and put it to use.

"There has always been a concern about Dutch disease, which is what triggered the way the fund was set up," Dyrdal says. "From the start there was a consideration of what the impact on the domestic economy might be if all the oil revenues were to flow straight into it. Historically that has been a dangerous policy. So the government set up the fund to avoid that problem."

The fund's management was outsourced to the country's central bank, Norges Bank, which operated independently from the national government. Under the fund's rules, the Ministry of Finance would determine its strategic asset allocation. It would set the portfolio's performance benchmarks and provide reports to parliament on the fund's performance. Norges Bank, in turn, would handle the daily trading activities of the fund, albeit within the parameters set by the Ministry of Finance's asset allocation models and performance benchmarks. It would offer the Ministry of Finance advice on its financial strategy. And most importantly, it would keep a close watch to make sure that the fund wasn't taking on too much risk.

The structure accomplished what the Norwegian government wanted, namely to protect the country's nest egg from being decimated by the global financial markets. The fund made slow and steady progress, earning annual returns of around 4 percent. However, its rules also held the fund back from making even more money during a time when those same global financial markets were booming. For example, it missed out on the 1990s Internet stock market explosion because of its prohibition on investing in equities. Obviously, that boom resulted in a bubble that popped all over the world. But there was still a lot of money to be made on the Dow Jones Industrial's run-up from 3,000 to 10,000. And Norway blew its opportunity to capitalize.

So, in 1998, as international stock markets were taking off, and every country, it seemed, was making money off its money, Norway started a multiyear project to reform the way the Petroleum Fund operated. It began to give Norges Bank more flexibility to operate by allowing it to buy stocks. The fund would still have to keep a keen eye on its risk exposure. The idea was to be a long-term investor. The fund would use indexing to calculate what equity positions to take, and its investment style would be completely passive—meaning that it simply followed its indexing models rather than deviating to take bold positions in companies that the fund's managers felt were undervalued. The mix of the fund's assets would still be tilted conservatively, with only 40 percent in equities and 60 percent in government bonds. But it was a start. In 2000 the fund loosened up further by adding emerging-market stocks to its holdings. And in 2002 it started buying corporate bonds. Little by little, the Norwegian government was easing up on the reins and letting its investment vehicle run.

However, the most significant changes at the Petroleum Fund started in 2004, when Norway instituted a series of ethical guidelines designed to make the fund's holdings more morally virtuous. To Norwegians, the move fit perfectly within the country's culture. But throughout the rest of the global investment community, the decision was met with more than a little skepticism and eye rolling. After all, the goal of investing wasn't about charity or doing good deeds, it was about making money, pure and simple. The group that ended up with the most money at the end of the game won. That's the way finance worked. But that's not the way the Norwegians saw it.

"Norway has always been an egalitarian society," says B. Espen Eckbo, a finance professor at the Tuck School of Business at Dartmouth University who was born in Norway and has advised the Oil Fund on its corporate governance strategies. "The economic system they have now goes back to the period after the Second World War. At that time Norway was very poor. And in response to this poverty the country organized itself in a social democratic way. So every year the government, the labor organizations, and the business organizations hold a huge negotiation to establish national wage increases. It's a unique system that's set up to be very egalitarian. To Norwegians, this premise is not controversial in any way. So if you expand this thinking, the idea that the country's investments would focus on good governance and ethics is completely logical."

The fund's new ethical guidelines started out by stating that it "should not make investments which constitute an unacceptable risk that the fund may contribute to unethical acts or omissions, such as violations of fundamental humanitarian principles, serious violations of human rights, gross corruption, or severe environmental damage." The fund was required to screen out any companies that made military weapons and munitions or were even tangentially tied to international weapons manufacturers. It also was required to get rid of companies that were considered to be "an unacceptable risk of contributing to" human rights violations, particularly forced labor and child labor, environmental damage, political corruption, and "other particularly serious violations of fundamental ethical norms."

The rules took the decision of which companies to include and which to exclude out of the fund managers' hands and gave it to the government. The Ministry of Finance created a Council on Ethics and used its recommendations to determine which companies didn't make the grade. None of this was to be done behind closed doors. Indeed, the Ministry of Finance was required to disclose its decisions and the council's recommendations to the public.

Since then, the fund has blacklisted dozens of companies. It booted major global defense contractors like Alliant Techsystems, BAE Systems, Boeing, European Aeronautic Defence and Space Company, General Dynamics Corporation, Honeywell International, Lockheed Martin Corporation, Northrop Grumman, Poongsan Corporation, Raytheon Company, Singapore Technologies Engineering, Textron, and United Technologies Corporation. Because of environmental concerns and human rights violations, it dropped mining outfits such as Barrick Gold Corporation, Freeport-McMoRan, Rio Tinto, Sterlite Industries, and Vedanta Resources and its subsidiary Madras Aluminum Company. It kicked out Wal-Mart because of its abuses of workers' rights, including prohibiting union organizing, gender discrimination, and child labor violations.

The reform efforts yielded some results, such as an agreement among seed companies like DuPont and Monsanto Company to reduce child labor abuses in the cottonseed industry. So Norway decided to add to the fund's ethical portfolio by using its capital to advance environmental causes as well. The fund has a plan in place to spend £2.2 billion, or nearly 1 percent of its assets, in companies that the Ministry of Finance believes are environmentally friendly and involved in sustainable growth. Norway is particularly focusing on water management issues, investing in companies in industries and geographical regions that are dealing with problems related to water scarcity, water pollution, and other water-related risks. And the fund is developing a strategy to use its investment strength to encourage companies and countries to fight climate change.

The fund, which is one of the most transparent, least secretive investment vehicles in the world, operating under stringent disclosure requirements, also became a shareholder activist, aggressively pushing the businesses it invests in to follow healthy corporate governance practices. It petitioned American companies such as Sara Lee Corporation, Clorox Company, Cardinal Health, and Parker

Hannifin Corporation to separate the jobs of CEO and chairman, which will reduce potential conflicts of interest between the companies' management and boards of directors. (So far the companies have ignored the fund's entreaties.) It opposed the merger of German car manufacturers Volkswagen and Porsche for a litany of reasons, including Norges Bank's beliefs that minority shareholders would be treated unfairly, that there were too many conflicts of interest in the deal, and that the strategic logic behind the combination was dubious. The fund even filed a lawsuit to block the £2.7 billion takeover of Constellation Energy Group by MidAmerican Energy Company, which is owned by Berkshire Hathaway, the conglomerate controlled by famed Wall Street investor Warren Buffett, because Constellation received an offer from the French power company Électricité de France that the fund deemed more attractive.

After Norges Bank filed the Constellation Energy lawsuit, Corporate Governance Chief Anne Kvam, who heads up its ethical investing group, said, "We are one of the biggest shareholders and take these necessary steps in order to safeguard our financial interests."

As a way to express the fund's new aggressive attitude and identity, the government even decided to change the fund's name. The Petroleum Fund moniker had been focused on where Norway's money came from. But Norwegian officials wanted something that reflected the fund's purpose: namely, providing for the well-being of Norway's citizens. So they chose a descriptive, though far more cumbersome, name, the Government Pension Fund Global. As you'd expect, that technocratic string of words didn't exactly catch on in the financial community or the media. So people started simply referring to it as "the Oil Fund," essentially undoing the entire reasoning behind the renaming in the first place.

But more important than the cosmetic name change, Norges Bank and the Ministry of Finance completely restructured the way the Oil Fund operated. First, in 2007, the Ministry brought in Slyngstad, a lawyer and economist who'd worked at Norges Bank since 1998, to run the fund. It then took off the handcuffs and allowed Slyngstad to be more creative in his investment choices. It revised the fund's asset allocation target to 60 percent stocks from 40 percent. It gave the fund more leeway to invest in emerging markets, and Slyngstad immediately set aside £1 billion to invest in companies in India. It allowed the fund to explore investments in alternative asset classes, which now could take up as much as 5 percent of the portfolio, and Slyngstad started looking at infrastructure projects and private equity. The fund even set aside £10 billion to buy landmark commercial properties in the United States and the UK. By the time Slyngstad was through reworking the Oil Fund, it had a diversified portfolio of assets that included shares of thousands of different companies from all over the world.

GETTING ICED BY NORWAY

Despite the Oil Fund's emphatic stance on pursuing ethical investing practices, it has still managed to rile Norway's friends and neighbors with its wealth. In particular, it infuriated Iceland in 2006 when the Oil Fund bet hundreds of millions of dollars against the overheated Iceland economy and almost crashed the tiny island's banking system. But this just proves that when it comes to making money in the shadow market, even deeply principled nations like Norway are willing to risk frosty diplomatic relations even with their close allies to get ahead.

In the early half of the last decade, Iceland experienced a massive economic boom, which was triggered in part by a government privatization program that freed the national banks from state control. By 2003, the privatization was complete, and Iceland's banks started growing fast. They competed aggressively for loan business at home. They invested in the capital markets. And they started buying foreign finance companies—primarily in Sweden, Finland, Luxembourg, and the UK—to gain access to new nearby commercial markets. As Ingimundur Fridriksson, governor of Iceland's central bank, pointed out during a June 2007 address to a UBS financial conference in Thun, Switzerland, in 2000 the total assets of the country's three largest banks were roughly the size of the nation's GDP; by 2005, the assets of those same three banks were *eight times* the nation's GDP. The bulk of this growth was funded through inexpensive debt that was available to these banks because of a global overabundance of capital. But as they piled on the leverage, the banks also were increasing their risk of default if interest rates rose and cash became more expensive.

By the second half of 2005, word quietly started circulating through the financial markets that Iceland's banks may not have had enough capital to continue paying for their growth plans and refinance their debt load. Among the people paying attention to this chatter were the portfolio managers at Norway's Oil Fund. They examined the numbers and realized that the rumors were correct. Iceland's banks and, in turn, its economy had become overheated from too much cheap capital. The country was just waiting for a fall. To the Oil Fund's investment professionals, to *not* do something about this would be criminal. So they did. Starting in the middle of 2005, they began selling short (which is stock exchange terminology for betting against) more than £200 million worth of bonds issued by Iceland's two largest banks, Kaupthing Bank and Landsbanki. Then they waited for everyone else to catch up to what they already knew.

The financial markets didn't let Norway down. In February 2006, the global debt rating agency Fitch Ratings downgraded Iceland's outlook to "negative" from "stable" because of a "material deterioration in Iceland's macro-prudential risk indicators, accompanied by an unsustainable current account deficit and soaring net external indebtedness . . . In the absence of a more balanced policy response, Fitch believes that the risks of a hard landing have increased, raising concerns about how well the broader financial system would cope in such a scenario." In plain English, the country looked like it was headed for a meltdown. In response, the cost of insuring the debt of Iceland's largest banks against default became increasingly expensive and the value of Iceland's currency, the krona, started to crash, which caused a sell-off in currencies of seemingly unrelated countries that the market suddenly deemed overvalued as well, like Hungary, New Zealand, Poland, South Africa, and Turkey. Then, in March, a Merrill Lynch analyst in London named Richard Thomas issued his own broadside against the soundness of Iceland's banking system, writing, "We think the banks should be compared less with other European banks and more with emerging-market banks, since the systemic risks we see in Iceland have much more in common with emerging markets."

Finally, in April, Norges Bank Investment Management revealed publicly in an annual filing that the Oil Fund had bet hundreds of millions of dollars against Kaupthing and Landsbanki in late 2005. That was pretty much all that Iceland's financial system could bear. The Iceland Stock Exchange, also known as ICEX, collapsed. In less than two months, the index of blue-chip ICEX stocks fell more than 20 percent. Soon the entire Icelandic economy was crumbling as the nation succumbed to outright panic. Government officials lashed out at everyone they could possibly blame for their problems. They hollered at hedge funds and Wall Street firms. But mostly they were furious at Norway for profiting from their pain. It didn't matter that things were coming unstuck because the country was in legitimate economic trouble. Icelanders were furious at their neighbors to the east, whom they blamed for triggering the crisis. "We must protest against this action," Iceland's then prime minister Halldór Ásgrímsson implored, speaking to the Reykjavík newspaper *Morgunbladid*.

Ironically, the only reason that Iceland was even aware that Norway had bet against the bonds issued by its banks was because of

Norway's insistence on ethical investing. The Oil Fund is unique among global investment vehicles in that it has no secrets. It regularly discloses its investment positions and its books are transparent. So everyone in the investment community knew that Norway had shorted Iceland, although precisely how much Norway made on the trade remains a mystery because the fund does not disclose its gains and losses on each position. But it's safe to assume that the profit was handsome. Indeed, looking at the trading patterns in credit default swaps in late 2005 and early 2006, it appears that numerous hedge fund traders saw the same thing Norway did and cleaned up as well. But there's no way of knowing for sure what anyone else was up to during that time because so much of the financial world is shrouded in secrecy. That's the way the shadow market works. Except in Norway.

MAYBE GREED REALLY IS GOOD, OR SHOULD BE

Beyond the issue of whether it was "ethical" for Norway to bet so aggressively on its neighbor's demise another question remains: does ethical investing actually generate competitive rates of return in the financial markets? Examining the Oil Fund's recent performance, the answer remains elusive. Like so many investors, the fund got slaughtered in 2008 when stock markets worldwide tanked. On the strength of record oil prices that soared above $100 a barrel, the Norwegian government gave the fund roughly $50 billion (£35 billion) that year, the most it had ever contributed. But Slyngstad admits to having misread the financial markets, and rather than sitting on the sidelines as the global economy spiraled out of control, he plunged the fund's capital into bailing out a series of American and European banks and finance companies, including the failed Wall Street firm Lehman Brothers. The fund lost roughly a quarter billion pounds on those positions alone. In addition, to reach its goal of having 60 percent of the fund invested in equities, Slyngstad and his team kept buying American and European stocks, even as those markets were collapsing.

As a result, the Oil Fund had its worst year ever in 2008, losing £64.5 billion, or 23 percent of its value. Basically, it killed off a dozen years' worth of investment gains in twelve months. Even worse for Slyngstad was the way the losses fell. It turned out that the fund's bond positions fared pretty well, falling just 0.5 percent. But its stock positions were down a whopping 41 percent. This isn't surprising considering the MSCI World Index lost 42 percent and the Dow Jones Stoxx 600 Index of European companies dropped 46 percent. Still, the results were deeply disturbing to the Ministry of Finance, which slashed Slyngstad's 2009 pay by 35 percent to around £350,000.

However, as 2008 gave way to 2009, the stock market pendulum started to swing back in the Oil Fund's direction. After a sluggish opening to the year, it began picking up steam in the spring. The trickle of returns quickly turned into a torrent as global stock markets started rebounding from an extended dismal period. Indeed, the Petroleum Fund earned a 13 percent return on its investments in the second quarter of 2009, making it the best three-month period in the fund's history, and overall gained 26 percent for the year. In other words, whether it's investing ethically or not, the Petroleum Fund appears similar to other investment vehicles in at least one respect. Its success and failure remain tied to the whims of the financial markets. And that makes the Petroleum Fund worth watching for international investors, particularly if they're interested in mixing ethical stands with strong performance.

"The Oil Fund has an extremely diversified portfolio that's based on indexation," Dartmouth's Eckbo says. "This is the best way to generate steady returns in the stock market. Then it uses whatever influence it can to push the companies it invests in to behave a certain way. The fund can have good quarters and bad, but basically it's a long-term national savings plan for future generations. Norway is kind of a boring investor in this way because it just wants to spread its money around the financial markets while at the same time keeping an eye on the issues that are important to it."

The capital generated by oil and gas has given Norway's 4.6 million citizens what is generally considered to be the highest quality of life in the world. Norway hauled in £47 billion in oil revenues alone in 2008. The oil and gas sector accounts for roughly 25 percent of the country's gross domestic product. And the ancillary businesses and intense foreign capital investments that typically come along with the petroleum industry have helped finance the growth of other parts of Norway's economy, particularly in high technology. In all, the business has kept Norwegians wealthy. Norway's per capita gross national income was £60,135 in 2008, according to figures from the World Bank, making its citizens among the wealthiest in the world, along with the residents of Liechtenstein and Bermuda. Also in 2008, Norway's gross domestic product per person was nearly £41,500, compared to £32,500 in the United States, £26,000 in neighboring Sweden, and £25,000 in the UK. Its unemployment rate typically hovers around a mouth-watering 2 percent, meaning just about every Norwegian who wants to work can find a job.

And then there's the country's unbelievably generous health care and social security systems, which are funded by oil money and Norway's astronomical income taxes, which are among the highest in the world. In return, Norwegians can count on cradle-to-grave care from their national pension system. All citizens have health insurance that is paid for by a combination of the state, the employer, and the individual. Medical treatments, including medications and hospital stays, are all free, paid for through the health insurance system. If you have a long-term illness, you still receive your full salary. Pregnant Norwegian women who work full-time are entitled to a year of paid maternity leave, plus they are *required* to stop working three weeks before their due date. New fathers are *required* to take four weeks of paid leave from work after their child is born. Parents can share their year of paid maternity leave, so both mothers and fathers can spend time at home with their baby. And just for fairness, Norwegian women who give birth but don't work are given a cash grant by the government. Meanwhile, at the other end of the age spectrum, the retirement age in Norway is sixty-seven. After that, every Norwegian receives pension payments for the rest of his or her life. The amount is based on how much the person earned during his or her lifetime. But everyone is guaranteed a generous minimum payment.

Of course, none of this is cheap. Norway spends more on health care per capita than any country in the world other than the United States. Its taxes are high, with a top income tax rate of nearly 50 percent and a flat corporate tax of 28 percent. It is also among the most expensive places on the planet to live or visit. A McDonald's Big Mac costs nearly £4.75. A beer at a pub in Oslo is more than £5. An average hotel room anywhere in the country goes for £100 a night. But all that being said, is it any wonder that Norway is routinely found at the top of lists calculating the quality of life in different countries? A 2009 survey by the UN ranked Norway the "best place to live" on earth. No shock there.

Still, despite its tremendous wealth and health, it's not as if Norway has managed to decouple its economy from the rest of the world. Indeed, as the market crises of 2008 and 2009 spread, the Norwegian government was forced to dip into the Oil Fund to stimulate the country's economy. The Ministry of Finance came up with a £10 billion plan for the Oil Fund to inject capital directly into the nation's banks by buying Norwegian corporate bonds. Then it used the fund again for another £17 billion economic stimulus package. The government even tapped the Oil Fund for a £1 billion cash transfer to cover a looming budget deficit. But none of these measures could stave off the inevitable. By May 2009, the Norwegian economy had slipped into a recession for the first time since 1993. How the mighty had fallen.

THE BIGGER PURPOSE

Of course, nobody was crying for Norway in 2009. With the country continuing to extract valuable natural resources from its North Sea holdings and the Oil Fund putting the nation's increasing wealth to work, its recession wasn't particularly violent and didn't last long compared to what much of the world suffered through. That's the benefit of a government having enough capital to manage a country's economy. Indeed, the oil fund was up 4.6 percent in the first four months of 2010 alone, which is more than its target for the year, Dyrdal says.

The real question facing the Oil Fund now is where to go from here. In many ways, it's on the leading edge of an experiment in "ethical investing" that's become increasingly trendy in the global financial markets. So the Oil Fund's success, or failure, is bound to be closely watched.

But from a geopolitical perspective, even more important than the Oil Fund's ability to generate returns will be the manner in which Norway uses its wealth to influence world affairs. But regardless of how high minded the purpose may be, a mixed political agenda is still very different from a strictly economic one. And in the financial markets, where scores are given only for measurable performance, political agendas often mean controversy.

The country has already shown that it's capable of leading the shadow market in nearly collapsing its neighbor, as it did with Iceland, and that it's willing to take sides in controversial intractable battles, like the Israeli-Palestinian conflict, where it has shown sympathy for the Palestinian cause and accused the Israelis of violating human rights. As investors in financial markets and global citizens, it's important to keep an eye on what wealthy nations like that are doing. And anyone who owns stock in a company that's also owned by the Oil Fund has to understand that aggressive shareholders will be pushing the company to behave in ways that may be ethical—even admirable—but may not be helpful to the bottom line.

For example, in August 2009, Norges Bank Investment Management, which oversees the Oil Fund, published a report called "NBIM Investor Expectations: Climate Change Management," in which it spelled out how it wants the companies it invests in to behave when it comes to climate change. In a series of bullet points, the fund explained how it wanted the businesses to comb through every aspect of their operations to reduce their contributions to climate change and to participate in research and explore opportunities in their industries to cut their carbon output. In some instances, this could be extremely costly to the companies in question. But the Oil Fund wasn't concerned whether its requirements hurt these companies' short-term financial performance because it was convinced that over the long term, reducing carbon emissions would be a financial boon for these businesses (though Oil Fund managers were vague on precisely how that would happen). For now, the fund just wanted its companies to do what it told them to do. "NBIM expects companies to develop a well-defined climate change strategy in line with the standards set out in this document," the report stated bluntly. Companies that did not go along would not receive a penny.

So Norway showed the world how to use the power of capital to make a difference environmentally. The trouble is, it's not so easy to consistently seize the higher ground. And in some cases, the Oil Fund has shown a willingness to get down in the mud with everyone else. Take its exploitation of Africa. An October 2009 report by Norwatch, an investigative news service that focuses on Norway's business dealings, found that the Oil Fund is deeply involved in "the plunder of valuable natural resources in occupied Western Sahara." Since 1975, Morocco has occupied Western Sahara, violating rulings by the UN Security Council and the International Court of Justice. Since then, Morocco has proceeded to extract and export phosphate rock from the area it seized. The

Norwatch report found that the Oil Fund had invested hundreds of millions of pounds in eight major fertilizer producers from the United States, India, Australia, Spain, and Venezuela that buy more than £500 million worth of phosphate rock each year that Morocco extracted from Western Sahara. Other so-called ethical investing funds have divested their interests in these companies. But not the Oil Fund. In 2006 it temporarily divested its holdings in the Texas oil company Kerr-McGee Corporation to protest its extraction of oil from Western Sahara. Phosphate, however, was just fine, apparently.

This little example of hypocrisy demonstrates how difficult it will be for Norway to remain ethically clean as it becomes an increasingly important player in the shadow market. Eventually it will have to make choices about whether to pursue ethical or financial interests. And although the Oil Fund's managers say they intend to maintain the moral high ground, it's not always so easy. In this way, predicting what countries like China or Abu Dhabi will do is fairly easy. But Norway remains something of an enigma. For all of the Oil Fund's transparency and disclosure, it's still hard to know precisely what it's up to. That's the challenge for investors—and the rest of the world.

CHAPTER 8

Colonizing Europe in the Twenty-first Century

The part of the planet that has suffered most from the rise of the shadow market is "Old Europe." The financial crisis of 2008 and 2009 exposed that. With wealthy countries such as China, India, and South Korea successfully weathering the disaster, and even America stirring by the end of 2009, Europe looked almost like an anachronism; a withered former empire that was no longer wearing its age very well. Financial experts spoke openly of a return of "Eurosclerosis," a term economists used in the 1980s to describe Europe's relatively high rates of unemployment and low rates of growth compared to those of the United States. Back then, it was believed that the "structural rigidities" in European economies, like powerful labor unions, were holding the continent back. But now the problem was much simpler. Europe was running out of money.

Then, on 14th April 2010, the Icelandic volcano Eyjafjallajokull erupted and shut down much of Europe for nearly a week as a massive volcanic ash cloud covered the northwestern portion of the continent, preventing aircraft from flying safely in and out of major destinations such as London, Paris, Amsterdam, and Berlin. More than 100,000 flights were cancelled and 10 million passengers were stranded. The European Commission estimated that the European travel industry lost as much as £2 billion. And that doesn't include the uncountable ancillary economic damage Europe suffered from the unexpected weeklong stoppage.

What a seemingly quick comedown for the continent. Leading up to the crash, from 2000 to 2007, Europe appeared as if it might be in economic ascension again. Ireland had transformed itself into the Celtic Tiger, with an economy that was exploding like Silicon Valley during the 1990s Internet boom. Plus, more mature countries such as France, Germany, and the UK were experiencing prolonged periods of low unemployment and sustained growth. But if you peeled back the numbers, the picture was far more troubling. For example, European workers were less productive than their global counterparts. During the first decade of the twenty-first century, the growth rate of Europe's worker productivity was half that of America's and lagged far behind emerging powerhouses like China and India. And Europe's exports were shrinking. In 2004 the "Eurozone," or the sixteen countries that use the euro as currency, accounted for 31 percent of world trade. But by 2008, the figure was down to 28 percent, as other expanding markets, such as China, India, Brazil, and Russia, asserted themselves.

Then the global financial crisis hit, and European economies started to spiral out of control. By February 2009, industrial production in the Eurozone had plummeted nearly 20 percent. It was the steepest decline since 1990, when the Eurozone started keeping records. Even worse, Europe's gross domestic product was also falling at a quickening pace. And prices were dropping so fast that the entire continent was at risk of deflation. In short, Europe was no longer growing economically, it was contracting. The economies of countries that had seemed on the rise, like Spain, Ireland, and Greece, all shrank in 2009 and were expected to continue shrinking in 2010, according to projections from the World Trade Organization. It was a mess.

"Europe unfortunately is shrinking as a geopolitical actor," says Singapore-based globalization expert Kishore Mahbubani. "Its economy is still too big to ignore. But the European Union is an economic superpower and a geopolitical mini-power. They are absolutely incompetent. It's like they're constantly rearranging the deck chairs on the *Titanic*."

What European countries are most concerned about is their obvious loss of influence in the global arena. In 2009, world leaders decided that the G20, rather than the G7, would be the dominant economic body in governing the global economy. The G7 was an exclusive group dominated by the United States and European countries. The G20, however, included emerging powers such as China, India, and Brazil, which severely diluted Europe's position at the negotiating table. European foreign policy experts fear that the G20 structure will eventually devolve into a G2, where countries line up behind America or China. This would effectively cut the UK and Europe out of the economic diplomacy loop. But there was nothing it could do to stop the G20's emergence. It had already lost that power.

So what happened to Europe, the continent that had dominated the world economically and politically for centuries? The answer is that, like so many dynasties, each European empire eventually lost its way. The last one had been the British Empire, which at its height in the 1920s controlled more than 25 percent of the world's land mass—a territory roughly 150 times larger than Britain itself. But two world wars in less than a quarter century can decimate a continent, which is what happened to Europe. By the time the 1950s arrived, the United States and the USSR were squaring off, while the UK and the rest of Europe were still cleaning up, in large part depending on American aid. Since then, Old Europe has largely been trying to find its place in the New World. Today the largest European economies, like the UK, France, and Germany, have been reduced to using the shadow market's tactics to protect themselves. It's all they have left.

THE EMPIRE STRIKES OUT

For Britain, what really stings is that it didn't have to end up this way. When oil was discovered in UK waters, the country could have taken its new-found wealth and saved it for a rainy day—like today. But it didn't. And now it's paying a price for that decision.

In 1970 British Petroleum discovered the huge Forties oil field about one hundred miles northeast of the Scottish city of Aberdeen. A year later, Shell found the Brent field farther north, not far from the coast of the Shetland Islands. Those discoveries were followed in quick succession by the Beryl, Piper, and Ninian oil fields. In time, four hundred oil and natural gas fields would be located in Britain's North Sea territory. As a result, by 1980, the UK was pumping more than a half million barrels of oil and gas a day. And petroleum production was accounting for roughly 4 percent of the country's GDP. To the shock of many Britons, their country had suddenly become an oil state.

However, Britain was also going through a horrific economic shock. The country was mired in a brutal recession. By the middle of 1980, inflation had reached 20 percent. Unemployment was skyrocketing, so that by mid-1982, three million people, or nearly 13 percent of the British population, were out of work. This was the nation's highest level of unemployment since the 1930s. Overall, the economy had dipped to negative growth. Britain was shrinking.

In order to combat these challenging conditions, the government headed by Prime Minister Margaret Thatcher decided to dip into its oil wealth to provide benefits for its increasing number of unemployed citizens, while also cutting taxes to stimulate growth. At the time, there were calls to use the country's oil wealth to create a pension fund for future use. In particular, Scottish officials believed that Scottish residents were owed special consideration, since the natural resources were technically in Scotland's offshore territories. However, Thatcher's government argued that the UK was a single country, not a confederation of independent nation-states, and therefore its oil wealth needed to be used for all of the British people who were suffering from the dismal economy. In the end, the Tory argument carried the day.

Combined, oil producers have pumped almost £250 billion into Britain's coffers. But today there's literally nothing to show for it except for the estimated 380,000 jobs that have been directly and indirectly created by the UK petroleum industry. The government has no records showing precisely what happened to the money. Many UK economists speculate that it simply disappeared into a black hole of unchecked wasteful government spending programs.

Scientists estimate that the oil industry has already extracted thirty-five billion barrels of oil and gas from UK fields. However, seismic reports show that there's still another twenty-seven billion barrels beneath the sea floor waiting to be tapped. So there's still time for Britain to do something with its nest egg if the country wants to. The New Economics Foundation, the politically progressive London think tank that specializes in economic, environmental, and social issues, points out that more than 8 percent of the taxes the UK collects come from oil. So, the group says, this money could be easily siphoned off into an investment fund to finance renewable energy projects.

The foundation's suggestion that Britain create some kind of oil legacy fund has been greeted with little enthusiasm in the UK parliament so far. But it has gained support among Scottish government officials, who are once again clamoring for the UK to do something with its oil windfall other than spend it. A 2009 study by the Scottish government found that Scotland's stake in North Sea petroleum wealth would increase the average income in the country by 30 percent. Scotland is now determined to get its fair share or at least force Westminster to set aside some of the money for future savings or energy conservation projects.

After the results of the Scottish government study were announced, Brian Adam, who represents Aberdeen North in the Scottish parliament, said in a speech: "In the 1970s requests for an oil fund were turned down. A repetition of this failure by [the British government] in the twenty-first century would be unforgivable."

So far, however, the UK hasn't done anything to preserve its oil wealth. As a result, the country essentially gave up its ability to become a player in the shadow market. Rather, once-mighty Britain has put itself in the position of asking the shadow market for help in closing its yawning budget gap. Economists estimate that by 2010, the country's deficit will reach £180 billion, or 12 percent of its GDP. That would be the highest percentage for any country in the G20—worse even than the United States. So the British government knew it had to start getting creative to bring in some money.

In May 2009, UK officials began approaching sovereign wealth funds and other wealthy investors about possibly participating in the privatization of the nation's state-controlled banks. UK Financial Investments, which manages the government's 70 percent stake in the Royal Bank of Scotland and its 44 percent ownership position in the Lloyds Banking Group, has said that it plans to unload its stakes over the next five years. What's more, in October 2009, Britain's prime minister, Gordon Brown, announced plans to raise as much as £15 billion in cash by selling off a series of government-owned assets. Most conspicuously, the UK would unload its share of the popular Channel Tunnel (nicknamed the Chunnel) high-speed rail link between Paris and London, which is owned by the British-French entity called Eurotunnel.

"We've reached only the halfway point on the road to rebuilding the global economy," Brown said during a press conference to announce Britain's proposed sale of its share of the Chunnel. "And we'll have to be just as radical to make sure that the next decade doesn't become a lost decade. Each country will have choices before them that it will have to look at. In Britain's case, I can tell you we will not shrink from the difficult and tough choices that are necessary for our economy to grow and play its part in the development of the world economy."

In addition, Brown said that the government would look to sell the Dartford Crossing bridge and tunnel, which straddles the River Thames east of London, as well as its stake in Urenco, a European company that makes equipment used in uranium enrichment, and an investment portfolio containing real estate and some student loans. Some critics complained that Brown wasn't likely to attract good prices for the country's assets because he was putting them on the market at a time when there wasn't much demand or capital available in the global economy. However, he generally received praise from the investment community for at least trying to do *something* in the face of such a dire economic situation. To the financial markets, letting the nation's economy crumble because the government ran out of money would have been seen as negligence bordering on the criminal. Indeed, even after Brown was voted out of office in May 2010 and replaced as prime minister by Conservative Party leader David Cameron, the new government quickly confirmed the plan to sell public assets.

"We recognize that there are structural problems," says Paul Donovan, the London-based deputy head of global economics at UBS. "The government is spending too much money, period, and a one-off asset sale doesn't stop that. But anything that reduces the overall debt number makes the UK's treble-A position more sustainable. Maintaining the treble-A position is extremely important given that Sterling [the pound] is the third most important reserve currency in the world and that's completely contingent on a continued treble-A position. So there are different aspects behind the government's thinking than simply what it should keep and what it should sell."

THE FRENCH KISS OF PROTECTIONISM

In October 2008, French president Nicolas Sarkozy explained to the world in no uncertain terms how France planned to deal with the emerging power of the shadow market. In a fiery speech before the European Parliament in Strasbourg, France, the French leader implored his compatriots to follow his country's lead and create sovereign wealth funds that wouldn't be used to invest abroad, but rather to protect each country's national economy from unwanted invasions from what he termed foreign "predators."

"I don't want European citizens to wake up in several months' time and find that European companies belong to non-European capital," he told the delegates. "Europe mustn't be naïve, mustn't leave its companies at the mercy of all predators, mustn't be the only one not to defend its interests, not to protect its citizens."

Sarkozy had good reason to be concerned. Like the rest of Europe, France was in the midst of a brutal economic stretch. The Paris CAC 40 stock index had shed more than 40 percent in a year. The nation's banks were struggling to find financing. The Bank of France was projecting that the country would tumble into its first recession in fifteen years. The country's GDP was contracting. French consumer confidence was at a fifteen-year low. So it was likely that wealthy foreign investors, particularly from China and the Middle East, would start seeing attractive bargains in French businesses, many of which could now be snapped up for a third of the price they were selling for just six months earlier.

This also wasn't the first time Sarkozy had warned against the dangers of sovereign wealth funds buying European businesses. Indeed, on the eve of a trip to Saudi Arabia in January 2008, he attacked countries that were eager to invest in France but hadn't opened their markets to French capitalists. But his comments to the European Parliament marked the first time that he called for a European-wide mobilized solution. Two days after his speech, Sarkozy put his country's money where his mouth was. To great fanfare, the French president formally unveiled his proposal to establish a sovereign wealth fund that would be used solely to support French companies that the government had deemed significant to the nation's economy or security. As he explained to his countrymen, in passionate remarks that echoed the themes he'd hit in Strasbourg, the move was necessary to protect the nation's key businesses from falling prey to the siren song of foreign capital.

"I will not be the French president who wakes up in six months' time to see that French industrial groups have passed into other hands," he said. "What oil producers do, what China does, what Russia does, there is no reason that France should not do, in the service of an industrial policy worthy of the name."

And with that, Sarkozy created the £18 billion (€22 billion) Fonds Stratégique d'Investissement, or Strategic Investment Fund, as it's called in English. The fund would be managed by the state-owned bank Caisse des Dépôts et Consignations, which had a long history of investing for the government and other parts of the public sector. It would be headed by Gilles Michel, a top executive at the French carmaker Peugeot Citroën and before that at the building materials supplier Saint-Gobain. The fund's guidelines were spelled out clearly. Its primary goal was to make investments to promote the development of all sizes of French businesses. It would participate in any government efforts to stabilize troubled large companies that, if they went under, could damage the French economy. It would invest with a long-term time horizon, acting more as a partner with its businesses than as an aggressive shareholder pressing for returns. The fund would be overseen by a policy committee, which would include economists, business leaders, and members of the social welfare community.

In essence, Sarkozy had turned the concept of the sovereign wealth fund on its head. Most countries typically viewed their SWFs as vehicles they would invest to make money overseas and then return the capital back home. The idea was to be a financial investor; to find bargains in the market and capitalize. That was the way to help your country, by making as much money as possible as quickly as possible. So if there were bargains to be had at home, have at them. But in general, that was the sole criterion for investing. Would the position be profitable? Typically, they weren't designed to prop up a nation's businesses or its economy. In Norway, which obviously was flush with cash and in a very different economic situation than France, the Oil Fund was strictly prohibited from investing in Norwegian businesses because the country feared the corrosive effects of using its wealth to protect the nation's businesses and economy.

But the French Strategic Investment Fund was designed specifically for domestic investment. The entire point was to intervene in France's economy to protect French businesses and encourage innovation by pumping in gobs of cash. Considering France's traditional protectionist economic reputation, many global economists considered Sarkozy's idea to be a "very French" solution. But many financial market insiders were skeptical of its long-term benefits to the French economy.

"Protectionist moves like that cause confusion in the about what a country's economic goals really are," says IDEAglobal currency strategist Kevin Chau. "In a free and open system a government isn't regularly intervening by spending money to rescue businesses. When that's the plan we start to get concerned. It's a subversion of the free market."

The Strategic Investment Fund's first investment was around £85 million for 20 percent of the aerospace firm Daher, which makes parts for the nuclear and defense industries, as well as carmakers. It then bought 8 percent stakes in both Valeo, a struggling car parts manufacturer, and Gemalto, the world's largest maker of so-called smart cards, and 5 percent stakes in both Technip, an equipment producer for the oil and gas industries, and Nexans, which makes industrial copper and fiber optic cables. It also made sizable investments in smaller French companies that weren't publicly traded. All of the purchases were made for undisclosed prices, showing that France at least knew how to play the investing game. And by the summer of 2009, Michel was pledging to spend £800 million over the next six months to help the French motorcar and aerospace industries. In particular, he mentioned that aeroplane manufacturer Airbus and defense contractor the Safran Group could receive financing from the fund, as could carmakers Peugeot Citroën and Renault. Michel also said that the country was going to create a subsidiary of the fund that would specialize in making investments in small and medium-sized companies. It even signed an agreement with the Mubadala Development Company, the £9 billion sovereign wealth fund from Abu Dhabi, to coordinate investments in France.

And the money kept flowing. In October the fund invested £15 million in Dailymotion, a video-sharing website that was France's version of YouTube. And then in January 2010, the fund helped the state-owned nuclear power conglomerate Areva raise £900 million by taking on its 26 percent stake in the French mining concern Eramet.

It will take years to determine whether Sarkozy's experiment is a financial success. But as a start, it appeared as if his plans were moving in the direction he intended. For international investors looking for safe overseas opportunities, this was a wonderful development. After all, France's government had put a safety net under the country's major industries. So all of a sudden investing in French companies came with a built-in protectionist insurance policy. These businesses couldn't fail. Maybe they wouldn't produce outstanding returns. But for safety-minded investors what was important was that they couldn't go bust. And best of all, the insurance was completely free—that is, as long as the Fonds Stratégique d'Investissement held enough money to continue artificially propping up France's private sector.

DEUTSCHLAND ÜBER ALLES

Germany naturally had a completely different take on how to handle the emergence of the shadow market than France did. In fact, the German economic minister, Michael Glos, responded to French president Nicholas Sarkozy's speech in Strasbourg by promptly telling anyone who'd listen that the French do not speak for the Germans when it comes to how the European economy should operate.

"The French proposal that the state should take stakes in European industry so as to protect it from foreign state takeover goes against the successful principles of our economic policy," Glos announced in the German-language newspaper *Frankfurter Allgemeine Zeitung*.

Rather, German chancellor Angela Merkel had another plan in mind. And in much the same way that Sarkozy's Strategic Investment Fund could be considered *très français,* or "very French," Merkel's ideas offered a "very German" take on how to get a handle on the dramatic shifts in the global financial markets. Specifically, Merkel proposed a law that would enable the German government to review any attempt by an entity not based in the European Union to buy 25 percent or more of a German company. Under the law, if the German officials conducting the review determined that the company was important to the country's national security, the government could veto the deal. An analysis by the New York law firm Debevoise & Plimpton concluded that the industries that could be affected by the law included telecommunications, railways, container ports, airports, and gas and electric grids, as well as the more apparent sectors such as aerospace and any sort of defense contracting.

The new law was immediately slammed as extraordinarily protectionist by officials from the United States and several members of the European Union, including France. But as you'd expect, the most strident comments came from the obvious target of the legislation: Middle Eastern sovereign wealth funds, which were already deeply invested in Europe. Not surprisingly, ministers from throughout the Persian Gulf were absolutely outraged over the entire concept and lashed out at Germany.

"If somebody comes up with regulations that make it difficult for someone from certain geographical locations to invest in Europe or the West, people will take their investment somewhere else," warned Dubai World chief Sultan Ahmed bin Sulayem. "I think it's dangerous when this money and liquidity is so badly needed. We are investors, and we are free to go wherever we want. If you squeeze us, we will go elsewhere."

Bader Al Sa'ad, who heads the Kuwait Investment Authority, was equally blunt when he spoke directly to the German people after Merkel's new investment law was proposed: "We are very surprised by the Germans' fear of sovereign wealth funds. We have been in Germany for more than forty-five years. We still consider Germany an economic anchor in Europe, even in the world. We still like to invest in Germany. But in the future, any regulations on sovereign wealth funds in Germany could limit our engagement in your country."

With these warnings ringing in their ears, German government officials quickly rushed in front of the cameras to try to explain the country's thinking and assure the world that it remained open for investment.

"Germany has had very good experience with Arab investments since the 1960s through funds from the Kuwait Investment Authority," said Germany's finance minister, Peer Steinbrück. "The UAE has considerable investments in Germany, but laws cannot differentiate between good and bad guys in terms of procedures. Regarding sovereign wealth funds, Germany sets specific rules to make sure that none of the tremendous volume of capital flying around the world poses a negative role to our economy and to the security of our country."

In the meantime, behind the scenes, German officials also started quietly dismantling key portions of the bill. It turned out that Merkel had chosen an awful time to put restrictions on any investment in Germany. Its GDP in 2009 slid roughly 6 percent. Exports were falling. Unemployment was rising. In short, the country needed capital. In March 2009, the German carmaker Daimler raised £1.5 billion by selling a 9.1 percent stake to an Abu Dhabi investment fund. And yet, in the middle of all this, here was the national government provoking the very investors who wanted to put money into the nation's economy.

In the end, Germany was saved from itself by the European Union, which took a dim view of the protectionist measure. Europe's parliament reviewed the law and determined that the requirement that German officials could veto a takeover only if the potential deal threatened the public order or safety of the German state would be construed very narrowly. How exactly could a cash investment threaten the public order or safety of the German state? The wording was loose enough that it could apply to just about any investment in a German company or to very few investments, depending on how you wanted to interpret the meaning. So, by ruling that German officials had to use the strictest definition of the word *threaten,* the European parliament freed Germany to pass a law that seemed to have real teeth in protecting the domestic economy while still enabling German officials to approve most takeovers. A briefing by the London law firm Freshfields Bruckhaus Deringer for its Chinese investing clients concluded, "It is therefore in practice rather unlikely that the German government will ever use the new law to prohibit any transactions, except in cases where critical and unique infrastructure assets were sold (e.g., the sole national railway operator)."

In short, international investors were once again welcome in the German Republic. To the rest of the world, this was an important sign about the growing might of the shadow market. If a large, rich, and powerful country like Germany couldn't slap restrictions on it, then who could? It was a dramatic display of power that was lost on no one in the investment community who was paying attention. Protectionist policies were no longer going to work, at least not by countries that can't dictate their own economic futures. The only real way for the countries of the West to play the shadow market was to open up their markets, engage the wealthy nations diplomatically and economically, and let the cash flow. Fighting this inevitability was useless because the shadow market was going to go where it wants to go regardless of what anyone else wants it to do. There was a significant lesson here for investors trying to figure out how to navigate this new world. When a country is fighting the forces of global capital, it's wise to take your money in another direction until the dust settles. The battle will result only in a painful, sloppy, unwinnable conflict. And the opportunities will return only when the fighting stops.

"Germany is struggling to find the right policy," says Dr. Peter Wand, a partner at the law firm Debevoise & Plimpton, who studied the implications of the changes in German law for the firm's multinational clients. "The government sees certain problems and is trying to react. Whether it is the right reaction, I'm not sure. The primary trigger for the amendments to the Foreign Trade Act was a concern that sovereign wealth funds were attempting to acquire key public infrastructure items, such as telecom and energy networks. Germany was looking for a means to restrict that, the same way countries like the US and the UK can. It was an attempt to level the playing field. The question is whether this was the best way to do it. For example, there definitely was a measure of economic patriotism involved, which always is a proxy for protectionism. But in a crisis legislation is fueled by angst, politics, and intensive lobbying, which is what we've seen. Sovereign wealth funds, which used to be the primary target, aren't even that much of a concern anymore—the politicians are much more into hedge fund bashing. Whether sovereign wealth funds or hedge funds actually are a problem, I have my doubts. And whether any of the proposed measures really will solve anything, I'm not so sure. But they are an effective way to maintain a political majority."

A NEW GREEK TRAGEDY

Despite everything that countries like France and Germany have done to protect themselves from the economic power of the shadow market, Europe's biggest risks actually come from within—particularly among the countries that use the euro as their currency. As of 2010, there were sixteen nations and four territories using the euro: Andorra, Austria, Belgium, Cyprus, Finland, France, Germany, Greece, Ireland, Italy, Luxembourg, Malta, Monaco, the Netherlands, Portugal, San Marino, Slovakia, Slovenia, Spain, and Vatican City. Looking at this list, it's clear that these places are highly diverse in the size and scale of their economies. But all are linked through their use of the same currency. The strength of the euro requires contributions from each member of the group. The problem is that some of these nations have high-risk, developing economies that are susceptible to dangerous financial bubbles. And without the shadow market's mounds of capital to contain its problems, trouble in a relatively insignificant economy could spread easily to the rest of the EU and set off a full-fledged crisis. That's what happened to Greece in early 2010—and it nearly triggered the collapse of all of Europe.

For decades Greece was considered a highly risky bet in the financial markets because its government took on so much debt to fund the country's day-to-day operations that it often seemed to be on the precipice of default. At the time it joined the European Union in 2001 its debt load was greater than its GDP. But by Greece's joining the EU, the financial markets now viewed it as part of a stable economic system, and the country was able to turn things around financially by using the strength of its new economic alliance to refinance its debt at more attractive rates.

Suddenly the government had room to operate. And the lower interest rates encouraged Greek banks to lend even more aggressively than they had been before. Not surprisingly, in a relatively short amount of time, the Greek economy was taking off.

The problem was that Greece hadn't actually done anything to warrant the lower interest rates. The Greek economy was operating just as it had been before. All that had changed was that the country now was a member of the EU. And because of that, the financial markets suddenly were underpricing the risk baked into bonds issued by a financially shaky country. What's more, this phenomenon wasn't specific to Greece. Other economically questionable European countries such as Spain, Portugal, Ireland, and Italy also were using the strength of the euro to create their own national economic booms.

Trouble arose in late 2009, following the US meltdown, when investors began trying to predict where the next shoe would drop. Quickly they focused on the economically vulnerable European Union, where unemployment was skyrocketing to double-digit levels. Of particular concern were the large amounts of debt taken on by weak countries—namely, Greece. By late January 2010, rumors that Greece no longer could pay its debts were reaching a crescendo. The country had to raise more than £30 billion by the end of June or face default. The price of insuring Greek bonds against default was at an all-time high. By all appearances, the country was running out of money and time. Hedge funds and other trading outfits started lining up against it by shorting Greek bonds or buying credit default swaps that accomplished the same task. A lot of people in the financial community were betting that a collapse was imminent.

By February, short positions on Greek sovereign bonds were rising dramatically. All of this activity indicated that numerous savvy international investors were getting in on the game as well, following the smart money and helping to push Greece over a cliff. The Greek government realized that to avert a meltdown it needed to raise money quickly. But to do that, the country would have to issue bonds, and there was no guarantee that buyers would materialize for such risky debt. So Greece turned to the one place everyone in the world eventually turns to when they need cash: the shadow market. In the past, wealthy investors from the Persian Gulf, who for years have been very active in Europe, would likely have soaked up Greece's debt. But this time the Middle East was in the midst of dealing with its own crisis in Dubai, and Greek officials knew that their old friends would have little interest in bailing them out as well. So instead Greece cast a hopeful gaze toward the country with the deepest pockets in the world: China.

In late January 2010, Greek financial officials leaked to the *Financial Times* their plans to ask China to buy more than £20 billion worth of bonds during Greece's upcoming "road show" presentations to investors in Asia and North America for its debt sales. Up until then, China's main ties to Greece were in shipping because the bulk of China's export cargo was transported on Greek ships. But now Greece wanted to step up the relationship considerably by having China rescue the country and become a primary financial partner. The feeling, however, was not mutual. In fact, China was reluctant to get involved with Greece or any other geopolitically insignificant risky country outside its sphere of influence in Asia. As word of Greece's plans to coax China to buy its debt filtered through the capital markets, Chinese officials moved to shut down any speculation about their interest in solving Greece's financial problem. Instead, they said, this was an issue that Europe should handle on its own.

"Let European governments and the European Central Bank rescue Greece," Yu Yongding, an influential Chinese economist who has served as an adviser to the People's Bank of China, told *China Daily*. "China can try its best to help Greece via the EU or the IMF, which has an institutional framework in place for such problems."

So the solution was going to have to come from within the EU.

A consensus quickly formed around an idea for a series of loan guarantees worth tens of billions of pounds that would be backed mainly by Germany and France, although the countries failed to come up with a final agreement on a bailout package. In the meantime, EU officials demanded that Greece rein in its out-of-control spending. The country promised to slash its budget deficit to 8.7 percent by the end of 2010 and below 3 percent by 2012. To accomplish this, Greece would cut up to £8 billion in expenses by freezing government worker salaries, cutting entitlement spending, increasing the gasoline tax, and closing the country's gaping tax loopholes. The Greek people, of course, resented these extreme measures and launched nationwide strikes and other civil actions to voice their displeasure, all of which added to the economic chaos. Greek customs and tax officials shut down ports and border crossings with a two-day work stoppage and the civil servants union held a day-long strike to march on parliament in protest.

Not that Greece's attempts at belt tightening or the complaints of the Greek people made the rest of Europe more sympathetic about the bailout package. Indeed, across the continent Europeans were bitter about having to reach into their own pockets to help a country out of a mess caused by its profligate ways. Polls in Germany, which had the largest economy in the EU, found that the vast majority of Germans opposed providing financial assistance to Greece. It was hard to begrudge Germany for being reluctant to get involved in a Greek rescue deal. After all, it's not as if Greece had ever been straight with the EU about its financial condition. To the contrary, it turned out that back in 2001 when Greece was seeking to become a member of the European Union, the country used complex currency swap agreements to borrow billions of dollars, while still remaining within the EU's deficit spending limits. The deals, which were arranged by Goldman Sachs, helped Greece qualify for EU membership. Greece had been lying to the EU for years. Why should it be trusted now?

In the end, however, it didn't matter whether or not the Europeans trusted Greece. The EU had to do something. Because lurking behind the questions about how to best handle this crisis was the suspicion that Greece just represented the start of an awful trend among EU countries with immature, overheated economies. Would this Greek tragedy play out across Europe? Spain, Portugal, and Ireland also had used complex financial securities and aggressive bookkeeping tactics in order to overspend wildly and appear on paper to be safe bets for investors. What was to prevent those nations from collapsing as well and bringing the entire EU down with them?

As Europe dithered over finalizing the Greek bailout package the crisis continued to spiral out of control. On 22nd April, the EU's statistical authority revealed that Greece's 2009 budget deficit was even wider than had been estimated, 9.4 percent of the country's GDP up from 2.7 percent in 2008. The debt rating agency Moody's Investors Service responded by downgrading Greek debt. Any remaining investors who were hoping to score on a turnaround fled for the exits. Yields on ten-year Greek government bonds headed up toward 9 percent, or nearly three times what Germany was paying. Greece was left with no other option but to beg.

On 24th April, Greece's finance minister, George Papaconstantinou, formally requested an emergency €50 billion (£40 billion) bailout from the EU and IMF. A short time later, the debt rating agency Standard & Poor's cut Greek debt to junk status and, as feared, the crisis now appeared to be spreading to Ireland, Portugal, and Spain, where bond prices were falling steadily and yields were rising, meaning the countries had to spend increasing amounts of money to borrow capital. So Europeans were reluctant to throw their precious cash down a seemingly bottomless pit in Greece because there could be other handouts coming for other troubled nations. However, the alternative was no less appealing, since Greece's economic collapse could drag down the entire continent with it before Ireland, Portugal, or Spain imploded.

By early May it had become clear that Europe's hesitance to face Greece's economic problems head-on had only exacerbated the crisis and made the solution that much more costly. Had Greece been able to secure China's financial support back in January it might have been able to avoid the emergency before the crisis turned into a full-blown continental disaster. Europe's foot-dragging only compounded the problem.

Now, however, the IMF was taking charge. It came up with a €30 billion (£27 billion) loan program to stabilize Greece and coordinated another €80 billion in loans from the European Central Bank. But in order for the Greeks to get the money they would have to accept some strict financial terms designed to get the nation's economy back on its feet. The austerity measures required Greece to raise taxes, significantly cut wages for public sector workers, freeze pay for private and public sector employees, slice pension payouts, slash military spending, start an emergency fund to be used whenever the economy reached another crisis point, and publicly disclose the losses at the largest state-owned corporations, which economists believed might nudge Greek government officials to sell off these businesses. To pitch the plan to his people, Greece's prime minister George Papandreou gave a televised address in which he stated, "I want to tell Greeks very honestly that we have a big trial ahead of us." And then he added, "These sacrifices will give us breathing space and the time we need to make great changes."

Unfortunately, the Greek people weren't buying it. Instead, they became furious. They felt put upon by politicians who had lied to them. And they adamantly did not want to give up their expensive social safety net in the name of saving the country's economy. Soon, the relatively tame protests of a month earlier turned ugly and deadly. On 5th May 2010, more than one hundred thousand protesters showed up in central Athens as part of a nationwide strike and demonstration against the proposed austerity measures. As the marchers made their way through the city, angry marauding youths went on a rampage, setting vehicles and businesses ablaze before fire bombing a bank building. When it all was over three people inside the bank were dead, shards of glass covered the streets, and black smoke billowed from trash burning on the sidewalks. Meanwhile, people across the globe watched in horror as the onslaught played out on live television. Whatever sympathy the world may have had for Greece vanished in the sea of brutality.

Beyond this tragically violent outburst, however, the bigger problem for Europe was that Greece no longer was the sole issue. As feared, the crisis had metastasized to other markets. European banks were having trouble getting their hands on the capital they required to operate, so loans quickly became more expensive and harder to get. By all appearances the initial stages of a credit crunch were taking hold. Officials at the IMF and European Central Bank suddenly realized that they were in a race to get out in front of the tsunami before it slammed into Europe. The only problem was that accomplishing this would take significantly more capital than the €110 billion in loans they'd already arranged for Greece.

So on 10th May, the European Union and IMF dramatically upped the ante. They agreed to a bailout package totaling nearly €750 billion (£650 billion) specifically designed to pump liquidity back into the financial markets. The European Central Bank then announced that it stood ready to buy European government bonds to keep cash flowing, and the US Federal Reserve said it would assist the ECB by opening a currency swap line that would enable the central banks to trade euros for dollars. The program was called "shock and awe" after the strategy used by the United States in the second Iraq war, and it was designed to show that economically weak countries such as Greece, Spain, and Portugal had all the financial backing they needed. The irony that "shock and awe" hadn't exactly played out the way America had hoped seemed lost on the European economists mired in a desperate fight to simply keep the EU afloat.

Still, the question remained: Would the plan work? Many Europeans were skeptical. Indeed, it took some personal prodding from President Barack Obama to get German chancellor Angela Merkel to sign on and a lot of cajoling by the IMF to keep the package together. Then, after the deal was done, the CEO of

Deutsche Bank, Josef Ackermann, went on a German talk show and said that he doubted Greece would ever be able to repay its debts. He was hardly alone in the financial community. Indeed, even as the European Central Bank was buying €13 billion (£11 billion) worth of bonds in the first week of the bailout program, major currency investors and hedge fund managers were lining up against the euro, betting that it had even more room to fall. Finance officials in South Korea, Russia, and Iran all said that their countries were shifting away from the euro in their reserve holdings. And the biggest bond fund in Asia, the Global Sovereign fund run by Kokusai Asset Management, announced that it was slashing its euro holdings. Meanwhile, the rest of the world was left to wait and see if Europe could stave off a calamity or if the West had just thrown a trillion dollars down the drain.

Of course, it was here, in the desperate search for capital, that the power of the shadow market was again revealed. Why? Although European banks and financial institutions were having trouble getting their hands on cash in the winter and spring of 2010, by no means was there a worldwide credit crunch. In fact, the major players of the shadow market were throwing money around even as Europe sank deeper into the muck. For example, China bought $17.7 billion (£11.7 billion) worth of US Treasury bonds in March 2010 alone. Think about that for a second. In a single month, China spent more on Treasuries than the ECB did in its first round of bond buying in a financial emergency. But that's not all. In early May 2010, as the IMF and EU were desperately trying to come up with capital to save Greece and the rest of Europe, Qatar set up a £650 million fund to invest in Indonesia; Singapore's Temasek Holdings and China's Hampton Asset Holdings bought £400 million worth of bonds from the US gas company Chesapeake Energy Corporation; and the UAE invested £325 million in constructing a port on the Black Sea in the nation of Georgia. And that was just during a couple of weeks in early May.

Eventually, before Europe collapsed, China decided to step in. Why? Because Europe is China's biggest export market, and the country couldn't afford to allow the continent to go under. In January 2011, Chinese finance officials announced that they would start buying debt issued by European nations, including bonds belonging to struggling countries such as Spain, Portugal, Ireland, and Greece. China's vice premier, Li Keqiang, basically went on a shopping spree across Europe. In the UK, Chinese energy and car concerns spent £2.5 billion on deals with British companies. In Germany, Li inked £3 billion in purchase agreements with Volkswagen and Daimler. And in Spain, Li spent £4.5 billion on a stake in an oil field. That's the way the shadow market works. It's fickle and ruthlessly bottom-line-oriented. It bought US bonds when Europe was hemorrhaging because Treasuries were a better investment. When Europe got on its hands and knees, then it was time to consider a deal.

"Europe can't go on the way it has been," says Yale economic security specialist Paul Bracken. "It's not the contagion or the social safety net. It's just that people are going to look at the books and realize that Italy's been cooking them worse than Greece. Who doesn't know that? Every business I know of knows that. So they're not going to expand business in Italy because you've got to pay people off. Then you have Greece, Spain, Portugal, and Ireland, which are a mess. They're bleeding jobs. I was in Germany recently talking to this senior guy at Siemens and he said the company is overstaffed in Europe by a third, that if they could get away with it they'd fire a third of their European workforce. . . . This is a real long-term problem."

GASSING UP FOR THE FUTURE

Still, all is not lost for the nations of the EU, at least from an economic standpoint. Remarkably, it turns out that Europe still has a valuable natural resource that hasn't been exploited yet: natural gas. In the autumn of 2009, geologists and engineers from

Italy and Norway took a field trip to Oklahoma City. Their aim: to learn new techniques for extracting natural gas from layers of shale, a black rock made up of minuscule pieces of clay and other minerals. Since natural gas shale had been found in several sedimentary basins throughout Europe, energy companies were leasing vast tracts of land all over the continent to drill for it. But when it came to technology, European firms were about twenty years behind their counterparts in the United States and Canada, which have been researching and drilling for shale gas for decades. So the Norwegians and Italians, who represented the firms Statoil and ENI, were visiting drilling sites in Oklahoma, Texas, and Pennsylvania on a fact-finding mission. They simply wanted to learn.

Energy analysts estimate that natural gas extracted from shale could severely reduce Europe's dependence on Russia for its natural gas. The best guess is that European natural gas reserves could increase by as much as 40 percent between 2010 and 2030. If this resulted in increased natural gas use, it would reduce the threat of increased global warming. Natural gas is considered one of the cleaner energy sources because it emits fewer greenhouse gases than coal or oil. And the discovery of extensive natural gas fields in European shale rock could encourage more countries to try to develop technology to use cleaner burning natural gas in cars and buses. The global consulting firm IHS CERA estimates that outside of North America, there's enough recoverable natural gas available from shale to provide more than two centuries of natural gas consumption in the United States. But even more important, any new findings could help power Europe, which is fighting through dwindling natural gas reserves.

ExxonMobil already has begun natural gas exploration operations in Germany. The French firm Total partnered with Devon Energy Corporation of Oklahoma City to drill wells in France. ConocoPhillips is hunting for natural gas in Poland. Italy's ENI is working with Quicksilver Resources of Fort Worth, Texas, on projects in Italy. As these and other projects start to hit pay dirt,

European countries will be given a new lease on life through the wealth provided by unexpected revenue streams. Plus, any natural gas discoveries would provide Europe with a diplomatic wedge to use against Russia, which supplies about a quarter of the continent's natural gas and hasn't been shy about cutting it off to make a political point—even in the dead of winter, when natural gas is crucial to heating homes. Russia, with its two sovereign wealth funds holding a combined £110 billion, certainly knows how the shadow market game is played.

For instance, in January 2009 Russia's national gas company Gazprom shut down supplies running through the Ukraine, leaving roughly a dozen countries scrambling for heating fuel. The move actually had nothing to do with Europe; Russia was trying to punish the Ukraine for supposedly not paying its bills and siphoning off Russian gas in its pipelines. But the Europeans were caught in the middle. With the development of shale gas the continent wouldn't be in that kind of vulnerable position.

Not that the development of shale gas reserves is risk free. Indeed, there is a growing body of evidence showing that the most common method of extracting shale gas, which is known as hydraulic fracturing, or fracking, can be ruinous to the local environment, particularly the groundwater.

So will shale gas emerge as Europe's savior? Or will it just be another fleeting hope, but one that leads to environmental devastation? Only time will tell. Right now Europe is playing catch-up with wealthy shadow market countries that either control the resources the continent requires or have the cash to buy the assets before Europeans can get their hands on them. But who knows, perhaps someday soon, emerging shale gas exporters from Europe will become an important component of the shadow market too. Stranger things have happened. Just not yet.

CHAPTER 9

Now On Sale!
Everything Must Go!

Pittsfield is a rugged but picturesque New England industrial city nestled in the heart of the bucolic Berkshire Hills of western Massachusetts. It's the seat of Berkshire County, which is the westernmost part of Massachusetts, abutting the New York state line. The town is a little more than two hours due west of Boston and just a little over two hours north of New York City. In many ways, it has an identity all its own, separate from the rest of the Bay State. Pittsfield's loyalties are often divided between Boston and New York. It's probably the only place in the state where the governor can get ribbed for being a Boston Red Sox fan by his barber, a New York Yankees fan.

Largely rural with broad swaths of wide open space, Berkshire County has the distinction of being the biggest county in Massachusetts in terms of acreage but the smallest in population. Over the past few centuries, countless writers and artists—from Edith Wharton to the modern naturalist painter Walton Ford—have called the area home. Herman Melville wrote *Moby-Dick* at Arrowhead, his house in Pittsfield. For decades, Norman Rockwell lived and worked in Stockbridge, and each December, on a Sunday afternoon before Christmas, hundreds of people turn out to see a physical reenactment of Rockwell's famous 1967 painting *Stockbridge Main Street at Christmas.*

The Berkshires are also a vacation wonderland. In the summer, people from all over the Northeast US swarm the region because there's so much to do. The area is filled with lakes and rivers, and the Appalachian Mountain Trail meanders through like a slow-moving snake. And then there's all that culture. Tanglewood, the summer home of the Boston Symphony Orchestra, brings in thousands of classical music fans during the season. The Williamstown Theater Festival has an equally illustrious history and is the summer-stock theater of choice for top Broadway and Hollywood talent. Plus, there are the Jacob's Pillow Dance Festival, the Berkshire Theater Festival, the Barrington Stage Company, Shakespeare & Company, and many other performance spaces, as well as world-class museums like the Sterling and Francine Clark Art Institute and the renowned modern art complex MASS MoCA. The autumn brings out different kinds of tourists called leaf peepers, who wander around and stare in amazement at the incredible variations in hues of red, orange, and yellow found in the changing foliage. And then winter means downhill and cross-country skiing, ice-skating, sledding, snowshoeing, even ice fishing, followed by some hot chocolate in front of a roaring fire.

As long as you can appreciate the fickle New England weather, the Berkshires are a wonderful place to live. I know, because my wife and I chose to move to the small town of Great Barrington several years ago after finally deciding to leave New York City, which is 120 miles to the south and where we'd been for over a decade. We live in a century-old house on a hill just above Main Street. For exercise I ride a bike over undulating terrain, hike through marshy forests, or just wander around the steep inclines and declines of our neighborhood. My wife relishes shopping for the local fresh produce at the multitude of farm stands and farmers' markets in our area. Our son took his first swim in Lake

Mansfield, which is around the corner from where we live. To say that the Berkshires have crept into our blood would be an understatement. It's home.

But there is a snag. Since Berkshire County has little industry to speak of, life isn't easy for the people who grew up here. In order to live comfortably, many recent arrivals to the area, like us, have brought their work with them from someplace else. You can't count on just finding something to pay the bills. Jobs are scarce and typically seasonal. When the tourists are around, everyone has money in his or her pocket. But when they're gone, belts tighten.

It wasn't always this way. From the late nineteenth century to the mid-twentieth century, Berkshire County was a thriving industrial region. The rivers were dotted with manufacturing plants and paper mills that employed thousands of workers. The Berkshires weren't a ritzy place to live back then, with fancy theaters and high-end restaurants. Instead it was a simple blue-collar area. Fathers went off to work in the morning, and mothers stayed home and tended to the children.

At the center of the community, smack bang in the middle of the county between Great Barrington and Williamstown, on Route 7, was the "big city": Pittsfield. And at the center of Pittsfield was General Electric. Pittsfield was a company town, and GE was the company. At its peak in the 1960s, GE employed at its various plants roughly three-quarters of the workers living in the city. Just about everyone in Berkshire County knew someone who worked at GE in Pittsfield. The man who owned my home, Bernie Gibbons, was a shop steward at GE and worked there his entire life. Many people did, and their children often followed them. That's the way it was in those days.

"I can remember seeing the cars line up in the morning at the bottom of our hill as the men would head off for their shifts, and then watching them come back home up the hill when their shifts were over at night," says my eighty-year-old next-door neighbor Don Goranson. He and his wife, Natalie, moved to Great

Barrington in the 1950s to work as teachers in the local school system and never left. Like so many people of a certain age in Berkshire County, they had many friends who spent their lives at GE.

"It was a very predictable life, which made people feel comfortable," Don says. "That's why the GE people were so fiercely loyal to the company. Even Bernie [Gibbons], who was always fighting with them over one union thing or another, was incredibly loyal. You couldn't say a cross word about GE to him. He could say whatever he wanted. But you couldn't. It was like family to him. I think that's the way it was for a lot of people who worked there."

However, those good times didn't last. As the recession of the 1970s sank in, GE, like many large American industrial companies, started closing operations and retrenching. Pittsfield was one of the towns that GE abandoned. Little by little, the company announced plant closings and layoffs, with each step receiving banner headlines in the local newspaper, the *Berkshire Eagle*. The people of Pittsfield were forced to watch their city decay as GE fled the area and nothing ever came in to take its place. By the late 1980s, Pittsfield was a town left for dead. An all-American city wrecked by a multinational conglomerate with an all-American image. It's a horribly sad story, but a familiar one, too.

THE COMPANY TOWN

The story of GE and Pittsfield began in 1903 with an inventor named William Stanley, Jr. Stanley was born in Brooklyn in 1858, the son of a wealthy lawyer. After attending Yale University, he took a job as an electrician, serving as an apprentice to Hiram Maxim, the inventor of the machine gun who already was considered a pioneer in the electrical industry. As Maxim's assistant, Stanley ran one of the country's first electrical installations at a store in New York City. That's how he caught the attention of the industrialist George Westinghouse, who hired him to serve as the chief engineer at his factory in Pittsburgh.

In the 1880s, Stanley started developing his idea for an electrical transformer. At the time, electric lighting was very expensive and dangerous and not a feasible replacement for gas or kerosene. The obvious way to reduce the cost of electrical power would be to create a single central station (which Stanley called a transformer) that could efficiently deliver the current over an expanded area. And Stanley was determined to build it. In the meantime, his relationship with Westinghouse was falling apart. By the spring of 1885, Stanley's health also started failing. His doctor told him that he could no longer withstand the environment in Pittsburgh and suggested that he relocate to a quieter area in the country.

Stanley picked the bucolic town of Great Barrington in western Massachusetts. He built a laboratory there with financial backing from Westinghouse. In the summer of 1885, Stanley set to work trying to design his transformer. In less than a year, he had created not only the device but a system to power an entire town. To celebrate his discovery and the return of spring to the Berkshires, Stanley decided to give Great Barrington a gift. As an experiment, he powered up his transformer and fired electrical currents from his lab across three-quarters of a mile down to Main Street. And with that, in March 1886, Great Barrington became the first downtown in America to have electric lights.

Although Stanley believed his discovery was miraculous, Westinghouse was less impressed. So Stanley established his own business called the Stanley Electrical Manufacturing Company about twenty miles up the road from Great Barrington in the city of Pittsfield. In 1903, Stanley sold his company to Thomas Edison's General Electric Company, which soon began to produce small transformers, flat irons, and electrical fans at its Pittsfield facility. But over time, the operation grew. During the Great Depression, the company started making large high-voltage transformers that could be used to power massive public works projects like the

Hoover Dam. By the 1950s, GE was building the largest electrical transformers in the world. To keep the growing company happy in Pittsfield, the city bent over backwards to accommodate GE's needs.

"GE could basically get whatever it wanted," says Daniel C. Dillon, a former Pittsfield city councilor and former twenty-five-year GE employee whose family worked for the company for roughly eighty years. "They had a lot of influence. They wanted an abutment cleared and it was done. They wanted a zoning change, no problem. And they were involved in everything. They were on the city council, the chamber of commerce, the Rotary Club. They were extremely generous with charitable giving and had volunteers on just about every agency in Pittsfield. So they built up a lot of goodwill in town, which is why the town was so eager to make them happy."

"Politically you didn't just have to work with the GE executives, you also had the labor organizations, which had a lot of clout," says Remo Del Gallo, the mayor of Pittsfield during GE's heyday in the 1960s whose family owned Del Gallo's Restaurant, a popular neighborhood bar across the street from the GE plant. "You're talking about thousands and thousands of people who worked for GE, were loyal to GE, and looked out for the company's interests. And you needed their votes. That really was the base of their power."

With such a cosy relationship, GE decided to locate many of its key operations in Pittsfield. Not only did GE build transformers there, but it also put its plastics and advanced materials divisions in the city, making it one of the company's key industrial centers. GE's rising executives, including future chairman Jack Welch, regularly cycled through Pittsfield, spending a few years at the company's facilities there as part of their training.

During the 1950s and 1960s, as GE grew, Pittsfield was a storybook version of the ideal American city. Unemployment was low. The city's schools were considered top-notch. There were upscale department stores and shops lining North Street, the city's main commercial drag. For GE employees, job security was a given. Not only were you basically employed for life, but GE also took care of you. You could buy all the appliances your family needed at steep discounts. Local stores offered discounts to GE employees. If you needed soil for your yard, GE would give it to you for free from its own piles of backfill that were left over from the company's constant construction projects. If you had to move because the company had transferred you but you couldn't sell your house, GE would buy it and sell it for you.

Life was good in Pittsfield until the 1970s, when the recession brought GE's success to a screeching halt. With the oil crisis in full swing, the market for major electrical transformers dried up as American companies tried to limit their power consumption. So GE's transformer business slowly evaporated, and in 1986 the company's Pittsfield transformer plant was shut down. At the same time, the company decided to relocate its advanced materials operation. Suddenly, the talk of Pittsfield wasn't about job security, it was about layoffs and how they were killing the city. And with that, the Pittsfield diaspora began.

At Pittsfield's economic peak between 1950 and 1970, the city had more than 57,000 residents. But it's been in a steady decline ever since. By 1980 Pittsfield's population had fallen to 52,000. By 1990, it had dropped to 49,000. By 2000, it was 46,000. And by 2009, it was below 43,000, meaning that Pittsfield lost 25 percent of its residents in a slow trickle over forty years. Today Pittsfield is a shell of its former self. Troubled neighborhoods are filled with drugs and guns. Abandoned houses sit rotting with yards overgrown with weeds. In 2003, the author and documentary filmmaker Joanna Lipper wrote a book called *Growing Up Fast,* which was about the raging problem of teen pregnancy in Pittsfield, where more than sixty teenage girls give birth each year. To many Pittsfield residents, this was no longer their fathers' city.

Not only that, but GE left another, more troubling legacy than just job losses. It turns out that for decades the company was poisoning the city's water and soil with toxic polychlorinated biphenyls, otherwise known as PCBs. The company dumped PCBs into the Housatonic River, which winds through much of Berkshire County. And remember that topsoil the company gave its employees? Most of it was loaded with PCBs. In the end, a vast swath of Pittsfield surrounding the GE plant was designated as a Superfund environmental cleanup site. What a mess.

Then, in the autumn of 2007, Pittsfield finally received a lifeline. It came from a highly unlikely source. As GE was getting ready to divest its last operation remaining in Pittsfield, the famous GE Plastics laboratory, a group of Saudi Arabian investors from the petrochemical company Sabic (Saudi Basic Industries Corporation), which is 80 percent owned by the Saudi crown, stepped up and bought the business for $11.6 billion (£5.7 billion). The move saved one thousand area jobs at two sites: one in Pittsfield, and the other less than an hour away in Selkirk, New York, outside of Albany. Pittsfield residents were thrilled and relieved by the news. Finally, something was going their way.

The press conference at the Cranwell Country Club to announce the deal was a sight to behold. Deval Patrick, the Massachusetts governor, was there, as were all of the city's local politicians and many of the GE Plastics employees who now would be working for Sabic. What was so odd about the scene was that Pittsfield's lily-white blue-collar workers were literally embracing the Arabs who were taking over their business. Berkshire County, with its rural background, has a very hardcore politically conservative constituency full of traditional, conservative Republicans. For many of these people, the idea of associating with Saudis in business, much less working for them, would normally be considered anathema. But here they were hugging them in thanks for saving so many local jobs.

"It is so nice to see this heart-warming welcome from the governor and the entire community," said Sabic chairman Mohamed Al-Mady. "It's very welcoming."

So Pittsfield was nearly killed off when General Electric picked up and left without so much as a good-bye, and then was partially saved by some investors from Saudi Arabia. Unfortunately, it's not that unusual a story. Plenty of small towns and villages across the United States, the UK, and Europe have experienced the jolting sadness of industrial decay. In Pittsfield, the sense of abandonment is acute. All of the jobs not affiliated with GE Plastics are gone. The soil and water are poisoned. The city is still trying to dig its way out of the mess GE left behind.

Over the years, I've spoken to countless former GE workers and a few people who work at the Sabic plants. The conversations are remarkably similar. On some level they're angry at GE for what it did to Pittsfield, but they're thrilled that a major multinational like Sabic appreciated GE's skilled industrial workers. They don't care that Sabic is owned by the Saudi government. But they are sad that a US company didn't see the value that Sabic did. So many people say that they think this is a symbol of a larger problem: that the West—America, Britain, Europe—is selling itself off piece by piece. And in many ways, they're right.

HERE, THERE, EVERYWHERE

In the summer of 2009, executives from several South Korean manufacturing companies toured the city of Dayton in western Ohio. They weren't there to look at the scenery. They were scouting potential business opportunities in an area that's been decimated by redundancies in the car industry. This was not a one-off thing. Rather, it was part of a growing trend that's happening all over the country. In 2007, South Korean companies invested £6.5 billion in the United States, up from £800 million in 2003. During that time, Hyundai Motors built a car manufacturing plant near Montgomery, Alabama. Samsung unveiled a factory to make semiconductor chips in Austin, Texas. And Kia Motors launched plans to construct a plant in West Point, Georgia. And it's not just South Korea doing the investing. In 2010, China's Anshan Iron & Steel Group invested $175 million (£110 million) in the Steel Development Corporation in Mississippi; Singapore's sovereign wealth fund Temasek Holdings invested $500 million (£300 million) in Chesapeake Energy Corporation, an Oklahoma natural gas producer. And BYD Company Limited, a Chinese maker of energy efficient technology such as electric cars and solar panels, established its North American headquarters in Los Angeles.

Regardless of their size, all of these investments are important to their communities because they mean jobs and an influx of cash. For example, in September 2009, a South Korean company called Uni-Chem bought a shutdown semiconductor plant in Eugene, Oregon, and converted it to make solar cells. The $50 million price tag may not have landed the deal on the front page of the *Wall Street Journal*. But in Lane County, where unemployment was running at nearly 13 percent and twelve thousand jobs had been lost in the previous year, the one thousand new jobs at the plant were welcome news.

When one pieces together all the disparate numbers, it becomes clear that corporate America is increasingly selling off pieces of itself to foreign entities because those entities have the capital to spend. In 2009, for the first time ever, the Chinese government and Chinese companies bought more US assets than the other way around. According to statistics compiled by the financial data firm Dealogic, China spent $3.9 billion (£2.4 billion) on US assets, while the United States spent $3 billion on Chinese assets. What does this mean? It means that when the Virginia power company AES wants to raise $2 billion in capital, it knows where to turn: China, which in November 2009 bought a 15 percent stake in AES, along with a 35 percent stake in AES's global wind generation subsidiary.

It's not just China and Korea doing the buying, either. India also has been pouring money into the United States, with companies like the information technology services conglomerates Wipro and Infosys Technologies snapping up US workers and properties as fast as they can. In October 2009, Wipro's chairman and chief executive officer, Azim Premji, told Bloomberg News that the company was planning to hire more American workers to take advantage of a rebound in the technology market and favorable economic conditions. Then, a month later, Infosys bought McCamish Systems of Atlanta for $58 billion (£35 billion). Meanwhile, also in November 2009, a collection of Indian companies signed partnership agreements with US counterparts: Tata Communications with Tyco Telecommunications, HCL Security with Cisco, Cadila Pharmaceuticals with Novavax, Apollo Hospitals with StemCyte, and Infosys Technologies with Microsoft.

These kinds of arrangements are being encouraged around the world by the US Commerce Department's "Invest in America" program. Invest in America is only a few years old because up until 2007, the United States didn't even have a formal plan for attracting foreign investments. It didn't have to. America could take care of itself, and if foreigners wanted to invest too, so be it. But as the economy started to turn sour in 2008, it became clear that the country would need to compete with other Western countries for the foreign capital that could help rescue its struggling businesses. So attracting foreign investors became a paramount concern. Soon the US government was pushing its new program, which was designed to serve as a conduit between potential investors, government offices, and companies in the private sector. Today Invest in America organizes events across the globe and even has a highly functional website that provides all the support a prospective foreign investor could want, including copies of state-by-state regulations and specific names and telephone numbers of key contacts. The website also can be viewed in Chinese, Japanese, Korean, Russian, German, French, and Spanish.

Not surprisingly, today there are tens of thousands of Americans working for companies like India's Tata Group conglomerate or the Chinese appliance maker Haier. Yet surveys show that if given a choice, an overwhelming 90 percent to 95 percent of Americans would prefer to work for an American company. But in the new globalized world, that may not be possible anymore. The West needs international capital to save it. However, each time America, Britain, or a European nation accepts foreign investments, it raises questions about the death of the West. And if the so-called American empire can't save itself, who can?

Obviously, none of the issues raised here is simple. What has the United States become? Or the UK or the Eurozone? What do they want to be? What are their places in the world? The shadow market is forcing the West to look in the mirror and assess where it's been and where it's going. It's a constant tug-of-war. On the one hand, Westerners aren't comfortable with the idea of foreign countries and companies buying up their businesses and properties. But at the same time, the West can't survive without them. America, in particular, owes trillions of dollars all over the world, so it can't just walk away from the table now. Instead it's got to play the cards that it's been dealt and fight its way back into the game.

The United States remains an awesomely powerful country with an enviably dynamic economy. The shadow market knows this and wants to have access to it. It's not as if countries such as China or Saudi Arabia are going to buy up America's farmland or forests. Rather, they're going to focus on buying US businesses or partnering with them to gain access to skilled workers and the valuable Western market. For instance, China is working with General Electric and the State of California to build high-speed rail lines across the West Coast. But it's not just large-scale projects attracting international attention. There also are smaller Chinese operations making money all over the United States, from a soy sauce plant in Georgia to a telecommunications company in Texas to a Chinese-built shopping plaza in Wisconsin. So there will be opportunities to get rich as Western companies of all types increasingly engage with wealthy nations from across the world. In fact, if America makes the right choices, it could straighten itself out financially and buy back its empire. There's no guarantee that the United States will be able to do it. If it doesn't, it will find its future in Pittsfield.

But What About Me?

At its core, the emergence of the shadow market is the story of geopolitical power shifting from West to East. Just as America's rise as a global superpower in the twentieth century showed, in our world wealth begets international influence. The shadow market is now the wealthiest force in the global economy. The numbers prove it: the investments by SWFs, the financing provided by shadow market banks and state-owned companies, the capital flows being deployed for nationalist purposes. So it's only natural that power will follow the money. Indeed, the coming realignment is going to leave the world virtually unrecognizable from what we know today. The real authority will no longer lie with Western banks and well-heeled investors from the United States, Britain, and Europe but with wealthy nations and bulging nationalized investment funds from the Middle East and Far East.

In specific terms, this means that while the US and UK fret over what to do about their lost jobs and ever mounting debt, massive developing countries with cash to burn and amped up consumer markets—like China, India, and the nations of Southeast Asia—and prosperous countries that are stocked with valuable natural resources—like the petroleum states of the Persian Gulf and Africa—have already started to assert their political and economic influence over the global economy. Indeed, the main reason why these countries are in such a strong economic position is that they either hold so much Western currency and debt, or control so much of the natural resources that the West requires, that we have become beholden to them, not the other way around.

The bottom line is that the United States may still have the largest economy on earth, but it no longer can dictate its own economic destiny. Although shocking, this development should come as no surprise. It's simply what happens when you wake up one morning to find that you're trillions of dollars or pounds or euros in the hole and you have no idea how to pay it back. If this debt was owed to a more aggressive collector, like the mob, a couple of enforcers would probably be on their way over to break our thumbs. However, in global finance, retribution comes slower and in more subtle forms. But it's no less painful.

How painful? Take a look at the work on future economic projections being done by the British economist John Hawksworth, the head of macroeconomic research at the accounting and financial advisory firm PricewaterhouseCoopers. Depending on whom you ask, sometime between 2020 and 2030, China's gross domestic product will surpass America's, officially giving China the title of "world's largest economy." But that flip-flop is really just scratching the surface of the coming transformation. In Hawksworth's report, titled "The World in 2050," he shows how within a mere forty years, the entire planet will be economically turned upside down. In particular, Hawksworth's key finding is that by 2050, the combined GDP generated by the economies of a group of countries that he calls the Emerging Seven, or the "E7"—Brazil, China, India, Indonesia, Mexico, Russia, and Turkey—will be at least 25 percent *larger* than the economies of the G7, which is made up of Canada, France, Germany, Italy, Japan, the UK, and the United States. How drastic will this change be? Today the combined GDP of the E7 is more than 20 percent *smaller* than the combined GDP of the G7. We're looking at a complete reversal of the global economy as we know it.

To America and Americans, GDP is a particularly important macroeconomic statistic because it's probably the most effective gauge of how well positioned the US economy is to generate jobs. US financial regulators have traditionally been reluctant to intervene directly in the American economy by specifically getting involved in job creation. Instead they prefer to stimulate the economy by providing liquidity to banks and large companies and then let the private sector and the free market take care of the rest. This, in effect, creates an indirect jobs program where the government is one step removed from intervening in individual businesses. As a result, GDP has become America's primary way of grading its economic success in generating jobs. As long as the country's GDP is expanding, it is safe to assume that US businesses are growing healthily and increasing their payrolls, which means that they're adding workers.

Thus, one particularly troubling finding in Hawksworth's research is that the United States is not only going to eventually cede the title of "world's largest economy" to China, but by 2050 it's likely that India also will be generating a GDP that's as big, if not bigger, than America's. Obviously, in this new economic environment the West will be forced to confront certain painful fiscal realities. Among them will be whether the US can continue to spend far more on defense than any other nation on earth. According to a study by the Stockholm International Peace Research Institute, in 2009 America spent more than $660 billion (£420 billion) on its military, or £1,300 for every American; the next closest country was China, with estimated military expenditures of £64 billion, or about £50 for each of its citizens. And the next closest in terms of per capita spending was Saudi Arabia, with £26 billion in military spending, or £1,000 for every citizen. It seems nearly impossible that the US can maintain its current level of military spending without experiencing an economic collapse. Eventually, something's got to give—and it will affect America's diplomatic standing around the world, one way or another.

Even more striking than America's decline in relative economic strength is the coming loss of international influence of traditional powers like Japan, Germany, and Britain. These countries will likely be economically superseded not only by China and India but also by longtime economic backwaters like Brazil, and possibly even Indonesia and Mexico.

"If anything the trend is speeding up and things are changing even faster than we'd expected," Hawksworth says. "The base year for the first report we did was 2004 and quite a lot has changed since then. At the time we thought that the E7 would overtake the G7 by around 2040. But looking at conditions now I think the takeover point is going to happen earlier. Since 2004, China and India have grown faster than we'd expected despite the financial crisis, whereas the US and Europe obviously have tended to grow quite a lot slower and indeed have been going backwards for a couple of years because of the crisis. So the story has become even stronger."

At the center of Hawksworth's story is the deeply enmeshed codependent financial and economic relationship between China and America. As noted earlier in these pages, for most of the mid- to late twentieth century, the United States was considered so indomitable and its reach so vast that it could largely dictate geopolitical terms. Back then, understanding the global economy largely meant understanding the United States: its consumer culture, its corporate structure, its financial markets. But no more. Today much of the global economy is powered by the shadow market, with large chunks of capital zipping around the world and bypassing America—and the rest of the West—altogether.

To get access to these markets Western companies are going to have to start making products for these consumers," globalization expert Kishore Mahbubani says. "In the good old days all you had to do to be successful was to take McDonald's or Coca-Cola and saturate the market. That was the old model when the American economy was so dominant. But when your economy isn't as dominant you cannot assume that any product that works in America will succeed overseas. You have to get a sense of the differences in tastes and cultures."

In Mahbubani's mind, Western companies and workers need to be on the ground, physically, in booming overseas markets such as China, India, Korea, and Brazil in order to truly understand what these populations want and need. After all, these people represent the next wave of global consumers. A one-size-fits-all approach to manufacturing won't work anymore—whether it's cars, appliances, or personal technology—because these burgeoning economies are growing at different rates and require different products and innovations at different times. But there are immense opportunities to make money in these markets.

Indeed, the shift of employees to emerging markets is already starting to happen. In 2010, American companies created 1 million jobs in the US and 1.4 million jobs overseas, according to the Economic Policy Institute in Washington, DC. However, this isn't an old-fashioned "off-shoring" of jobs for cheaper labor. If you look inside the numbers, you'll find that these businesses are launching operations overseas not to cut costs per se, but to be closer to their growing customer base in the Middle and Far East. Recall that General Motors now sells more cars in China than in the US. Or consider that in January 2011, two US finance giants, JPMorgan Chase and Morgan Stanley, received permission from the Chinese government to form joint ventures with Chinese partners that will give them access to the country's booming securities market; the firms will join Goldman Sachs, Credit Suisse, UBS, and Deutsche Bank as the only Western financial companies operating in mainland China. At the other end of the spectrum, there's PharmaSecure, a tiny outfit, based in New Hampshire, that creates technological systems to prevent the distribution of counterfeit pharmaceuticals. The company's products work well, but it turns out there's more of a demand for them in developing nations where problems with such counterfeit drugs are rampant. So the bulk of PharmaSecure's fifteen employees are located in India, where they work with the government to monitor the nation's supply of medicine. These are only a sampling of the companies that have adapted to the shift in global power and consumer demand.

But in truth, for Western nations to compete they first need to get their own financial situations straightened out. With all the debt overhanging the US and Europe, it has been difficult for the West to stabilize its economies so its corporations can raise capital freely and drive innovation. An excruciating transformation is all but inevitable. In the United States, the painful bloodletting began to become apparent in late 2009 and early 2010 when the national unemployment rate crept above 10 percent for the first time in nearly twenty-five years. And what's more, that may have represented only the start of the process. Unfortunately, conditions could very well get even worse before they begin to get better.

"The US economy is enormously resilient," Yale's Paul Bracken says. "It's capable of reforming itself in the private sector in a very ugly, harsh way, where social wefare programs can't keep up. I mean, who would've thought you'd ever see four-day school weeks in Hawaii and other places. Next you're also going to see public sector cuts in pensions. I'm not advocating this, I'm just describing it. But breaking social contracts will be the name of the game for the next three or four years. Productivity is going to be the metric to watch. And in the end I think you will see huge new innovations in the US economy."

So there it is: a stark program for survival in a tough new world and a challenge to the nation. Do we have the stomach to make these difficult adjustments now in order to compete in the future? Time will tell.

GO EAST, YOUNG AND OLD CAPITALISTS

To succeed as investors in this vastly changed world, we have to learn to follow the money. I'm not talking about mindless racing down a blind alley chasing the latest hot stock. In most cases, that's throwing good money after bad, and it's resulted in more than a few lost fortunes. No, I mean finding the smart money, determining which way the trends are heading, and capitalizing on that insight. If you're a major player in the international financial markets, and global capital is funneling away from one area and into another, you'd be wise to figure out why, and if the reasoning makes sense, determine how to get in on it. Today, all investors must think on a global scale. We must learn to be patient, with investment time horizons of five or even ten years, to fully capitalize on these trends. The kinds of long-term changes that are happening right now don't take hold overnight. The shadow market isn't a place to shoot for a quick score. It's much larger than that. It's an economic entity that ultimately will force the entire world to rethink its assumptions. Investment portfolios will be changed forever because of its emergence.

So how do investors capitalize on these developments? The most obvious place to begin is by thinking about what the nations of the shadow market need in order to grow. In most cases, this means natural resources: oil, precious metals, food. Traditionally, investors would play these kinds of investments by buying futures and options in the commodities markets. An investor who believed that global demand for wheat was going to lead to higher wheat prices would buy wheat futures, which are a bet on the future direction of wheat prices. Futures give investors the right to buy a commodity at a set price within a certain timeframe. If the actual price of the commodity rises higher than the price stated in the futures contract, the investor makes money.

Investors can still buy commodity futures, but now there are simpler alternatives available: mutual funds, exchange traded funds (ETF), and exchange traded notes (ETNs) that track specific commodities or baskets of related commodities. Investors also can buy shares in companies that produce the underlying commodity. So if investors want to capitalize on the potential rising price of wheat, they could put money in a fund that invests in wheat or buy shares in a company such as Archer Daniels Midland, the world's largest processor of grains, which grows and sells a tremendous amount of wheat. Of course, this indirect strategy can pose a challenge, because companies' share prices can be affected by issues beyond, say, the price of wheat. But the point is that certain commodities are going to become increasingly valuable as countries such as China, India, and Brazil grow from the second world to the first. Investors should look to take advantage.

Commodities also perform another important role in investment portfolios: they are a highly effective hedge against the falling value of a currency. Assuming the shadow market forces the global community to move away from the US dollar in favor of a new worldwide reserve currency, the dollar's value is bound to slip, and that hedge will be essential. One way for investors to protect themselves is to own commodities, such as gold, that hold their value when the dollar falls. Mark O'Byrne, executive director of the British precious metals dealer Goldcore, notes that the "smart money"—big-name hedge fund managers like John Paulson, David Einhorn, and Paul Tudor Jones—already have started accumulating gold and gold-related stocks as long-term hedges against global volatility. But there still could be room for ordinary investors to make money in gold as well. O'Byrne projects that the precious metal's price will reach $2,400 (£1,500) per ounce within the next few years. Oil has become another popular hedging device.

In fact, the shadow market's demand for commodities has even brought once esoteric asset classes, such as farmland, into the mainstream. For years, major institutional investors such as BlackRock, Barclays, Franklin Templeton, and TIAA-CREF have been adding farmland holdings to diversify their investment portfolios. But so far it's been difficult for individuals to tap into this market, since the typical way to add farmland to your investments has been to literally go out and buy some. That's starting to change, however. In the summer of 2007, the investment firm Van Eck Global rolled out an agribusiness fund for US investors. It's basically an ETF that tracks the DAXglobal Agribusiness Index. The fund owns around fifty companies that participate in the global agriculture industry, from food producers to farming equipment manufacturers. Other firms are starting to follow Van Eck's lead, and there now are several ETFs and ETNs dedicated to investing in the industry. There are also upstarts like Agcapita, which runs two funds that invest directly in Canadian farmland. If Agcapita succeeds, it's only a matter of time before this model is repeated around the world.

Of course, right now, most of the money is flowing east, and there's no sign of that abating any time soon. So, naturally, much of the global financial community is focused on the wealthy emerging markets of the Middle East and Far East, where major investors are keen to get a piece of the action. But just like investing in natural resources, making money on a worldwide shift in capital flow isn't as easy as simply buying stocks and bonds from emerging markets. That's like throwing darts at a board. First you have to determine which specific markets you want to focus on because they're going to provide long-term growth with some semblance of stability. To succeed you must be very selective.

Just listen to David Riedel, the head of Riedel Research, which analyzes emerging-markets investments for a host of institutional investors, including the Van Kampen Funds. Riedel divides the taste for emerging-market investments over the past thirty years into three phases. The first, which lasted from the 1980s to the late 1990s, was dominated by the countries that produced cheap manufactured exports, like the Asian Tigers of China, Indonesia, Korea, Malaysia, Taiwan, and Thailand. Indeed, from 1985 to 1995, the fastest-growing economy in the world actually belonged to Thailand, which posted a compounded annual GDP expansion rate of 10 percent over that time frame. The first phase ended at the close of the twentieth century because overinvestment flooded the region with capital, forming a bubble that eventually triggered a financial crisis across Asia from 1997 to 1998. The second phase lasted from 2000 to 2009 and was marked by investments in commodities and raw materials as the demand for agriculture, energy, and infrastructure materials exploded. Soon capital was flooding into the commodity markets and triggering a boom in asset prices. The biggest beneficiaries were the oil producers of the Middle East and "frontier" countries like Brazil that had plentiful resources and didn't spend a lot of capital on infrastructure.

To Riedel, the third phase of emerging-markets investing starts now and will focus on domestic demand for products and consumer demographics. For example, looking at the BRIC countries of Brazil, Russia, India, and China, Riedel believes that Brazil, China, and India offer much better economic models than Russia. Why? Because Brazil, China, and India all have large populations with strong consumer cultures, so their economic development can be powered by their own consumer markets. The negative for China is an aging population, and for India it's a relatively small tax base that holds back its national investments in the economy. Russia, on the other hand, is not what Riedel's looking for in an emerging market. It has a shrinking population that's aging rapidly, and its economy is dependent on depleting supplies of natural resources such as petroleum, natural gas, coal, and precious metals. Riedel believes that countries like Indonesia, South Africa, and Turkey could surpass Russia as highly sought-after emerging-market economies, and that several of the ASEAN countries could become much more prominent players on the global stage.

Riedel believes that this global transformation should be more fully reflected in people's investment portfolios. He points out that until a very recently a majority of pension fund and major institutional investors in the United States allocated little more than 10 percent of their assets to international investing. That's *all* international investing—developed and emerging markets in Europe, Asia, South America, Africa, and Australia. The rest is dedicated to the domestic economy. This is starting to change as new global powers emerge. Already, relatively conservative investment shops, such as Pennsylvania-based Vanguard, the originator of index funds, are recommending that investors increase their international exposure to up to 40 percent of their equity portfolios. Riedel can see a day where investment portfolios in the United States are 60 percent international and a fifty-fifty split between international emerging markets and developed markets. But even if investors don't heed his advice and adjust their behavior, they still would be wise to start tuning in to what's happening in these regions. Because they're growing so fast that one way or another they're going to have a significant effect on Western economies.

"People need to be paying attention because these countries are going to be drivers of global earnings growth over the next three, five, and ten years," Riedel says. "You're already starting to see it in the way investors react to news coming out of China or Brazil. Even if you aren't investing there directly, you'd damn well better be paying attention because these countries tend to have a pretty big impact on your domestic market, and that influence is only going to increase."

One way for investors to support their domestic economy while also indirectly tapping into the growth of the shadow market is to buy shares of homegrown companies that are building inroads to the booming parts of the world. Take China, for instance, which is experiencing an enormous shift from a rural lifestyle to a modern, urban one. Since Westerners are prolific consumers, many US and European companies are well positioned to provide products to the Chinese market. Doing so avoids the potential risk of investing money directly in Chinese companies, since some economists posit that, with all the capital flooding the nation and the government's manipulative monetary policies, China is bound to experience a financial bubble in the not-too-distant future. That scenario, if it came to pass, could be particularly ugly because the Chinese economy doesn't require the same level of disclosure as its Western counterparts. Investors literally won't know what hit them.

Indeed, in 2009 and 2010, Chinese companies for the first time raised more money through initial public offerings than American companies did, but several of the IPOs—including one of the hottest companies in the bunch, pollution control equipment maker RINO International—have since run into serious financial trouble. RINO more than doubled its share price shortly after it began trading. But after RINO executives admitted to the US Securities and Exchange Commission that the company's financial statements were fabrications (in part because they had made up two contracts), the shares lost nearly all of their value. On 2nd December 2010, RINO's shares were delisted from the Nasdaq exchange. The company's fate could be seen as a cautionary tale for anyone thinking they can get rich quick in China.

That being said, investing in markets with strong financial disclosure rules doesn't eliminate the risks for investors either. Some of the biggest potential pitfalls in the market were to be found in troubled "old" Europe, particularly the flagging economies of Spain, Portugal, and Ireland. The problem in these countries wasn't transparency; the financial disclosure rules in the eurozone are among the most stringent in the world. Instead, it is that it will take years, possibly a decade, to recover from the financial crisis that hit in 2010.

The fallout is not limited to the economies that faltered. France, for example, continues to face the threat of severe economic stagnation, caused in part by the country's intense labor disputes. As the European economic system was wavering in late 2010, the French people protested the government's attempts to reform the economy, such as increasing the national retirement age to sixty-two; the degree of animosity triggered by these proposals was a demonstration of how unprepared France appears to be to compete in the twenty-first-century economy. Meanwhile, in Germany, Europe's biggest and most stable economy, the primary debate has become how much capital the nation eventually will have to provide to keep the euro together in some form; all of the government's spending and stimulus plans come weighted with the belief that Germany will eventually be called upon to bail out its neighbors.

Perhaps most ominously, in Britain there are real fears that the country's once booming economy could sink into oblivion for the next ten years or so, conjuring images of the "lost decade" Japan experienced in the 1990s. The prospect was first raised publicly in November 2009 by Adam Posen, a senior member of the Bank of

England's monetary policy committee. The parallels between Japan in the 1990s and Britain in 2009 were fairly clear. Both countries went through periods of exuberant growth that were largely fueled by inexpensive loans and housing investments. When the party ended the countries were left with crumbling banks and crippling national debt. For Japan, the scenario led to ten-year period of anemic growth. Now Britain is wondering if that will be its fate as well.

"The United Kingdom has an uncomfortable parallel with the Japanese financial system when the Japanese economy began to recover in the mid-1990s and was unable to sustain it," Posen said in a speech at the Peterson Institute for International Economics in Washington, DC "The closer one looks, the more worrisome this specific parallel becomes, given the concentration of the UK banking system in a few major, mostly still troubled banks, and the relative underdevelopment of alternative nonbank channels for getting capital to nonfinancial businesses."

As the economies of Western Europe whipsaw, it's inevitable that some investment bargains will shake out—which explains why shadow market countries like China and the oil states of the Persian Gulf are busy hunting through the economic rubble. But for ordinary investors, there are probably more ample opportunities for returns in the "new" Europe, particularly in Poland, Hungary, and the Czech Republic, where the overhang of the crisis hasn't been as severe.

Of course, Britain and mainland Europe aren't alone in being concerned about their troubled economies and loss of global influence. With the nations of the shadow market in ascension, America too was looking at a humbling decline in global economic authority in the coming years.

Perhaps most important, the shadow market has changed the way the West has to view the world. New forces are at work in the global economy that are different from anything we've ever experienced. So we have to keep our eyes open to the ramifications of *everything* going on around it. A decision by China or Kuwait to buy up massive tracts of farmland in Africa may happen thousands of miles away, but it has geopolitical and environmental consequences that reverberate across the globe. This is what makes keeping track of the shadow market so tricky. Few of its activities play out on the front pages of newspapers or in the headlines blaring from news channels. The truly important information takes time to piece together. But like an optically twisted drawing by M. C. Escher, if you examine the data long enough, the picture within the picture reveals itself.

Investors from across the globe are discovering that they must be much more calculating about both the economic and political impact of shadow market players on the global financial markets. First and foremost, anyone with a portfolio that's based primarily in domestic stocks and bonds probably should geographically diversify his or her holdings right away. This isn't about nationalism or patriotism. This is about survival. In an uncertain economic environment, it's essential to be where the action is, and the action isn't necessarily where it used to be. But it's not so simple to just say "Invest in emerging markets."

For example, if you believe that one of the keys to the economic future will be alternative energy technology, you almost have to invest with Chinese companies on some level. Why? Because the Chinese government is throwing money at green technology development in a way that all but ensures that the country will be a major player in all facets of the industry. Chinese solar manufacturers are using this capital infusion to drive down the cost of solar panels to nearly uncompetitive levels. In January 2011, Evergreen Solar, a leading developer of solar technology that makes the silicon chips used in solar panels, shut down its plant in Massachusetts, made redundant eight hundred workers, and moved its operations to China. In announcing the decision, Evergreen's CEO Michael El-Hillow bluntly stated that China had become the leader in solar manufacturing in large part because "solar manufacturers in China have received considerable government and financial support and, together with their low manufacturing costs, have become price leaders within the industry." To compete, Evergreen was following the money east.

The same scenario is playing out in the global race to develop an electric car, where Chinese manufacturers are receiving tremendous financial support from the government to develop the fuel cell technology that will make electric cars ubiquitous throughout the world. In 2009, China's leaders adopted a plan to transform the country's car industry. Their goal: to produce 1 million electric vehicles per year by 2020. The government felt comfortable with this bet because the nation's car manufacturers lagged so far behind their competitors in the US, Europe, Japan, and Korea that they might as well try to dominate the next-generation technology that is poised to replace the internal combustion engine. Since then, the Chinese government has announced plans to spend £9 billion subsidizing the push. By comparison, in March 2009 the US Department of Energy unveiled a program to allocate $2.4 billion (£1.6 billion) in grants to private enterprises working on fuel cell technology for hybrid and electric vehicles. More than a year later, the government had released only 10 percent of the money, according to a study by Pike Research, a clean technology research and consulting firm.

Obviously, it's not a level financial playing field when it comes to the development of environmental technology. With all of that cash floating around, China invariably is going to become a center for green innovation. There's no sense denying this transformation; a much better plan is to try to take advantage of it. As an investor in an uncertain economic environment, it's critical to be where the action is, and the action isn't necessarily where it used to be. When it comes to green technology, the action is in China, at least for the time being. So, investors interested in participating in this industry most likely will need to be there as well.

Along these lines, everyday investors, considering their pensions and other shareholdings, should prepare for the day when the United States is no longer the world's largest economy. It is not just a conceptual shift but, really, an act of the imagination. If possible, they should make a point of traveling to China or India or Brazil to see the changes for themselves. They should probably invest in the commodities that are most prized by wealthy developing countries. Whether you're buying metals or shares of companies that mine them, the commodity markets are going to play an important role in turning countries like China and India into modern superpowers capable of challenging America. To not capitalize would be a huge mistake. These are rising civilizations.

We're talking about oil, coal, natural gas, copper, iron ore, lumber, even water. And we're talking about companies that produce necessary items such as energy generation equipment, construction and farming machinery, and green technologies like solar panels and wind turbines. Regardless of your political beliefs, to be witness to this global transformation and not capitalize would be a monumental mistake. Because this isn't about politics; it's about economics. These countries are rising. The trend is real.

And in the end, that's really the point. We can argue over whether the development of the shadow market is good or bad, whether political or economic hardball is unfair, but that misses the bigger picture of what's going on. The shadow market simply *is*. It's a force in the world that we all have to deal with. We can try to get to grips with it. Or we can fight it. But there is no stopping it.

Acknowledgements

To explain an entity as diffuse as the shadow market, a writer must cover widely varied economic and geopolitical terrain. So it's hardly surprising that in the course of my research, I ended up speaking to countless different sources with broadly diverse fields of expertise, from financial engineering to national security. In light of the sensitivity of the subject matter, the vast majority of these conversations had to be done on background because so many experts were reluctant to have their names appear in print for one reason or another. Nonetheless, each of these conversations helped me put together a comprehensive picture of the shadow market's murkily powerful reach. To everyone who took my calls and patiently answered my questions, however prodding or naïve, I offer a hearty thank you. This book could not have happened without you. Literally.

The key people who helped me develop this project were my literary agent, Kris Dahl of International Creative Management, and my editor, Colin Harrison of Scribner. Kris patiently shepherded this book through several permutations before we landed on the right one with the concept of the shadow market. Through it all, she never lost faith that we'd eventually produce something important. For that, I truly owe her my thanks. Also at ICM, Laura Neely was a pleasure to work with and did a fantastic job of making sure that every single detail was taken care of promptly and smoothly.

ACKNOWLEDGMENTS

On the publishing end, I could not have asked for a better partner than Colin Harrison. From our first meeting, Colin had a clear idea of where the story needed to go and a plan to take it there. He was a constant presence, from the start of my research to the last sentence in the manuscript. This book is his accomplishment along with mine. Scribner's Kelsey Smith and Katie Rizzo were terrific about pulling together all of the loose strands and keeping track of the nuts-and-bolts of the manuscript. Phil Bashe displayed an extremely thorough and nuanced touch in copyediting the manuscript. And last, I'd be remiss if I didn't thank Alice Mayhew of Simon & Schuster for forcefully suggesting that I pursue this story over other ideas I was tossing around. If you ever get that kind of advice from someone like Alice, take it.

Several professional and personal friends also assisted on this project, whether they were aware of it or not. The idea for the book originated innocently enough when Doug Most, whom I've known since we were starting out in journalism together seventeen years ago, asked me to write a feature story about the private equity business for the *Boston Globe Magazine*. Robin Rauzi, a former editor on the op-ed page of the *Los Angeles Times,* encouraged me to expand my thinking about what was happening in the global economy in 2007 and 2008 and gave me a forum to explore my ideas. Along the way I also received enormously useful feedback from Chris Nagi, a managing editor at Bloomberg and one of the savviest minds in financial news today, and Dr. Dan Neilson, an economist and professor at Bard College at Simon's Rock. Steve Vilot introduced me to an improbably large number of key players in finance and publishing circles at his Sims Barber Shop in Great Barrington, Massachusetts, which is apparently a major nexus of the universe. And my dear friends Andrea Buchman and Hans Reuchlin provided me with invaluable support and encouragement throughout the entire process.

But most of all I want to thank my family for being my rock through all the twists and turns these past few years. My mother, the late Carol Weiner, who so badly wanted to see me become an author, was an inspiration to me each morning as I went to work. My father, Carl, was an eager sounding board for my ideas and even provided some important context with his overseas adventures. My brother, Glen, as always pushed me to fully think through each of my ideas during our regular hours-long conversations and offered surprisingly valuable insights that helped the story. My sister-in-law, Randi Hecht, a tremendous editor in her own right, added to the mix by helping me see the parts of the narrative that would grab readers.

Then there's my wife, Paige, my most trusted confidante and most loyal fan, who put up with the tumultuous process and enabled this book to get done by simply taking care of *everything* from the moment I started working on it. There are no words to describe how much she means to me. And finally, there's our son, Jake, who made the whole effort worthwhile by being all I ever could have wished for—and so much more.

Notes

Wherever possible, I've tried to include attributions to my research sources within the text. The following notes represent sections where I was unable to include attributions in the text. Please refer to the bibliography for the full sourcing information.

PROLOGUE:
THE FUTURE HAPPENED YESTERDAY

Lou Jiwei's remarks to the Clinton Global Initiative were reported by Xinhua and appeared in *China Daily* on December 3, 2008. The details of the Kuwait Investment Authority's cash injection into the nation's stock exchange were reported by Rania El Gamal on the website ArabianBusiness.com on December 16, 2008. The statistics on China's and Japan's holdings of US debt came from the report "Major Foreign Holders of Treasury Securities" by the Department of the Treasury and Federal Reserve Board on February 26, 2010. Statistics on sovereign wealth funds came from the website run by the Roseville, California, research firm the Sovereign Wealth Fund Institute.

CHAPTER 1:
MONEY IS A WEAPON

Though few experts dispute that China's economy will eventually surpass the American economy, precisely when this will happen is still in debate. Albert Keidel of the Carnegie Endowment for International Peace predicted that it would happen by 2035 in his report "China's Economic Rise—Fact and Fiction." John Hawksworth at PricewaterhouseCoopers predicted it would happen by 2020 in his report "The World in 2050." And Justin Yifu Lin of Peking University and the World Bank projected that by 2030, China's GDP will be two and a half times larger than America's GDP in an article in the *Harvard Business Review*'s Chinese edition that was excerpted by *China Daily*. So, nailing down a specific year when China surpasses the United States depends on who's doing the prognosticating. Fareed Zakaria's comments appeared in *Newsweek* in his piece "The Capitalist Manifesto: Greed Is Good (To a Point)" on June 13, 2009. The figures on currency trading reaching $3 trillion a day in 2007 were provided by the Progressive Policy Institute. The bulk of the information on the Mexican peso crisis of 1995 came from a research report prepared by the Federal Reserve Bank of Atlanta called "The Mexican Peso Crisis" and from *In an Uncertain World: Tough Choices from Wall Street to Washington* by Robert E. Rubin and Jacob Weisberg.

CHAPTER 2:
HOW TO SPEND $4 TRILLION

The data on private equity assets under management were from the report "Private Equity 2009" by IFSL Research. The data on hedge fund assets under management were reported in the BarclayHedge Alternative Investment Databases. The statistics on the size of private equity deals and funds raised by private equity firms from 1996 to 2006 were provided by Charles Uhrig of Raymond James & Associates in his report "Recent Trends in the Mergers & Acquisitions and Private Equity Markets," which was presented at the University of Florida on August 31, 2007. China's gold position was announced by Xinhua during an interview with Hu Xiaolian, head of the State Administration of Foreign Exchange, on April 24, 2009. Lou Jiwei's comments about the disagreements over regulating sovereign wealth funds were reported by the *New York Times* in the story "Overseas Funds Resist Calls for a Code of Conduct" on February 9, 2008. The details about the attempts of hedge funds to lobby Congress in order to avoid regulation were reported by the *New York Times* in the story "Hedge Funds Step Up Efforts to Avert Tougher Rules" on June 22, 2009.

CHAPTER 3:
THE LAND OF GIANTS

Details of the BRIC summit in western Russia were reported by Reuters in the story "BRIC Demands More Clout, Steers Clear of Dollar Talk" on June 16, 2009. The results of Ernst & Young's December 2008 story on global wealth were reported by the *Indian Express* in the story "Emerging Countries to BRIC up the Holes in Global Economy" on December 24, 2008. Goldman Sachs economist Jim O'Neill's view on the growth of BRIC nations over the next twenty years was reported by Reuters in the story "Crisis Speeds BRIC Rise to Power: Goldman's O'Neill" on June 9, 2009. The World Bank's revised projections for global economic growth in 2009 and 2010 were reported by the *New York Times* in the story "World Bank Cuts Forecast for Developed Economies" on June 22, 2009. The findings by McKinsey & Co. about China's consumer class appeared in the report "The Coming of Age: China's New Class of Wealthy Consumers" in 2009. China's emergence as the largest auto market in the world was reported by Reuters in the story "Chinese Auto Market Overtakes US" on January 8, 2010. The statistic that 1 percent of China's 560 million city dwellers can breathe air that would be deemed safe in Europe was reported by the *New York Times* in the story "As China Roars, Pollution Reaches Deadly Extremes" on August 26, 2007. The results of the study on birth defects by China's National Population and Family Planning Commission were reported in English by Reuters in the story "China Birth Defects Soar Due to Pollution: Report" on October 29, 2007. The statistics on China's facilities for the elderly and results of the *China Youth Daily* survey were reported by *China Daily* in the story "Youth Feel Pressure of Looking After Aging Parents" on June 29, 2009. The statistics on China's worker protests and labor arbitration cases were reported in the China Labour Bulletin research report "Going It Alone: The Workers' Movement in China (2007–2008)" on July 9, 2009.

CHAPTER 4:
CHINESE HARDBALL

The statistics about capital flows and assets on Beijing Financial Street were provided by the Bureau of Commerce of Xicheng District, Beijing. The data on China's foreign exchange reserves were reported by Xinhua on January 15, 2010. Joseph Stiglitz's remarks about China's large amount of financial reserves came during a talk in Shanghai on March 16, 2009, and were reported by the *Wall Street Journal*'s blog China Real Time Report. Chinese Vice Premier Wang Qishan's comments about the dollar were reported by Xinhua on July 30, 2009. Zhou Xiaochuan's report on a global reserve currency was called "Reform the International Monetary System" and was published by the People's Bank of China on March 23, 2009. Australian politician Barnaby Joyce's remarks about China buying up pieces of Australia's mining industry were reported by the *New York Times* on June 2, 2009. Qin Gang's comments on the Rio Tinto case were reported by Xinhua in a story called "China Welcomes Foreign Enterprises to Invest in China" on July 16, 2009.

CHAPTER 5:
TOO SMALL TO FAIL

Information about the evolution of Bader Al Sa'ad's investing style at the Kuwait Investment Authority was supplemented by the *Wall Street Journal* story "How a Gulf Petro-State Invests Its Oil Riches" on August 24, 2007. The statistics on Kuwait's and Abu Dhabi's standings on Standard & Poor's Oil Price Vulnerability Index came from S&P's report "Gulf Cooperation Council Credit Survey: How the Region Is Weathering the Storm" in June 2009. The details on Dubai's request for a six-month stay on Dubai World debt came from the government of Dubai's statement "Government of Dubai Announces Restructuring of Dubai World." The UAE's comments about the Dubai crisis were reported by *Khaleej Times* in the story "UAE Offers More Funds to Banks" on November 30, 2009. Moody's opinion of the restructuring of Dubai came from the Moody's report "Dubai World Unlikely to Harm UAE, Abu Dhabi Ratings" on November 30, 2009. Details about the US Commerce Department's opinion of America's nuclear energy deals with the UAE came from a report by the US-UAE Business Council called "US-U.A.E. Agreement for Peaceful Nuclear Energy Cooperation: Advancing Mutual US and U.A.E. Security and Economic Interests." The International Food Policy Research Institute's call for an international code of conduct on agriculture deals appeared in the report " 'Land Grabbing' by Foreign Investors in Developing Countries: Risks and Opportunities" in IFPRI Policy Brief 13 in April 2009. Andry Rajoelina's comments appeared in the story "The Korean Company Stuck in the Middle of Madagascar's Unrest" on the *Foreign Policy* magazine blog on February 10, 2009. The targets and goals of global money managers investing in agricultural land appeared in the report "Seized! The 2008 Landgrab for Food and Financial Security" in the GRAIN briefing in October 2008.

CHAPTER 6:
ROGUE OIL

The details of the Lockerbie bombing case came from various news accounts as well as voluminous amounts of court documents. Of particular help were the court's ruling on the initial judgment and first appeal, as well as the letter by Libya to the UN Security Council and the final appeal filings by Abdel Baset Ali Mohmed al-Megrahi. Al-Megrahi's statement upon leaving Scotland was printed in full by aljazeera.net on August 20, 2009. Libyan ambassador Abdulati Alobidi's threat that al-Megrahi's death in a Scottish prison would have "catastrophic effects" on Libya's relationship with the UK came from the notes of a meeting at Meridian Court on March 12, 2009. Qatar's decision to intervene on al-Megrahi's behalf was reported by the *London Times* in the story "Qatar Raised Al-Megrahi Release During Talks with Alex Salmond" on September 4, 2009. Saif al-Islam al-Gadhafi's response to the Scottish court's decision to release al-Megrahi was reported by the *Herald* (Scotland) in the story "I Think the Scottish Justice Secretary Is a Great Man. Why Be So Angry About an Innocent Man Who Is Dying?" on August 28, 2009. The push by British Petroleum to secure the release of al-Megrahi was revealed by the *Wall Street Journal* in the story "BP Lobbied U.K. on Benefits of Libya Prisoner-Transfer Deal" on September 5, 2009. Jack Straw's acknowledgment that al-Megrahi's release was tied to trade deals was reported by the *Daily Telegraph* in the story "Jack Straw Admits Lockerbie Bomber's Release Was Linked to Oil" on September 4, 2009. Lord Trefgarne's comments about oil contracts moving "more swiftly" after al-Megrahi was released were reported by *The Independent* in the story "Lockerbie: Now It's Payback Time" on August 22, 2009.

CHAPTER 7:
BEWARE THE DO-GOODERS

The decision by the Oil Fund to review its Israeli holdings and Finance Minister Kristin Halvorsen's comments were reported by Reuters in the story "Norway's Oil Fund's Israel Holdings Under Scrutiny" on January 6, 2009. Larry Catá Backer's comments came from his report "Sovereign Wealth Funds as Regulatory Chameleons: The Norwegian Sovereign Wealth Funds and Public Global Governance Through Private Global Investment" in the *Georgetown Journal of International Law,* vol. 41, no. 2, 2009. The historic details of the cost and conditions of Norway's oil industry came from the *Time* magazine stories "Oil: The North Sea Rush" on May 14, 1973, and "Oil: High Costs, High Stakes, on the North Sea" on September 29, 1975. The Oil Fund's ethical guidelines are spelled out in a report called "Ethical Guidelines" issued by Norges Bank on December 22, 2005. The Oil Fund's short position in Iceland in 2005 and 2006 was reported by Dow Jones Newswires in the story "Norway Makes a Big Bet on Iceland Turmoil" on April 10, 2006. The reaction of Iceland's then prime minister Halldór Ásgrímsson to Norway's short position was reported in the *Economist* in the story "Asset Backed Insecurity: Sovereign Wealth Funds" on January 19, 2008. Norway's standing as the "best place to live" in the world was reported by the BBC on October 5, 2009. The information on Norway's dealings in Western Sahara was reported by Norwatch in the story "Rich Plunder" on October 6, 2009.

CHAPTER 8:
COLONIZING EUROPE IN THE
TWENTY-FIRST CENTURY

The opinions of Scottish member of parliament Brian Adam on forming an oil fund were posted on his blog Brian Adam MSP—Working for You on September 29, 2009, under the heading "1970s Paper Reveals Oil Ownership Would Boost Scottish Income by 30%." The quote by investor Jim Rogers was from the transcript of an interview with personal finance journalist Martin Hutchinson on DailyMarkets.com on September 17, 2008. The details of French president Nicolas Sarkozy's proposal for a sovereign wealth fund were from the transcripts of speeches and press releases provided by the Strategic Investment Fund. Kuwait's response to Germany's sovereign wealth fund plan was reported by Reuters in the story "Kuwait's KIA Warns Berlin Not to Regulate Wealth Funds" on May 18, 2008. Dubai's response to the plan appeared in *The Independent* in the story "Head of Dubai World Threatens to Take His Money Out of Europe." Germany's decision to backtrack on its hard-line stance was reported by gulfnews.com in the story "Germany Says It Is Open to Foreign Investments" on May 23, 2008. Greece's push to have China buy its debt was reported by the *Financial Times* in the story "Joining the Queue for China Cash" on January 26, 2010. The opinions of Chinese economist Yu Yongding on China's buying Greek debt appeared in *China Daily* in the story "Avoid Risky Greek Debt Buy, Says Yu" on January 29, 2010. The data on natural gas reserves outside of North America came from the IHS Cera research reports "Gas from Shale: Potential Outside North America?" on February 5, 2009, and "Shale Gas Outside of North America: High Potential but Difficult to Realize" on April 16, 2009.

CHAPTER 9: NOW ON SALE! EVERYTHING MUST GO!

The bulk of the historical information about William Stanley's development of the electrical transformer and the relationship between General Electric and the city of Pittsfield came from documents stored in the vast local history section of the Pittsfield Athenaeum. Specifically, Pittsfield's difficulty in recruiting policemen and firefighters and the calculation that in the late 1960s roughly three-quarters of Pittsfield's workforce worked for GE were reported in the *Berkshire Eagle* in the story "GE and Pittsfield: Once a Major Presence, the Company Is Now Gone" on September 2, 2007. GE's historical employment figures in Pittsfield appeared in the *Berkshire Eagle* in a graph attached to the story "GE Workers Battle Blues with Party" on September 22, 1990. The description of William Stanley's personal background came from *Invention & Technology* magazine in the story "William Stanley's Search for Immortality" in the Spring–Summer 1988 issue. The details of the economic conditions in Lane County, Oregon, were reported by the *Oregonian* in the story "South Korean Company to Buy Eugene Hynix Plant, Hire 1,000" on September 25, 2009. The findings by Dealogic that China bought more US assets than vice versa in 2009 were reported by *USA Today* in the story "Chinese Buy More US Assets Than US Buys in China" on January 17, 2010. The partnership agreements between US and Indian companies were announced in the Indian business newspaper *Business Standard* in the story "Indian Firms Ink 8 Deals with US Counterparts" on November 25, 2009.

NOTES

EPILOGUE:
BUT WHAT ABOUT ME?

David Riedel's views on the development of emerging markets were spelled out in the 2009 report by Riedel Research Group called "David Riedel: Emerging Markets Entering the Third Phase." The details of the speech by the Bank of England's Adam Posen before the Peterson Institute for International Economics were reported by the *New York Times* in the story " 'Lost Decade' Feared for British Economy" on November 20, 2009.

Bibliography

Acher, John. "Norway's Oil Fund's Israel Holdings Under Scrutiny." Reuters, January 6, 2009.

Arends, Brett. "Farmland: The Next Boom?" *Wall Street Journal*, September 24, 2010.

Adams, Jonathan. "Exuberance in Taiwan as Ties with China Warm." *New York Times,* May 13, 2009.

Adams, Lucy, and Ian Ferguson. "'I Think the Scottish Justice Secretary Is a Great Man. Why Be So Angry About an Innocent Man Who Is Dying?'" *Herald* (Scotland), August 28, 2009.

Association for the Study of Peak Oil and Gas. Newsletter no. 25, January 2003.

Atsom, Yuval, Jennifer Ding, Vinay Dixit, Ian St. Maurice, and Claudia Suessmuth-Dyckerhoff. "The Coming of Age: China's New Class of Wealthy Consumers." Insights China by McKinsey & Company, 2009.

Backer, Larry Catá. "Sovereign Wealth Funds as Regulatory Chameleons: The Norwegian Sovereign Wealth Funds and Public Global Governance Through Private Global Investment." *Georgetown Journal of International Law,* vol. 41, no. 2, 2009.

Barboza, David, Christopher Drew, and Steve Lohr. "G.E. to Share Jet Technology With China in New Joint Venture." *New York Times*, January 17, 2011.

BBC News. Interview with Bill Rammell. September 1, 2009.

BBC News. "Norway 'The Best Place to Live.'" October 5, 2009.

BBC News. "Prime Minister Gordon Brown's Statement on the Decision by Scottish Ministers to Release Abdel Baset Ali Mohmed Al Megrahi on Compassionate Grounds." September 2, 2009.

BBC Radio 4. Interview with David Milliband. September 2, 2009.

BBC Radio 4. Interview with Mohammad Sayalah. September 1, 2009.

BBC Radio 4. Interview with Shukri Ghanem. February 24, 2004.

BIBLIOGRAPHY

Beattie, Alan. *False Economy: A Surprising Economic History of the World*. New York: Riverhead Books, 2009.

Bernstein, Shai, Josh Lerner, and Antoinette Schoar. "The Investment Strategies of Sovereign Wealth Funds." Harvard Business School working paper 09-112, April 2009.

Blitz, James. "Li Backs U.K. Call for Greater Trade Ties." *Financial Times*, January 12, 2011.

Blumenstein, Rebecca, and Laura Meckler. "Chinese Firms Set Sights on U.S. Investments." *Wall Street Journal*, January 27, 2011.

Bookstaber, Richard. *A Demon of Our Own Design: Markets, Hedge Funds, and the Perils of Financial Innovation*. Hoboken, NJ: John Wiley & Sons, 2007.

Bradsher, Keith. "China Racing Ahead of U.S. in the Drive to Go Solar." *New York Times*, August 25, 2009.

Bryanski, Gleb, and Guy Faulconbridge. "BRIC Demands More Clout, Steers Clear of Dollar Talk." Reuters, June 16, 2009.

Brzezinski, Zbigniew, and Brent Scowcroft. *America and the World: Conversations on the Future of American Foreign Policy Moderated by David Ignatius*. New York: Basic Books, 2008.

Business Standard Staff. "Indian Firms Ink 8 Deals with US Counterparts." *Business Standard*, November 25, 2009.

China Daily Staff. "'Bribery Is Widespread' in Rio Case." *China Daily*, July 15, 2009.

China Daily Staff. "GDP Could Be 2.5 Times That of the US by 2030." *China Daily*, May 3, 2008.

China Daily Staff. "Secrets of Chinese Steel Mills Found in Rio's Computers." *China Daily*, July 14, 2009.

China Labour Bulletin. "Going It Alone: The Workers' Movement in China (2007–2008)." Hong Kong: July 9, 2009.

China Real Time Report. "Ahead of the Class: Stiglitz on China's Savings Hoard." *Wall Street Journal*, March 16, 2009.

Chu, Kathy. "Chinese Buy More US Assets Than US Buys in China." *USA Today*, January 17, 2010.

Cooper, George. *The Origin of Financial Crises: Central Banks, Credit Bubbles, and the Efficient Market Fallacy*. New York: Vintage Books, 2008.

Cotula, Lorenzo, Sonja Vermeulen, Rebeca Leonard, and James Keeley. "Land Grab or Development Opportunity? Agricultural Investment and International Land Deals in Africa." London/Rome: Food and Agriculture Organization of the United Nations, International Fund for Agricultural Development, International Institute for Environment and Development, 2009.

Dale, Heather. "Management on a Huge Scale." *Global Pensions,* April 11, 2008.

Dean, Jason, Andrew Browne, and Shai Oster. "China's 'State Capitalism' Sparks a Global Backlash." *Wall Street Journal*, November 16, 2010.

Dickinson, Elizabeth. "The Korean Company Stuck in the Middle of Madagascar's Unrest." Passport blog, February 10, 2009.

Dobrowolski, Tony. "Sabic to Remain at GE Site." *Berkshire Eagle,* September 23, 2007.

Douglass, Sarah E. "Identifying the Opportunities in Alternative Energy." Wells Fargo Bank. San Francisco: 2005.

Dubai World. "Statement from Dubai World." November 30, 2009.

Economic Times Staff. "Moody's Urges Debt-Laden Dubai World to Sell Assets." *Economic Times,* February 15, 2010.

Ecomomist Intelligence Unit. "The GCC In 2020: Outlook for the Gulf and the Global Economy." A Report from the *Economist* Intelligence Unit—Sponsored by the Qatar Financial Center. London: March 2009.

Economist Intelligence Unit. "Foresight 2020: Economic, Industry, and Corporate Trends." A Report from the *Economist* Intelligence Unit—Sponsored by Cisco Systems. London: March 2006.

Economist Staff. "A Very European Crisis: The Sorry State of Greece's Public Finances Is a Test Not Only for the Country's Policymakers but Also for Europe's." *Economist,* February 4, 2010.

Economist Staff. "Asset Backed Insecurity." *Economist,* January 19, 2008.

El Gamal, Rania. "Kuwait Gov't Could Start Bourse Fund Next Week." ArabianBusiness.com, December 16, 2008.

Evans-Pritchard, Ambrose. "Investors Flee Iceland Banks as Economy Heads Toward Forecast 'Hard Landing.'" *Telegraph,* March 14, 2006.

Fallows, James. *Postcards from Tomorrow Square: Reports from China*. New York: Vintage Books, 2009.

Faulconbridge, Guy, and Michael Stott. "Crisis Speeds BRIC Rise to Power: Goldman's O'Neill." Reuters, June 9, 2009.

Ferguson, Niall. *The Ascent of Money: A Financial History of the World*. New York: Penguin Press, 2008.

Financial Times Staff. "Joining the Queue for China Cash." *Financial Times,* January 26, 2010.

Fishman, Ted C. *China Inc.: How the Rise of the Next Superpower Challenges America and the World*. New York: Scribner, 2006.

Fitch Ratings. *Fitch Ratings Revises Iceland's Outlook to Negative*. February 21, 2006.

Fitz-Gerald, Keith. "Jim Rogers Interview: How the Federal Reserve Will

Fail and the One Sector Every Investor Should Be In." DailyMarkets
.com, September 17, 2008.

Foster, Vivien, William Butterfield, Chuan Chen, and Nataliya Pushak.
*Building Bridges: China's Growing Role as Infrastructure Financier for
Africa.* Washington, DC: International Bank for Reconstruction and
Development/World Bank, 2008.

Fridriksson, Ingimundur. Turbulence in Iceland's financial markets in 2006.
Keynote address to the UBS conference "Annual Reserve Management Seminar for Sovereign Institutions." June 4, 2007.

G20 Working Group. "G20 Working Group 1: Enhancing Sound Regulation and Strengthening Transparency—Final Report." February 2009.

Gardner, John. *Recovery Grants to the EV Industry Not Stimulating – Yet.* Pike
Research, October 5, 2010.

Garnaut, John. "Who Is Hu? A Man of Integrity." *Sydney Morning Herald,*
July 10, 2009.

Gogoi, Pallavi. "Where are the Jobs? For Many Companies, Overseas." *Asso-
ciated Press,* December 28, 2011.

Government of Dubai. "Government of Dubai Announces Restructuring of
Dubai World," November 25, 2009.

GRAIN Staff. "Seized! The 2008 Landgrab for Food and Financial Security." GRAIN Briefing, October 2008.

Green, Chris, Andrew Grice, Oliver Duff, and Jonathan Brown. "Lockerbie: Now It's Payback Time." *Independent,* August 22, 2009.

Hagan, Erik. "Rich on Plunder." Norwatch, October 6, 2009.

Haider, Haseeb. "UAE Offers More Funds to Banks." *Khaleej Times,*
November 30, 2009.

Hawksworth, John. "The World in 2050: How Big Will the Major Emerging Market Economies Get and How Can the OECD Compete?"
PricewaterhouseCoopers. London: March 2006.

Hedge Fund Research. "Investors Return to Hedge Fund Industry as a New
Model Emerges." Hedge Fund Research. Chicago: January 20, 2010.

Hoffmann, Katie, and Margaret Brennan. "Wipro to Hire US Workers as
Spending Rebounds." Bloomberg News, October 15, 2009.

Human Rights in China Staff. "State Secrets: China's Legal Labyrinth."
Human Rights in China, June 12, 2007.

International Energy Agency. "World Energy Outlook 2010." Paris:
November 13, 2009.

International Working Group of Sovereign Wealth Funds. "Sovereign Wealth Funds Generally Accepted Principles and Practices—
'Santiago Principles.'" October 2008.

Invesco. "Private Sector Investment Fuels Infrastructure Expansion in

Emerging Markets." *Invesco Perspective*. Invesco. Atlanta: September 2008.

Jacques, Martin. *When China Rules the World: The End of the Western World and the Birth of a New Global Order*. New York: Penguin Press, 2009.

Johnson, Simon. "The Rise of Sovereign Wealth Funds." *Finance & Development: A Quarterly Magazine of the International Monetary Fund* 44, no. 3 (September 2007).

Kahn, Joseph, and Jim Yardley. "As China Roars, Pollution Reaches Deadly Extremes." *New York Times,* August 26, 2007.

Kaplan, Steve, and Antoinette Schoar. "Private Equity Performance: Returns, Persistence, and Capital Flows." MIT Sloan working paper no. 4446-03, November 2003.

Keidel, Albert. "China's Economic Rise—Fact and Fiction." Carnegie Endowment for International Peace, Policy Brief no. 61, July 2008.

Kotter, Jason, and Ugur Lel. *Friends of Foes? The Stock Price Impact of Sovereign Wealth Fund Investments and the Price of Keeping Secrets*. Board of Governors of the Federal Reserve System, International Discussion Papers no. 940, August 2008.

Krauss, Clifford. "New Way to Tap Gas May Expand Global Supplies." *New York Times,* October 9, 2009.

Krekel, Bryan. *Capability of the People's Republic of China to Conduct Cyber Warfare and Computer Network Exploitation*. US-China Economic and Security Review Commission. Washington, DC: October 9, 2009.

Kurlantzick, Joshua. *Charm Offensive: How China's Soft Power Is Transforming the World*. New Haven, CT: Yale University Press, 2007.

Kynge, James, Geoff Dyer, and James Blitz. "China and Europe: Bear Gifts for Friends." *Financial Times*, January 14, 2011.

Lahart, Justin. "For Small Businesses, Big World Beckons." *Wall Street Journal*, January 28, 2011.

Leung, Elinor. *Suicidal Decision*. Calyon Securities, January 13, 2010.

Li Cui, Chang Shu, and Jian Chang. "Exchange Rate Pass-Through and Currency Invoicing in China's Exports." *China Economic Issues*. External Depart-ment of the Hong Kong Monetary Authority. Hong Kong: July 9, 2009.

MacLeod, Angus, Peter Jones, and David Robertson. "Qatar Raised Al-Megrahi Release During Talks with Alex Salmond." *London Times,* September 4, 2009.

Mahbubani, Kishore. *The New Asian Hemisphere: The Irresistible Shift of Global Power to the East*. New York: PublicAffairs, 2008.

Mallet, Victor. "Chinese Arrivals Take Spain by Storm." *Financial Times*, January 21, 2011.

BIBLIOGRAPHY

Maslakovic, Marko. *Private Equity 2009*. ISFL Research. London: August 2009.

———. *Sovereign Wealth Funds 2010*. IFSL Research. London: March 2010.

McConnell, Michael J. *Annual Threat Assessment of the Director of National Intelligence for the Senate Select Committee on Intelligence*. February 5, 2008.

McDonell, Stephen. "Hu Being Held in Shanghai Detention Centre." ABC News (Australia), July 12, 2009.

Megrahi, Abdel Baset Ali Mohmed Al Megrahi. "Al-Megrahi Statement in Full." Aljazeera.net, August 20, 2009.

Megrahi, Abdel Baset Ali Mohmed Al Megrahi. Grounds of Appeal and Written Submissions for the Hearing on Grounds of Appeal 1 and 2 Before the High Court of Judiciary, Scotland. Date of Arguments: November 2, 2009.

Michel, Serge, and Michel Beuret. *China Safari: On the Trail of Beijing's Expansion in Africa*. New York: Nation Books, 2009.

Milunovich, Steven. *Alternative Energy Perspective*. Bank of America Merrill Lynch. New York: October 6, 2009.

Moody's Investors Service. "Dubai World Unlikely to Harm UAE, Abu Dhabi Ratings." London: November 30, 2009.

Morris, Charles R. *The Trillion Dollar Meltdown: Easy Money, High Rollers, and the Great Credit Crash*. New York: PublicAffairs, 2008.

Morrison, Wayne M., and Marc Labonte. *China's Holdings of US Securities: Implications for the US Economy*. Washington: Congressional Research Service Report for Congress, July 30, 2009.

Norges Bank Investment Management. *NBIM Investor Expectations: Climate Change Management*. Norges Bank Investment Management. Oslo: August 14, 2009.

Norwegian Government Pension Fund—Global. *Ethical Guidelines*. December 22, 2005.

Notes of meeting between delegations from the Scottish and Libyan governments. Meridian Court, Glasgow. March 12, 2009.

OECD. *Sovereign Wealth Funds and Recipient Countries: Working Together to Maintain and Expand Freedom of Investment*. October 11, 2008.

O'Neill, Jim. *Building Better Global Economic BRICs*. Goldman Sachs Global Economics Paper no. 66. 2001.

Opinion of the Court delivered by Lord Sutherland in causa Her Majesty's Advocate v Abdelbaset Ali Mohmed Al Megrahi and Al Amin Khalifa Fhima, Prisoner is in the Prison of Zeist, Camp Zeist (Kamp van Zeist), the Netherlands. January 31, 2001.

Opinion of the Court delivered by The Lord Justice General in Appeal

BIBLIOGRAPHY

Against Conviction of Abdelbaset Ali Mohmed Al Megrahi against Her Majesty's Advocate. March 14, 2002.

Own, Ahmed A. Letter dated August 15, 2003, from the Charge d'affaires a.i. of the Permanent Mission of the Libyan Arab Jamahiriya to the United Nations addressed to the President of the Security Council. August 15, 2003.

Partnoy, Frank. *Infectious Greed: How Deceit and Risk Corrupted the Financial Markets*. New York: Henry Holt and Company, 2003.

Pei, Minxin. "Think Again: Asia's Rise." *Foreign Policy,* June 22, 2009.

Posner, Richard A. *A Failure of Capitalism: The Crisis of '08 and the Descent into Depression*. Cambridge, MA: Harvard University Press, 2009.

PPI Trade Facts. *Trade Fact of the Week: Currency Trading Totals $3 Trillion a Day*. Progressive Policy Institute, March 14, 2007.

Prasad, Eswar, and Isaac Sorkin. "Sky's the Limit? National and Global Implications of China's Reserve Accumulation." Brookings Institution, July 22, 2009.

Press Trust of India Staff. "Emerging Countries to BRIC up the Holes in Global Economy." *Indian Express,* December 24, 2008.

Raphaeli, Nimrod, and Bianca Gersten. "Sovereign Wealth Funds: Investment Vehicles for the Persian Gulf Countries." *Middle East Quarterly* 15, no. 2 (Spring 2008).

Read, Richard. "South Korean Company to Buy Eugene Hynix Plant, Hire 1,000." *Oregonian,* September 25, 2009.

Reuters Staff. "Chinese Auto Market Overtakes US" Reuters, January 8, 2010.

Reuters Staff. "Chinese Birth Defects Soar Due to Pollution: Report." Reuters, October 29, 2007.

Riddell, Mary, Simon Johnson, and Andrew Porter. "Jack Straw Admits Lockerbie Bomber's Release Was Linked to Oil." *Daily Telegraph,* September 4, 2009.

Riedel, David. "David Riedel: Emerging Markets Entering the Third Phase." Riedel Research Group. New York: 2009.

Roach, Stephen S. *Stephen Roach on the Next Asia: Opportunities and Challenges for a New Globalization*. Hoboken, NJ: John Wiley & Sons, 2009.

Ros-Lehtinen, Ileana. Ros-Lehtinen Comments on Signing of UAE Nuclear Agreement. House Committee on Foreign Affairs. May 20, 2009.

Roxburgh, Charles, Susan Lund, Matt Lippert, Olivia L. White, and Yue Zhao. "The New Power Brokers: How Oil, Asia, Hedge Funds, and Private Equity Are Faring in the Financial Crisis." San Francisco: McKinsey Global Institute, July 2009.

Rubin, Robert E., and Jacob Weisberg. *In an Uncertain World: Tough Choices from Wall Street to Washington*. New York: Random House, 2003.

BIBLIOGRAPHY

Schuman, Michael. *The Miracle: The Epic Story of Asia's Quest for Wealth.* New York: Harper Collins Publishers, 2009.

Sender, Henry. "How a Gulf Petro-State Invests Its Oil Riches." *Wall Street Journal,* August 24, 2007.

Setser, Brad W. "Sovereign Wealth and Sovereign Power: The Strategic Consequences of American Indebtedness." New York: Council on Foreign Relations Press, September 2008.

Setser, Brad W., and Rachel Ziemba. "Understanding the New Financial Superpower: The Management of GCC Official Foreign Assets." *RGE Monitor,* December 2007.

Sibun, Jonathan. "Norway Makes a Big Bet on Iceland Turmoil." Dow Jones Newswires, April 10, 2006.

Sky News. *Interview with Saif al-Islam Qaddafi.* September 7, 2009.

Slyngstad, Yngve. *Active Management of the Government Pension Fund.* Ministry of Finance Seminar Presentation. Oslo: January 20, 2010.

Smith, Leta. "Gas From Shale: Potential Outside North America?" IHS Cera Client Services Private Report. February 5, 2009.

———. "Shale Gas Outside of North America: High Potential but Difficult to Realize." IHS Cera Client Services Private Report. April 16, 2009.

Standard & Poor's. "Gulf Cooperation Council Credit Survey: How the Region Is Weathering the Storm." Standard & Poor's, June 2009.

State Street Corporation. "Sovereign Wealth Funds: Assessing the Impact." *Vision* 3, no. 2 (2008).

Steinbeck, Dan. "Mutual Trust Can Ride Over Challenges." Xinhuanet .com, July 30, 2009.

Stockholm International Peace Research Institute. *SIPRI Yearbook 2010 – Military Expenditure,* June 2, 2010.

Story, Louise. "Hedge Funds Step Up Efforts to Avert Tougher Rules." *New York Times,* June 22, 2009.

Stricker, Andrea. "A Smuggler's Use of the US Financial System to Receive Illegal Payments from Iran." *ISIS Report.* Institute for Science and International Security. Washington: October 23, 2009.

Swartz, Spencer, and Alistair MacDonald. "BP Lobbied U.K. on Benefits of Libya Prisoner-Transfer Deal." *Wall Street Journal,* September 5, 2009.

Tan, Clement, and Tommy Yang. "Made in China Now Has a Fast-Growing Sibling: Bought by China." *Los Angeles Times,* March 4, 2010.

Tan Yingzi. "Youth Feel Pressure of Looking After Aging Parents." *China Daily,* June 29, 2009.

Tett, Gillian. "The Story of the BRICs." *Financial Times,* January 15, 2010.

Thomas, Landon, Jr. " 'Lost Decade' Feared for British Economy." *New York Times,* November 20, 2009.

BIBLIOGRAPHY

Thomas, Richard. *Icelandic Banks: Not What You Are Thinking*. Merrill Lynch. London: March 7, 2006.

Tian Ying and Erik Holm. "Buffett Posts $1 Billion Profit on China Hybrid Carmaker BYD." Bloomberg News, July 31, 2009.

Time Staff. "Oil: The North Sea Rush." *Time,* May 14, 1973.

Time Staff. "Oil: High Costs, High Stakes, on the North Sea." *Time,* September 29, 1975.

Timmons, Heather. "Iceland's Fizzy Economy Faces a Test." *New York Times,* April 18, 2006.

Trudell, Craig. "GM's to Add Third Shift, 750 Jobs to Flint Pickup Plant." *Bloomberg News*, January 24, 2011.

Uhrig, Charles. "Recent Trends in the Mergers & Acquisitions and Private Equity Markets." Raymond James & Associates, August 31, 2007.

United Nations Security Council. Resolution 883 (1993) Adopted by the Security Council at its 3312th meeting, on 11 November 1993. November 11, 1993.

US-China Economic and Security Review Commission. "2009 Report to Congress of the US-China Economic and Security Review Commission." Washington: November 2009.

US Commerce Department Bureau of Economic Analysis. "Foreign Direct Investors' Outlays to Acquire or Establish US Businesses Increased in 2008." Washington: June 4, 2009.

US Department of the Treasury/Federal Reserve Board. "Major Foreign Holders of Treasury Securities." February 26, 2010.

US-UAE Business Council. "US-U.A.E. Agreement for Peaceful Nuclear Energy Cooperation: Advancing Mutual US and U.A.E Security and Economic Interests." April 8, 2009.

Velculescu, Delia. "Norway's Oil Fund Shows the Way for Wealth Funds." *IMF Survey Magazine,* July 9, 2008.

Von Bismarck, Max, Nicholas Davis, Albrecht Dürnhöfer, Irvin Sha, Maliha Shekhani, Bernd Jan Sikken, and Andrew Turnbull. "The Future of the Global Financial System: A Near-Term Outlook and Long-Term Scenarios." Cologny/Geneva: World Economic Forum, 2009.

Von Braun, Joachim, and Ruth Meinzen-Dick. " 'Land Grabbing' by Foreign Investors in Developing Countries: Risks and Opportunities." IFPRI Policy Brief 13, April 2009.

Wassener, Bettina. "World Bank Cuts Forecast for Developed Economies." *New York Times,* June 22, 2009.

Weisman, Steven R. "Overseas Funds Resist Calls for a Code of Conduct." *New York Times,* February 9, 2008.

BIBLIOGRAPHY

Whitt, Jr., Joseph A. "The Mexican Peso Crisis." *Federal Reserve Bank of Atlanta Economic Review,* January–February 1996.

Wiesmann, Gernt, and Victor Mallet. "Li Calls for Deeper Trade Ties with Germany." *Financial Times*, January 7, 2011.

Wines, Michael. "Australia, Nourishing China's Economic Engine, Questions Ties." *New York Times,* June 2, 2009.

Wise, George. "William Stanley's Search for Immortality: He Helped Make Household Electronics Possible for All of Us, but He Couldn't Invent Fame or Independence for Himself." *Invention & Technology,* Spring–Summer 1988.

Woetzel, Jonathan R. "Reassessing China's State-Owned Enterprises." *The McKinsey Quarterly,* July 2008.

Xin Zhiming. "Avoid Risky Greek Debt Buy, Says Yu." *China Daily,* January 29, 2010.

Xinhua Staff. "China's Forex Reserves Near $2.4 Trillion." Xinhuanet.com, January 15, 2010.

Xinhua Staff. "China's Gold Reserves Reach 1,053 Tonnes." *China Daily,* April 24, 2009.

Xinhua Staff. "China Urges US to Stop Accusations on So-Called Internet Freedom." Xinhuanet.com, January 22, 2010.

Xinhua Staff. "China Welcomes Foreign Enterprises to Invest in China." Xinhuanet.com, July 16, 2009.

Xinhua Staff. "CIC: Not to Invest Massively Overseas till Uncertainty Clears." *China Daily,* December 3, 2008.

Xinhua Staff. "Four Rio Tinto Employees Detained in China for Spying." Xinhuanet.com, July 9, 2009.

Xinhua Staff. "Mutual Trust Can Ride Over Challenges." Xinhuanet.com, July 30, 2009.

Xinhua Staff. "Rio Tinto Employees Charged with Bribery, Infringing Business Secrets." Xinhuanet.com, February 10, 2010.

Yu De and Hu Yilin. "The Secrets of China's Iron Ore Negotiations." *Economic Observer,* July 22, 2009.

Zakaria, Fareed. "The Capitalist Manifesto: Greed Is Good (To a Point)." *Newsweek,* June 13, 2009.

———. *The Post-American World*. New York: W. W. Norton & Company, 2008.

Zhou Xiaochuan. *Reform the International Monetary System*. The People's Bank of China, March 23, 2009.

Zuckerman, Gregory. *The Greatest Trade Ever: The Behind-the-Scenes Story of How John Paulson Defied Wall Street and Made Financial History*. New York: Broadway Books, 2009.

Index

About the Author

Eric J. Weiner has covered business and economics issues for fifteen years as a writer and editor. His critically acclaimed first book, *What Goes Up: The Uncensored History of Modern Wall Street as Told by the Bankers, Brokers, CEOs, and Scoundrels Who Made It Happen*, was published in September 2005 by Little, Brown and Company, and was selected as one of the year's best books by *Barron's* magazine and one of the "Year's Most Enriching Reads" by *Kiplinger's*. He is a former columnist and reporter for Dow Jones Newswires, and he has written for *The Wall Street Journal, Los Angeles Times, The Boston Globe, The Village Voice*, and countless other major publications. He also is a contributor to the news and opinion website *The Huffington Post*. He lives in Great Barrington, Massachusetts, with his wife, Paige, and their son, Jake.